The Author

Jean Renvoize is the author of three very successful related studies, **Children in Danger** (1976), **Web of Violence** (1978) and **Incest** (1982), all published by Routledge & Kegan Paul. She has also written four novels: **The Masker** (Secker & Warburg, 1960), **A Wild Thing** (Macmillan, 1970), **The Net** (Quartet; Stein and Day, 1974) and **Coming Apart** (Stein and Day, 1981).

GOING SOLO

Also by Jean Renvoize

Children in Danger: The Causes and
  Prevention of Baby Battering
Web of Violence: A study of Family Violence
Incest: A Family Pattern

GOING SOLO

Single mothers by choice

Jean Renvoize

Routledge & Kegan Paul
London, Boston, and Henley

First published in 1985
by Routledge & Kegan Paul plc

14 Leicester Square, London WC2H 7PH, England

9 Park Street, Boston, Mass. 02108, USA and

Broadway House, Newtown Road,
Henley on Thames, Oxon RG9 1EN, England

Set in Garamond
by Columns of Reading
and printed in Great Britain
by T.J. Press (Padstow) Ltd.
Padstow, Cornwall.

Library of Congress Cataloging in Publication Data

Renvoize, Jean.
    Going solo.
    Bibliography: p.
    Includes index.
    1. Unmarried mothers — Great Britain.   2. Unmarried
mothers – United States.   3. Unmarried mothers —
Netherlands.   I. Title.
HQ759.45.R46   1985   306.8'56   85-2244

British Library CIP data also available

ISBN 0-7102-0065-X

To Paul

Contents

Acknowledgments

It is impossible to thank individually all the people who have helped me during the preparation of this book, and in particular I regret not being able to thank publicly the many women who talked openly about their lives, their thoughts, their hopes and their children, but the price of such openness was a need for anonymity. Not all wanted it, and in a few cases the Christian name used is the original one, but usually I asked them to select a pseudonym to protect the privacy of their children as well as themselves. Enough details have been sketched in about their lives in the dramatis personae at the beginning of the book for readers to flesh out the characters, although again I have been careful not to give enough detail to make the women recognizable.

I would also like to thank in particular the following professionals who gave me the benefit of their experience: in America – Dr Ed Cohen, obstetrician/gynaecologist, Los Angeles; Dr Ted Nagle, gynaecologist, Department of Obstetrics and Gynaecology, University of Minnesota; Dr Hendrika Vande Kemp, clinical psychologist, Fuller Theological Seminary, Los Angeles; Dr Karin Meiselman, clinical psychologist, Pasadena; Naomi Scheman, associate professor of philosophy and women's studies, University of Minnesota; Janet Proctor, anthropologist and archaeologist; Elaine May, historian on the family; and Marilyn Fabe, author of *Up Against the Clock*; in Britain – Dr Tony Baker, child psychiatrist, St George's Hospital, London; Dr Bridget Mason, gynaecologist, London; Dr Elphis Christopher, psychosexual counsellor; Dr Catherine Peckham; Pat Verity, who runs a day nursery; Dr Raimond Gaita, Department of Philosophy, King's College, London; Philippa Brewster, of

Pandora Press; the Gingerbread organization; and Wyn Knowles, ex-editor of 'Woman's Hour', BBC. Several of the women I interviewed primarily as mothers were also psychologists, psychiatrists, or therapists. Dr Jane Mattes, psychoanalyst and psychotherapist, also founder of the Single Mothers by Choice group, is one such, and Dr Afton Blake, clinical psychologist, is another. I would also like to thank Jessica Curtis, who is President of Single Mothers by Choice, and through her the members of SMC whose experience was of great help to me. Both the Dutch mothers are specialists in child psychology and child education.

My American researches, which took me right across the States and back to Boston via Washington and New York, would not have been possible without the travel grant made to me by the Nuffield Foundation to whom I express, not for the first time, my gratitude for their generosity. I would also like to express my particular gratitude to Ned and Annie Alpers who gave me their hospitality and time, as did Karin Meiselman and her family, Janet Proctor and Susan Geiger, Joyce Moulton and Nancy Genn.

And finally, my special thanks to Paul Moody, who read my manuscript as it progressed and made several invaluable suggestions.

Introduction

Any woman having a first child is entering on an astonishing adventure that will profoundly alter her life. Whatever her previous ideas about parenthood have been, she will not only discover new aspects of herself, but her concepts about humanity, human relationships and human possibilities will alter and broaden.

Women who have babies within the comparative safety of a long-term relationship – legalized or otherwise – mostly give less thought before pregnancy to what difference having a child will make to their lives than unmarried women who make a deliberate choice to get pregnant. For the latter it is essential to be as fully aware of what maternity involves as is possible, and to help in developing such an awareness is the aim of this book. But women living with partners, too, ought to be far more aware than they usually are of the extent of the changes parenthood will bring, not only to themselves but also to spouses or lovers.

And it does not stop there – the relationship between themselves and their partners will alter dramatically as well, not necessarily for the better; their careers also will be affected, and their own inner life apart from their attachment to their nearest and dearest will become a threatened, precarious thing that will need to be guarded with almost as much loving care as they hope to give to their new baby. Today's women, married or otherwise, are leading very different lives to their mothers, and live in a different world. *Any* woman having a baby should have advance notice of what will be happening to her – the profound changes, the joy, the despair, the boredom and the fascination.

I interviewed mothers, prospective mothers, gynaecologists, psychiatrists, therapists, etc. in Britain, America and Holland in order to arrive at as broad an understanding of the growing movement of single parenting as possible. In general the picture in all three countries was very similar, but there were certain differences, usually of emphasis rather than of fact. Most of the children of these single women are still very young, not much more than toddlers, but I also interviewed a few mothers with older children, and I think their experiences will be of particular interest.

The contents page details what the various chapters contain, but, to summarize briefly, Part 1, called 'Theory', opens with a preliminary look at the growing 'phenomenon' of single parenting by choice, goes on to look more deeply at women, at men, at relationships, at marriage, and where the family is going. In Part 2, 'Practice', single mothers tell how they got pregnant, how maternity has affected them, and how they have dealt with it, while various professionals add their own views. In Part 3, 'Shall I, shan't I?', single mothers alone have the field – they pass on final messages about their own experiences, and offer advice to women wondering whether or not single motherhood is the right choice for them. Married women, too, especially those with careers or interesting jobs, will do well to think about these messages before embarking on what will probably be the deepest, and sometimes the most rewarding, change a woman can make to her life.

List of Mothers and Mothers-to-be

ADINA – (see Nora also) 28 at interview, a printer. She and Nora are a lesbian couple awaiting the birth of a child they have arranged to adopt. American.

AFTON Blake – 42 at interview, one son of 20 months, clinical psychologist. Had artificial insemination through the Repository of Germinal Choice, the Californian sperm bank that selects fathers from carefully selected highly intelligent men. American.

ANGELA – 29 at interview, one son of 4, PhD graduate student. Father a lover she lived with for a while but when the child was 9 months old she moved out. At the father's insistence they share joint custody and actual care of the boy. American.

ANNA – 32 at interview, two children – a boy of 5 and a girl of 2, studied child psychology and child education but at present on state support. Had same father for both children, a French lover she sees occasionally. Dutch.

CAROLYN – 31 at interview, 1 daughter of 1 month, theatre director. The father was a lover in an affair that was coming to an end. American.

CATHERINE – 35 at interview, one son of 5, actress. She got pregnant accidentally by a married man she was in love with, but did not expect to marry. She very happily decided to keep the baby and stay alone. New Zealander.

CHARLOTTE – 34 at interview, one daughter of $1\frac{1}{2}$, part-time researcher. Father is a long-standing homosexual friend. English.

ELIZABETH – 38 at interview, one son of 10, curator of West Country local museum. Very much wanted to have the child of a much older man with whom she had had (and still has) a long-standing affair. The father has always had an 'open' marriage with the full agreement of his wife, who sometimes has Elizabeth's son to stay with her. Elizabeth is therefore mainly alone, but runs her own life in her own style and likes it that way. English.

FELICITY – 39 at interview, one son of 2, medical researcher but now on social security. Father is a lover she wanted and expected to marry, but he fled on hearing she was pregnant. English.

FRANCES – 39 at interview, divorced, one daughter of 9, art gallery owner. Father is a lover she much respected but could not live with. American.

JAN – (see Stella also) 32 at interview, one of a lesbian couple with one son of 7 months. Jan is a trained worker in one of the caring professions. Father is homosexual brother of the non-biological mother, who donated his sperm for artificial insemination. American.

JANE – 31 at interview, one daughter of 7 months, lawyer. The child is adopted. American.

JANICE – 30 at interview, one daughter of 2, research assistant. Father and she had lived together in 'open' relationship before birth of baby, and continue still to do so. Child is in mother's name, father has no official rights though they share child care. English.

JENNY – 22 at interview, one son of nearly 2, currently working in wholefood co-operative. Was living with father when she became unintentionally pregnant. Would not have chosen to have a child. Now lives alone, sharing child with father on regular basis. English.

JESSICA Curtis – 38 at interview, two children – one boy of 14 from her marriage (she's divorced), and a daugther of $2\frac{1}{2}$, nurse in public health nursing, also President of the Single Mothers by Choice group. Pregnant through artificial insemination arranged through a doctor. American.

JOANNA – 44 at interview, one son of 4, graduate student studying cultural history in the Third World. The father is a university colleague, very carefully selected using a number of criteria, purely for conception purposes. American.

JULIA – 29 at interview, one daughter of 5, various jobs – office worker, health food shop, now lives on social security.

Had child by a lover she wasn't living with, but after the birth they lived together for three years though it didn't work out and they eventually parted. The father stays involved. English.

LAURA – 26 at interview, pregnant with first child. No particular job, but has own house which can be partly let off. The father is an old friend, 'earmarked' ten years ago when she was 16 as a likely father, but except for a brief period the relationship was purely platonic. English / Caribbean.

LYNN – 41 at interview, two daughters, one of 5 and one of 11 months, nurse. Pregnant through artificial insemination, once with fresh sperm arranged through a doctor, the second through a sperm bank. American.

MARION – about 34 at interview, member of Gingerbread, one son of 10 and one of 7, married but husband walked out on her four years ago. Was a hairdresser. English.

MARY – 31 at interview, one son of 21 months, nurse in children's nursery with newborn babies. Pregnant through artificial insemination through sperm bank. American.

NORA – (see Adina) 26 at interview, has a master's degree in child education, works with children. One of a lesbian couple, they are awaiting the birth of a child they have arranged to adopt. American.

PAT – 35 at interview, one son of 3, midwife. Father an old friend and ex-lover. American.

ROSA – 35 at interview, one son of 2½, specialist in child psychology and child education (called pedagogic studies in Holland). Father a Greek she met on holiday with whom she lived for a while with intention of becoming pregnant. Dutch.

SARAH – 45 at interview, one daughter of 4, languages teacher. Father a man she wanted to marry, but affair finished before child was born.

SERENA – 40 at interview, one boy of 3, acupressurist. Father is a European she was in love with but whose lifestyle was too different from hers for her to share it. American.

SHARON – No child as yet, but is considering whether or not to have one.

SONIA – 24 at first pregnancy by Israeli artist she was

living with, who insisted on their marrying when she became pregnant again ten months later. The marriage broke up after a few years, the husband took the children away to Israel, and though she fought hard she lost care of them. Then became pregnant by a lover she had already decided she didn't want to live with and resultant daughter is now 10. Worked in publishing, translating, dressmaking. English.

STELLA – (see Jan) 33 at interview, has had various jobs. Lives as part of lesbian couple with Jan; father is homosexual brother of the non-biological mother who donated his sperm for artificial insemination. American.

STEPHANIE – 40 at interview, one son of 3, psychoanalyst and psychotherapist. Father a lover who she knew in advance would almost certainly not be interested in the role of active fatherhood. American.

TAM – clinical social worker and therapist, no child as yet but is considering whether or not to have one.

Part I
THEORY

1
The 'phenomenon' of single parenting by choice

Throughout patriarchal mythology, dream-symbolism, theology, language, two ideas flow side by side: one, that the female body is impure, corrupt, the site of discharges, bleeding, dangerous to masculinity, a source of moral and physical contamination, 'the devil's gateway'. On the other hand, as mother the woman is beneficent, sacred, pure, asexual, nourishing; and the physical potential for motherhood – that same body with its bleedings and mysteries – is her single destiny and justification in life. These two ideas have become deeply internalized in women, even in the most independent of us, those who seem to lead the freest lives.
(Adrienne Rich[1])

Women having children without either marriage or some other stable connection with a man who is going to be the father is not a new phenomenon – what's new is seeing it happen among middle and upper-middle class white women. That means it's entering the realm where it gets talked about, written about, becomes socially acceptable; it becomes a phenomenon *to be discussed.* (Naomi Scheman, professor of philosophy and women's studies, personal communication)

The women's movement

It is impossible to look at the subject of single parenting by choice without considering what effect the women's movement has had and is continuing to have on women all over the world. In the next chapter I will explore the women's movement more fully: here I want to give a taste of how it has affected the women I have interviewed, and why I think the whole process of growth and change is exciting for women without necessarily being threatening to men and the future of the family.

Rosa (see a brief note about her and the other mothers on pages xv-xviii), a Dutch woman who specializes in child psychology and who as a single mother had a son when she was 33, tells how the new atmosphere felt to her, a young country girl. 'I met people who were different from everything I knew. It was in the late sixties and I was swallowing everything I could find; all the news about movements – student movements, women's movements – so much was happening everywhere! You had to be affected by it.' This 1960s revival of feminism, while stimulating a new consciousness among women, naturally produced a severe reaction from a number of men, but the more thoughtful of them and many of the younger generation attempted to face up to the implications behind the independence that feminists everywhere were insisting on. There was change in the air, and it gradually became clear that young women were preparing to pull the plug out on the dirty bathwater of thousands of years of resigned acceptance of male dominance. Some men were, and still are, terrified. Others saw that 'liberation' has two sides: they relished the thought that they could allow themselves to relax, to be tender, to cry; could freely admit they didn't necessarily feel macho and dominant without risking the loss of their own inner feeling of masculinity – whatever that might be.

New kinds of female/male relationships began to be forged: *Janice*, a medical research assistant, began an open relationship about eight years ago with the man who eventually became the father of her child, born two years ago. 'I never saw our relationship as something that was going to last until we were both dead, or even that it would last until my child was 17 or leaving home. When the time came when I wanted to have a baby we talked about it a lot: essentially it was going to be *my* child, but he too felt very committed to the idea. I knew I'd much rather have a child with support there, that it would be very difficult without that, but I also knew that if the support went away then I'd still have *her*. If that happened I'd have to find support from elsewhere, from friends . . . .'

This acceptance that coming together with a man no longer necessarily implies a partnership for life involves a change in attitudes easier for women who came to adulthood in the 1960s and 1970s than for my generation which grew up in the 1950s weighed down with a heavy load of old expectations, however bravely we tried to jettison them. *Anna*, a Dutch child psychologist/feminist, with two children, says, 'I don't see myself as a deviation from being married, but that having children on your own is just another possibility of how you can live. I don't feel myself different from married couples – I feel much more close to married mothers with children the same age as mine than to single mothers who have just had a baby. We have much more – how do you say? – in common.' Anna is at ease with her life, as are so many of the mothers I interviewed, and it was this I was least prepared for. I suppose that in my heart (because for my generation it would have been a fairly revolutionary thing to deliberately have a child out of wedlock) I expected to find a group of tough-minded, militant women somewhat on the defensive: instead I found mostly happy, fulfilled, strong but gentle individuals who gave out warmth and a readiness to share with others. These were women who had made their choice after much deliberation, mostly at a mature age, and who knew in advance that nothing in life comes free.

This sudden change in female consciousness – which led to women at the end of the 1970s and the beginning of the 1980s realizing that being in charge of their own bodies meant not only the possibility of saying 'no' to having children but also the possibility of saying 'yes' – was not easily acceptable by the feminists who had grown up in the 1960s and to whom child-bearing was yet another part of the 'male plot' to keep women down. Philippa Brewster, publisher's editor, expresses her own change of viewpoint from those early days of the renewed women's movement. 'At Greenham Common there are many women with children – there was even a baby born there – and they've shown that there is a new strain of thinking among feminist women, that you have to protect your children and that motherhood is very important, which is anathema to people like me who were denying motherhood earlier on, saying that it was motherhood that was oppressing women.' She went on to explain how, apart from a few hardliners, many erstwhile anti-child feminists now feel it incumbent on them to help their sisters who have decided to have children by taking on baby-minding and giving moral support, although this determined unselfishness sometimes causes a certain amount of resentment and self-searching.

Janice, who has lived for seven years with the father of her 2-year-old daughter, but who nevertheless has no doubt that the child is primarily *her* child – it having been conceived by *her* desire, born out of *her* body – answered me with slight shock in her voice when I asked her whose name the child carried. 'Mine, of course! She has my surname, not his. I mean I'm not married, so why the hell should I call her any other name than my own? As he and I live together people think it a bit strange, yes, but that's to be expected.'

Her partner seems to have taken her independent views in his stride, but such thinking is a challenge that men respond to in various ways. One of the more interesting, for instance, is the way male doctors have been increasing their control over the actual process of birth, coming as close as is physically possible for man to actually give birth himself. We will look later at the extraordinary interferences now becoming common in what normally should be a straight-forward process, ranging from last-minute pressure to accept epidurals which make women unconscious of sensation in their bodies below the waist, thus denying them much of the birth experience, to drips, hormones, monitoring systems, etc., all officially intended to ease the birth and to ensure the safety of the babies, but which are in fact totally unnecessary in the great majority of cases.[2] I remember some years back an American nurse telling me rather flippantly how the gynaecologist she worked for, whose 'birthing day' was Thursday, went each week down the line of his mothers-to-be pop-popping membranes to ensure conformity with his appointments schedule. This attempt to take over on an unprecedented scale what until recently has been a purely female business is apparently on the wane in America, but in Britain it has become frighteningly 'normal'. I personally needed unexpected help at the birth of both my children, which took place in a celebrated teaching hospital, and I shall never cease to be grateful for the expertise available to me, but while it is unquestionably true there is a strong case to be made out for having babies – especially first babies – in hospital within reach of emergency aid, all that most women will need from that hospital is a small room, a proper bed, a good, preferably familiar midwife, family and/or friends around her, and further medical expertise within bleep call a couple of minutes away.

The truth is that men have to come to terms with the fact that they are not indispensable to women's well-being; as women are changing, so must men too unless they want to find themselves out in the cold – straight as well as lesbian women are finding themselves more at home in the company of other women than in the company of males who are unwilling to let go of old habits of behaviour. The minority of women who are lesbian certainly do not consider their children's need for male models to be much of a problem: those I interviewed mostly had a number of male friends, often gay, who in a few cases had agreed to be the father of their children, and on whom the lesbians were partly relying to broaden the social background of their single families. As these women said, it would be all to the good that their children would grow up knowing a less aggressive kind of man than the standard head-of-family stereotype they are typically presented with in their school books and on most television programmes.

Men must also face the fact that on the whole their influence on their children (unless it is positively malign, as in sexual or physical abuse) has not been as powerful as they might like to imagine. For one thing, most fathers are rarely around, and even where both parents work the mother is still almost invariably the primary caretaker. Interestingly, it has been shown that daughters in particular can gain from growing up in a household without men: '. . . the single-parent mother-headed family may be a spur to occupational achievement in girls. Hunt and Hunt have found that girls in father-absent families are freed from the ideal-typical female socialization. These families establish a new type of female role model, blurring the traditional distinction between male and female roles and the instrumental/expressive division of labour by sex, because mothers are performing both roles and both types of tasks. Thus, father absence, in conjunction with modifications of the mother role, may remove some of the conventional barriers to female occupation aspirations and achievement. When girls are not socialized into sharply differentiated sex roles, they may be freed from the traditional restraints of female achievements.'[3]

What has given today's women the courage and the strength to try new ways of living has been the support of other women. Every mother I spoke to stressed how important some form of extended family is, whether it be blood-related or more often groups of friends who can be relied on to rally around or simply 'be there'. This type of mutual female support may have been traditional in the past, but in the nuclear family in which most of us were raised it has become rare and is only now being restored, a happy result of the consciousness-raising of the last decade or so. A doctor I talked to spoke of a professional acquaintance of hers who had a child when she was 38: 'She's cracked up, she hasn't anybody in the world to help her. The child is now about 8, and the mother had a breakdown because she was worn out, exhausted. There were friends, but no really close friends. There's another friend of mine, a single mother also, who had problems – they're the same sort of age group – and because they're my generation they're very much alone, they don't have the really close female friends that younger women seem to have.'

People need people, and since the sexual urge is pretty strong sexual politics will not prevent heterosexuals from forming couples and, temporarily at least, families. This is why I stated earlier that I don't think the future of the family is threatened, always provided – and this is a big caveat – that men as well as women are prepared to look afresh at themselves and at how successful families are formed. In the past people married each other, and sooner or later, without much thought, families just 'happened'; with today's almost automatic divorces they can 'unhappen' just as easily. Nothing can be taken for granted any more. If the traditional family dies out, it won't be solely because a number of independent women have broken the mould.

The nuclear family

Jenny, 22 years old with a small son, who found living in an isolated country cottage with her lover and her baby intolerable, said, 'We were living together; it was just as though we were married – though I was only 19 when I got pregnant and certainly was not going to get married to anyone then! – and I think I had to go through the experience of living in a little nuclear family set-up and having a baby to discover that that wasn't what I wanted. I don't think I could have found that out without actually doing it. I might eventually have settled into that pattern if I hadn't had a child so quickly, I don't know. I've still got such a lot to learn about myself, who I am.'

'*Will you have more children?*'

'I might in about ten years' time when I'm 30, maybe!'

Although the nuclear family has come under attack from many quarters, not without justification, one of the main charges aimed at new-type single mothers is that they are leading society towards the break-up of the family. Specialist in child psychology, *Rosa*, a very politically conscious woman, insists, 'Many of the other mothers in our group wanted to stop working when they had babies and become typical Dutch matrons, but for me having a child by myself is an alternative for the family way of having a child, and for me it is a political choice. It is not that I want to break up the family way, but as a feminist I think we have to change the way the family is now, with men doing *this* and women doing *that*. I want to give positive information about having children *without marrying*, *not* without having men around – that's not my intention – but to raise up children with more than the biological mother or father or both. I am arguing all the time that I want to break up the isolation of the family. It worries me, children being brought up isolated in small houses or flats, no grandparents, not many grown-ups and children around them. I grew up in a village and there were so many other people always, neighbours and relations and the parents of my friends: I think that's good. I want my child to notice other people and to know people who have different lives from mine.'

We are so used to the idea of families consisting of mother, father and two children that we tend to forget this grouping is a comparatively new phenomenon. When I asked anthropologist Janet Proctor if she thought the human habit of settling in families was innate or learned behaviour, and how far women's desire to have children was biological or socially conditioned, she said, 'When you ask me "is something biological?" I will always look at it from the species level. I'm not just talking from a Western Judeo-Christian point of view. You've got to take a much broader picture than contemporary modern industrialized Britain and America. A family consisting of a monogamous male, female and children isn't at all the norm, it's class and race-specific, something that comparatively few people have experienced. You've been talking about extended families and support groups as though they are a new thing, but it's not such an experiment – it's always been happening within a community framework since back before chimpanzees! No, the nuclear family is not the common species pattern, even in the contemporary world.'

So the changes we are going to be exploring in greater depth in the following chapters are not so much revolutionary as a reversion to an older pattern, a way of life that is in fact the norm amongst many of our contemporaries. This will give comfort to some, and appal others who for some reason apparently feel that all is well with this deeply disturbed twentieth century of ours. Progress is our keyword: retrogression has to be bad. Doesn't it?

But how did it start, this single-parent-by-choice business? New movements appear to be spontaneously generated, but behind the scenes early pioneers can always be traced, the unheralded originators of change. How far back do we go? There are plenty of women who have defied convention throughout the ages and borne illegitimate children with joy and love, but for our purposes I think we must draw the line at the arrival of the period when contraception became commonly available, giving to women a genuine choice which they did not have before.

Early pioneers and the gradual change in society's expectations

Between the two world wars one way out of the dilemma facing an unmarried woman who wanted both to have a child and yet to stay respectable was to adopt. Margaret Wood, now in her late forties, was adopted as a baby by the matron and owner of a maternity nursing home. Because of her mother's class and the societal expectations of the time, together with the fact that she was a practising Catholic, it had always been out of the question for her to consider having a child any other way, and she was 54 before she finally took the plunge of adopting a baby. Even then, Margaret feels, there must have been many difficult moments for her mother: 'I don't know what she went through, we never discussed it. But I do remember very occasionally when I would call her Mummy – of course she was known as Miss – people would go sort of "oh, your *mother*!" and there'd be a few raised eyebrows.' She seems to have been the kind of woman who today might well have become a single parent by choice: 'I simply don't think she ever wanted to be married. There was someone killed in the war, but it wasn't just that – she was already 30 by then, and she'd been a volunteer nurse in the trenches out in Belgium. She was just a straightforward, independent woman who felt she had something to give a child. She thought about it very clear-headedly, and eventually she went ahead and adopted.'

Wyn Knowles, who was editor of BBC's highly respected 'Woman's Hour' for many years, points out that social conventions were very different in the 1940s. 'In London there weren't so many outlets for getting to know people, especially for well-brought up young Catholic girls like me. In those days it was very much a matter of waiting until men approached you, there was no question of openly engineering a meeting, which would be thought very "fast" and forward. It was a question of waiting by the telephone if you met somebody, rather than you ringing them up. But change was coming fast. *Sonia*, who worked in publishing and was also a translator, fell in love with an Israeli artist and had no qualms about having a child outside marriage. It was the early 1960s, and conventional morality was loosening up, but for most people illegitimacy still remained something to be hushed up. 'I myself had no shame at all about having an illegitimate child – among my friends it was nothing so marvellous – but it wasn't so easy for my mother's generation to accept it. My mother herself was fine, though underneath I think she felt a bit unhappy, but I had a letter from a friend of hers whom I cared for, saying that I must think of the child, it would be a bastard and so on – this was twenty years ago, after all. Attitudes were still pretty Victorian in many ways then.'

The changing mores of the swinging sixties began with the more 'advanced' set, as they once would have been called – trendy photographers, writers, film stars. Vanessa Redgrave's name came up again and again amongst people I talked to about that period. *Frances*, who runs an art gallery in North-West America, says, 'It was being done then, it certainly wasn't unheard of. I mean, Vanessa Redgrave and other well-known people were doing it. My mother was terrified of telling her own mother that I was pregnant, but when she did my grandmother's response was, well, if Vanessa Redgrave can do it, so can Frances!' Their parents' reactions often surprised these mothers, then as now. Frances is still amused by one incident. 'I come from the New York area, and my parents had an experience that could only happen there. They love me, and they've put up with a fair number of my changes in good spirit. They reel back, then they come forward and support me, so they took the news well. They liked and admired the father, and they knew I could support a child on my own, and though they kept checking that I really knew what I was doing they accepted it. So one day they ran into a woman, who'd known me from a child, in a line at the movie theatre, and this woman said, how is your daughter? and they said fine, she's having a baby. This woman said, oh, I didn't know she'd got married again, and my parents said well no, she didn't, and the woman was somewhat dumbfounded – she wasn't horrified, she just stopped in her tracks. The next morning, the very first thing in the morning, my mother received a phone call from this woman who calls to assure her that she wasn't at all disapproving of my choice to have a child, in fact she thought it was the most courageous thing, they must be very proud to have such a courageous daughter, etc. etc. I said, mother, only in New York do you get points for having a divorced, unwed pregnant daughter!'

Wyn Knowles, running daily hour-long BBC programmes devoted to subjects of particular interest to women, remarked that more and better contraception resulted in 'a definite revolution in the 1960s' attitudes, and certainly we were able to be more daring in our programme (just as women's magazines were) about what we could discuss, and what advice could be given. There'd be great discussions about what should you do if you discovered your daughter was sleeping with her boyfriend, or what you should do when they came for the weekend – did you give them single rooms or what? Yes, we did get a certain amount of flak from older listeners whenever we did anything about sex, naturally you got shock-horror reactions, but it tailed off. We didn't do much on people like Vanessa Redgrave, though; we found that when the subject of unmarried mothers came up we'd get a pile of disapproving letters from people who'd say there are lots of couples who'd like to have a baby and can't, that it was self-indulgent to do it, and it was bound to be bad for the baby.'

This reaction is still common, and as we will see later selfishness and self-indulgence is an accusation thrown as freely at women who are married and who decide not to have children as at women who are unmarried and who *do* have children. Few people will label a married mother who is having difficulties coping with her present children selfish or self-indulgent when she gets pregnant yet again, though they may call her stupid, yet the resultant child will be infinitely more at risk than the kind we are discussing. It is fairly clear that these negative reactions are primarily based on a fear of society's current structure being undermined, rather than on open-minded compassion and concern for any particular child's welfare.

Stephanie, an American psychoanalyst and therapist, says that even at the end of the 1970s her friends were trying to talk her out of bearing a child. 'I thought about adopting, and I had pursued that idea quite seriously up to the point where I almost got a child from India. I wasn't comfortable with the idea of doing it alone – nice Jewish girls just don't go around getting pregnant out of wedlock!' Pressure is put on women from all directions to conform. There is still a strong media bias towards the image of the 'normal' family, and though there is now a general acceptance that many people are choosing to live together without legal recognition of their conjugal status, on the whole the media continues to assume a basis of mummy, daddy and children for their average family, ignoring the existence of huge numbers of single-parent families, whether they be a result of divorce, separation, unintended or deliberate illegitimacy.

For instance, at the time of writing the BBC is producing a series of sex education programmes for primary schoolchildren. In the 1970s a programme dealing with sex made for a similar audience resulted in a flood of outraged comment, VD clinics being anticipated for 12-year-olds. The new version apparently pulls very few punches indeed, showing full colour childbirth, nudist families enjoying themselves on a beach instead of posed art class nudes in order to demonstrate physical differences between the sexes in a naturalistic way, etc., and yet still there is an apparently unquestioned assumption that all children grow up in a standard family containing a mother, father, etc., though marriage is no longer necessarily implied. Mrs Mary Whitehouse, notorious for her attacks on demonstrations of ideas she considers morally unsound, 'was angry in the early years [of the sex programmes] that marriage and wedding rings were not firmly to the fore, but the BBC has always stood fast, saying the programmes are purely factual and in no way a social commentary. All the same, there are no one-parent families [in these new programmes] as they say teachers did not want them, and all the children are shown in happy, loving homes.'[4]

It is possible that in this very rapid summary I am

giving the impression I regard the changes in society about which I have written as being easily achievable, and even that they are already established to a considerable extent. This is obviously untrue: people in general kick as violently as they know how against any alteration in society's normal pattern which affects them personally, and here we are dealing with a fundamental transformation of female/male relationships and the structure of the family. Changes *are* happening, there is no turning back the wheel of time, but although on the surface social mores may transmute comparatively quickly, it takes far longer to overcome psychological barriers stemming from early family experiences in childhood.[5]

Between the beginning and the end of a period of change confusion is inevitable. We are living through a time when sex roles are no longer clearly defined. For some years now it has not always been easy to tell at a quick glance who is a boy and who is a girl, but though girls may wear unisex clothing and boys may dye their hair there are certain differences which cannot be ignored, although which these are may not be the ones we thought we cared about. Many automatic assumptions about ourselves and our sexual relationships have been abandoned. Certain expectations that even my generation were still brought up on – for instance, that you would find the perfect man (Mr Right to my mother's generation), marry him and have the perfect family – have been discarded except in romantic literature (the popularity of which, incidentally, should not be ignored, for a continuing myth such as this exhibits a deep desire which I suspect most of us still secretly subscribe to).

More and more women are accepting that the perfect man isn't going to turn up, so they go ahead without him, hoping optimistically they will produce the perfect family all the same. People will argue that you cannot have a 'family' at all without two parents, and we will look at this point later, but in my researches what has come through strongly to me is that recently there has arisen a new kind of child-centredness that is not reliant on the old-type full-time mother/part-time father family. Whether or not we worked, I and my friends were perpetually conscious of John Bowlby and his book *Child Care and the Growth of Love*; we brought up our children in the fear that we would harm our children if we didn't give them virtually every minute of our time, our attention, suppressing our own needs for the good of the child. This new generation is wiser – it knows full well that while a happy mother makes a happy child, a frustrated mother bored to tears over the sink may conscientously give her child twenty-four hours a day of her time, but if she does it is likely the child will grow up as neurotic as she is rapidly becoming herself.

There has developed, though, a kind of casualness in relationships that may or may not be a good thing. It can imply a lack of maturity, an inability to commit oneself to another because the concept of the self is still rather shaky, or it may imply the opposite, a strong sense of the self and a need to protect one's own 'space'. This casualness need not preclude a deep sense of caring and even commitment. Note the apparent casualness of *Mary's* description of how she decided to go ahead and get pregnant. Mary, a nurse who works in a children's nursery with newborn babies, has a child nearly 2 years old, and is clearly a devoted mother. She had always wanted children and had assumed she would have them early, just as her mother had. 'No, it wasn't social pressure – I've always had a very strong maternal instinct, I was always taking care of little babies whenever I could. I'd thought several times about having artificial insemination if I didn't find a man, and by the time I was in my mid-twenties – I don't know whether to call it the sexual revolution or whether it was just the feel of the country – I felt that when the time was right it wouldn't be such a big deal. When the first test-tube baby was born I thought, well, twenty years ago they would never have been able to do that; even if they could have done it scientifically they just wouldn't have dared actually do it, people would have gone nuts. So I thought, give it another few years, and I'm just not going to have to worry about what people think: by the time it comes to tell my kid how he was conceived it's not going to be such an unusual thing anyway. I wasn't giving up the idea of marriage, you understand, having a big family and all that, but I thought, OK, I'll give myself till 30, and if I'm not married then I will have an alternative. And that's just what I did.'

Now the change in social mores has arrived. It is no longer social death to be an unwed mother. Part-time researcher *Charlotte*: 'On the contrary – I found almost that it's so right on to be a single mother that I'm almost too proud of it! I find myself going around telling people they ought to do it, I'm so happy about it all, and I think that's rather dangerous because people might rush into it without thinking properly about it, just because it's suddenly the thing to do. No, in hospital and clinics nobody expressed any disapproval, in fact I got far more disapproval when I had an abortion years ago – then I remember one gynaecologist saying to me, how can you be so stupid, when there are women in this hospital with real illnesses and here you are wasting our time. *That* was awful.'

Some statistics on single parenting

Statistics can prove anything and nothing: later we will examine the available statistics on working mothers, one-parent families, children born out of wedlock, etc., but here are just a few indicating a remarkable social change. In America the new Census Bureau study shows that there are twice as many women having a child or being pregnant before marriage as there were at the end of the Second World War, and as many as 38.5 per cent of babies born to women under 20 were illegitimate.[6] The US Department of Health and Human Services showed that in 1980 an increase in out-of-wedlock births, which had risen by a record 11.4 per cent, was due to 'the substantial rise in the rate of single white women – 17.6 per cent'.[7] In Britain the Office of Population Censuses and Surveys reported that in the years 1979-81 10.4 per cent of families were headed by a lone mother, and 1.5 per cent by a lone father. Of these lone mothers, 2.2 per cent were single.[8] Between 1971 and 1981 the number of one-parent families rose by some 71 per cent.[9]

The accusation is frequently thrown at single mothers with careers that you can't both be a proper mother and have a career. Thus not only are the vast numbers of single mothers who don't have careers but who work at any job they can get because they have to ignored or condemned, but also huge numbers of 'properly' married women. In Britain ten million women are currently paid workers – this is 40 per cent of the work force. Of these 56 per cent work full-time and 44 per cent part-time, most of the last being mothers with young children.[10] The researchers of this particular study found that it was the norm for women to work before and after having children, thus demolishing the idea that it is a peculiar selfishness of single mothers by choice to work as well as enjoying motherhood. In America the situation is similar: more than half of all married women are working as against 30 per cent a generation ago. 'The figures for married women with children under 6 are even more striking: almost 19 per cent in 1960, close to 45 per cent in 1980.'[11] However, the recession is taking its toll: the latest HMSO General Household Survey shows that whereas in 1979 the proportion of couples where both husband and wife worked was 58 per cent, by 1982 it had fallen to 53 per cent. The situation is similar in all the countries I have examined.

In any case, comparisons between single families and standard families are becoming more and more meaningless as the divorce rates rise (one in two in America, one in three in Great Britain). One way or another, the difficulties of working while raising children affect most people nowadays, not least in basic day-to-day problems like how to get little Sarah or Johnny to and from school. 'Almost half of the nation's children will spend at least part of their early years in one-parent homes. . . . Yet most schools are still structured around traditional styles of family living. They haven't budged from bankers' hours that pose problems for working single parents' (A quote from the *New York Times*, 7 January 1979).

Is social class or race relevant?
Having a child out of wedlock is no longer a class-related activity – it is occurring in all layers of society, though to do

it quite deliberately – at present, at any rate – does seem to be primarily a middle-class choice. Anthropologist Janet Proctor added to her comment on the nuclear family: 'the phenomena you're talking about is class and race-specific, that it's a luxury for middle and upper-middle-class professional women, white, to decide to have children in the absence of a conventional family. But if you look at black women here in the States this is not unique at all. Though it's very complicated here because if a poor black American woman does get married she's going to miss out on certain benefits she'd get otherwise.'

Social welfare benefits, such as council housing, also play a similar role in Britain. In both countries there is a tradition of young black women bearing children before they marry – if they marry at all – which means that the question of social stigma does not arise in their own communities. Obviously social pressure wields an enormous influence on how people of any class or race behave. Girls from white working-class families probably still receive less education about contraception than their middle-class counterparts, but if they get pregnant the pressure on them to marry is profound. *Laura*, herself a black unwed mother, said, 'I hate to say this, but I think having a child by choice is very much a class thing. Like the women's movement in Britain was a very middle-class, educated thing, I think the single mothers' movement will be the same, along with the ones who would have done it anyway, the 17, 18-year-olds who get into a mess and don't realize what they're doing. I don't think among the working class you're going to find much of it, because they are brought up with the ethic that you leave school, you get married, you have your 2.2 [sic] children, your Ford Escort and so on. In their family they'd be looked down upon, they'd be totally isolated, and I don't think they'd do it. I find the shock/horror of my situation has come mainly from the working-class women I know, of my own generation too. But all the intellectuals say, oh, it's wonderful, it's fantastic!'

Dr Elphis Christopher, family planner and psycho-sexual counsellor, says, 'Most of the women I work with are in the lower socio-economic groups, and they've not really chosen to have babies in quite that way. They've often gone into relationships hoping they would work out, and if it doesn't then the baby may be the thing that's salvaged out of it. They may get themselves pregnant hoping to keep the man, but when he abandons them they're left with the child, which can produce quite enormous problems all round.' Pat Verity, who runs a state-owned day nursery: 'The younger mums using this nursery are people who are perhaps emotionally immature and are looking for emotional security, and they've been involved with somebody hoping for a loving relationship and it's failed, but they've got a baby out of it who they hope will love *them*. They just don't realize how demanding a baby is, how much you've got to give *them* and love *them*. I don't think they get deliberately pregnant, or if they do it's subconscious, it's more that they're looking for some loving affection because very often they're deprived in that area, and a baby is what they end up with.'

   The understanding of the class aspect of single parenting by choice is important, because people have sometimes said to me, why are you only looking at middle-class mothers? The reason is that it is almost entirely middle-class mothers I am told about – middle-class not necessarily by birth but by virtue of their education or what they have done with their own lives since they left school. What daddy did isn't the point – it is what they have done with themselves and who they have become that counts. Lenore Weitzman in her book *Sex Role Socialization* clarifies the American position with regard to the influence of class, and her comments hold true for Britain also. 'All the studies have found that persons in the higher social classes tend to be less rigid about sex distinctions.' Lower-class families are more conscious of the different roles the two sexes will later be expected to play, are more traditional than middle-class families and differentiate sex roles earlier. By the time working-class boys were 4 or 5 years old, they knew which toys were meant for boys and which were meant for girls, whereas middle-class boys did not have the same awareness until they were 6. 'Middle-class parents may encourage "traditional feminine behaviour" in their daughters, but they also encourage a degree of independence and assertiveness.' They don't mind their daughters being tomboys, and are glad to see them successful both in sports and in their studies. 'Lower-class parents are more likely to view such interests and achievements as "too masculine" and to discourage them. . . . In summary, then, middle-class parents are interested in seeing both their sons and their daughters develop a greater range of traits along both instrumental and expressive lines. In contrast, blue-collar parents encourage traditional sex role behaviour in both boys and girls.'[12]

This quotation shows fairly conclusively how much more difficult it would be for someone from a lower-class background to set out deliberately to break conventions which she had been brought up to respect, and that a girl with that kind of determination is probably in any case going to end up with the sort of career that will earn her, by the time she chooses maternity, the label of 'middle-class', regardless of her social origin. Obviously I have been talking in generalizations, and there will be exceptions; more to the point for the future is the probably inevitable fact that as single parenting by choice becomes more accepted generally, so will the lower socio-economic groups accept behaviour from their daughters that at present would distress them deeply.

A few notes about the mothers

When I talked to single mothers who had deliberately chosen maternity, what became obvious to me in the great majority of cases was that these were women who understood themselves pretty well. And the recurrent message they gave me to pass on to women who were considering whether or not to have a child was that the prime essential is to know yourself, to know who you are. That it's not on to have a child just for your own comfort – better go out and buy a puppy. At this point I do not want to look in depth at the personalities of the mothers I have interviewed, but I would like to clarify a few issues.

The 'puppy syndrome' is one accusation that is often thrown in one form or another at these mothers, usually by people who never query the reasons why *married* couples have children. Psychologist Hendrika Vande Kemp, who works in the Child Development Clinic of the Fuller Theological Seminary, and who had given the matter of parenthood a great deal of thought, admits to a bias because of her own profound religious beliefs, but her viewpoint represents that of large sections of the community. 'It's inappropriate for mothers to get their nurturing needs met by the child, and I see this happening often. You say that most of these women have careers so that they don't have to depend on their children in the way that a mother living alone at home might, but a career does not and cannot meet your nurturing needs. I don't think that having a career, and knowing who you are and all that, meets your relational needs, your nurturing needs. You cannot be whole apart from a relationship. Now that's a special bias I have, but that reflects my theological and theoretical thinking, that there is no such thing as a self-actualized person apart from relationships. I'm talking personally as well as professionally – I'd very much like to have a child myself, but there is no way I'd do it outside of marriage. So if I don't meet the right man. . . ,' she shrugs ruefully. 'It's painful, but it's what I believe. I think it has to be a question of whether you are dependent on your kids or another adult; you can't be dependent on yourself – that's a fallacy. That's the pop psychology of the sixties, the fallacy of finding who you are, of doing your own thing. Ultimately the Christian point of view is a relational one – I don't know it necessarily says you have to be married, but you have to be in significant relationships, you have to have a significant relationship with an adult male or female. It doesn't have to be sexual, you can be a fairly healthy fulfilled person without having sexual relationships.'

This view is countered by psychologist Karin Meiselman, who paradoxically is happily married with two children. 'It's kind of axiomatic in my clinical practice with women that I subscribe to the belief that one *can* be alone, that one can be perfectly OK, in a very good state, without having one central relationship or being married. When I work with women I strongly emphasize the proposition that you can prefer to have a central relationship, you can like that and be looking for it, without feeling that you drastically need it, that you must have it or you'll collapse. I think that to have a close, intimate committed relationship is important, it's something most people want, and when you're fortunate enough to find it it's very gratifying. At the same time I think it's extremely important for people to live by the principle that they don't have to have that, that it would be nice if they could get it, it might be their first choice, but that they could easily live with their second choice. You can live long periods of your life while not having a committed relationship without feeling you have to go out and desperately seek one, and perhaps fall into something bad. It's very imporant for people to feel whole and fulfilled without necessarily having their first choice.'

She went on to make a further point which I think is fundamental to why I have been so favourably impressed with the attitude of most of the mothers I have met (though in fairness to Dr Kemp I must add that many have retained a 'significant' relationship either with the father or, in the case of two sets of lesbian couples I interviewed, with a partner with whom they are sharing care of the child): 'In the sort of situation you're looking at, I assume that most of the women are starting out from a position of strength. They've purposely chosen to add a child to their life, it's not like they're starting out single parenthood by being deserted by a husband or left unwillingly an unwed mother, or something like that. There are a whole lot of single-parent families where the person is hurting from a ruptured relationship, and what you're looking at seems to me to be very different, that the mother is a person whose life is already pretty well together.'

Another charge often laid at these mothers' doors is that if they haven't been able to make a lasting intimate relationship with a man, they can't expect to make a sound relationship with a child. The *New York* magazine quotes psychologist Martin Cohen as saying, 'A mother's relationship with a child should not be confused with that of a mate. These are distinct roles that tap entirely different areas of strength. A relationship with a man is based on issues like power, sex, and sharing. Some women may have emotional problems that make it difficult for them to cope with those particular demands, but that doesn't mean they're not ready for parenting.'[13]

The mother/child relationship must have a different meaning for women than for men, because they have the physical possibility of becoming a copy of their mother, of carrying and giving birth to their own child, thereby becoming in one sense the primary figure of the mother that has remained part of their internal being, replacing their own internalized mother with their own enhanced self. It isn't necessary to become a mother in order to grow up, but it is certainly a great help. It was our own mother who first gave us care and love, 'with whom we form a symbiotic bond within which we do not yet know self from other. For each of us, whether a girl or a boy, it is a woman who is in this primary position in our inner life – a woman who is the object of our most profound attachment, a woman who becomes our first loved other.'[14] If the relationship with the mother has been a reasonably good one, then she will have, as Cohen says, many strengths to lean on when she herself produces a child. Becoming a mother forces you to grow, to become less selfish, less self-centred. For many of today's women, learning how to share ungrudgingly with a man is a very difficult process, not least because of a new awareness of the need to protect one's own 'space' if one is to continue to grow into a true maturity. Since men are facing the same problem, it is not to be wondered at that many of the women with whom I have talked have told me that while, before motherhood, they found it impossible to maintain a deep relationship with any of the men they met, now they find they are less demanding, more ready to share and to accept compromise. This does not mean a lowering of standards, only an adult acceptance that a 'perfect' partner does not come ready-made, that a great deal of work has to be done before two people can learn how to live together in real harmony without either sacrificing their individuality.

It is, incidentally, interesting that women seem to be able to cope better than men with living alone. Current research shows that single women live longer, have healthier lives, both physically and mentally, than married women, but exactly the reverse is true for men. When spouses die a widow's life span remains the same as it would have been, but a man's health and well-being is likely to deteriorate rapidly if he does not quickly remarry.[15] Women are resilient creatures, and the rewards of having a child, when it has been chosen and wanted, more than outweigh the problems and weariness that single parenthood inevitably brings.

Even so, all the mothers agree that to do it entirely alone without any kind of support would be intolerable. Support groups of some kind are an essential, and we will be looking closely at these, but part-time researcher *Charlotte*, who admits to 'being dotty about my baby', sums up the necessity: 'The main general problem is that it's rather a spiritual burden, having the responsibility for the whole thing yourself, basically being mother and father in one, earner and sole carer at the same time. It's a bit emotionally exhausting, carrying all the weight by yourself. You have to have someone you can share it with emotionally, someone you can ring up any time of day or night. Otherwise I think you'd be very lonely indeed, you'd have much more worry if you've no one to share it with. For me, it's my family, my parents and my sisters – for some mothers it's close friends. The main thing is there has to be someone you can unburden on to.'

Also, not all women have had the 'reasonably good' relationship with their mothers that I have just written about. For such mothers there can be a certain amount of danger in having children, though this would apply as equally to married as to unmarried women. A happy, secure background with two caring parents is a less common start to life than many people like to imagine; child abuse of one sort or another is only too frequent, in comfortably off homes as well as in impoverished ones.[16,17] Jessica Curtis, President of the *Single Mothers by Choice* group, was herself abused emotionally as a child. 'I was abandoned several times – I didn't suffer any physical deprivation, but my father left my mother when she was pregnant, my mother left me in the care of my aunt which wasn't so good, then my grandmother took me away for a year from when I was 6 months to 18 months and I didn't see my mother at all, then I went to a foster mother for three years and I only saw my mother on Saturdays during the day. After that I lived with her, but then she married a really abusive guy – a scary guy. He didn't raise his hand to me but he was just real scary – I had to live with that for eleven years. So I knew when I had a baby that I was at risk. It's one of the reasons I have people around me so that if I start going off the deep end they can point it out, because alone I wouldn't necessarily notice it. I have trouble maintaining informal support systems, so I have formal ones, like this household I live in' (Jessica owns her house and has various people sharing it with her), 'and the Single Mothers group. I feel that abuse happens mainly because you're at your wit's end, and I work very hard not to get there, not to over-stress myself. I enjoy my job, I'm not financially pressed, I've a lot of friends, and the group has a wonderful lot of women in it – if you met them you'd want every one of them for a friend.'

Without good models in their own lives, both of marriage and of parenting, women ought to make doubly sure that they know what they are doing before they embark either on marriage or on parenthood. Unfortunately few of us are properly prepared for the first, but that doesn't stop most of us from charging ahead – hence the appalling divorce rates. As for the second, at least – at present – single mothers by choice seem to be aware of what is going to be demanded of them. My fear, and one of the main reasons for writing this book, is that if the movement is commonly accepted without being fully understood, young, less mature women might leap into single parenthood as readily as they leap into marriage, with equally unfortunate results.

Single parenthood by choice versus marriage
There is a lot to be considered under this heading but, important as the subject is, it is not central to this book as for most single mothers the choice between single parenthood and marriage has never been a genuine option. And

this says a great deal for these particular women, for it is not that they haven't had their chances to marry but rather that they were not prepared to put a ring on their finger in order to achieve 'legitimate' pregnancy while knowing in their hearts that sooner or later the ring would be thrown away at the back of some drawer.

However, there are one or two points worth looking at in this opening summary. I take it for granted that few people would disagree with me that a child is highly advantaged if she or he is brought up in a happy home with two well-adjusted parents who love each other and their children, whose attitudes are open to change and who willingly let their children develop in their own way, giving minimum but sufficient guidance. But to assume that we are simply balancing such a model upbringing on the one hand against the admitted difficulties of coping single-handedly as a one-parent family on the other, is to grossly misrepresent the reality of 'normal' family life. During the lifetime of any family there are various stages of well-being, some of the stages being downright miserable in a great number of cases due to a whole variety of life events, such as unemployment, marital infidelities, death in the family, illness, boredom, etc.

Professor George Brown of Bedford College, whose work we will look at later in more detail, found in his well-known study on working-class women in Camberwell, London, that 42 per cent of those working-class mothers with children under 6 years of age were psychiatrically disturbed – that is to say that they suffered symptoms of depression severe enough to be classified as needing treatment if a psychiatrist were to examine them.[18] This is a frightening statistic, and it is true that as the children in the sample grew older the situation improved considerably, but the fact remains that marriage did not ensure contentment for these women. Nor does it for any of us. This is a trite statement, but it needs to be reiterated, because people when considering single parenthood by choice will insist on talking about marriage as though it is synonymous with general happiness and unimpaired growth all round, when all of us know perfectly well this is not so.

Even if such a state of bliss were possible, however, it

would not necessarily be best for the child. A child has to learn how to cope with life, with disappointments, anger, frustration – an adolescent brought up in Utopia and then exposed to life as it normally is would be sadly unprepared to deal with it. As Lillian Rubin writes in her wise and illuminating book *Intimate Strangers*,

there is no perfect parenting, no possibility of meeting and assuaging every anxiety a small child experiences. It's simply not in the nature of life, may not even be desirable . . . Such misguided attempts at protection may offer some momentary comfort, but they also deprive the child of the joy to be experienced in the developing independence, of the sense of safety that comes with knowing a self exists and can be relied on, of the pleasure of becoming acquainted with that emerging self.[19]

Typically single mothers by choice explore every issue of motherhood before they make their decision – how successful they will be in the long run in raising their children is too early to tell as yet, but in contrast to many married mothers they mostly enter their pregnancies as fully prepared as it is possible to be before the reality bursts upon them. And when they do have their children at least they will not be faced with the squabbles and tensions that often arise between married couples over the upbringing of their offspring. In fact it is often considerably easier to solve a problem alone than to have to battle against someone else who wants a different solution from yours! Sharing is not always all it is cracked up to be.

There is one aspect of marriage, though, that gives married partners a considerable advantage over single women, and that is that sex is regularly available. I had originally underestimated the problems some women have in conceiving, and had thought in terms of single women simply asking men to act as stud on one or two occasions, and hey presto! you had a pregnant mother. Of course it is not as simple as that, but it is not only the common physical problems which many men and women face in achieving pregnancy that can bedevil a single woman wanting to conceive – there is also the slightly weird fact that, for married and single women alike, the body can and does play its own subtle games. Just as married women, who after years of trying finally abandon attempts at pregnancy and arrange the adoption of a child, quite often find themselves pregnant after all, so several of the single mothers I interviewed told me that they had made repeated unsuccessful attempts to conceive, sometimes over a long period, but then one day – after an occasion when they hadn't planned it at all – they found themselves unexpectedly pregnant.

In any case, finding a man who is prepared to knowingly act simply as stud has proved an almost impossible task for most of these women – at least from among the men they would be prepared to accept as fathers for their children. As a result, artificial insemination was often resorted to – though sometimes it was chosen because of fear of possible legal complications over care of the child, or personal feelings about having sex with an uninvolved partner, or lesbianism – but even when such a choice has been made it is not necessarily easy for a single woman to persuade a doctor to inseminate her, and in some countries neither artificial insemination nor adoption is available to unmarried women.

I have quoted Dr Hendrika Vande Kemp's feelings about the morality of single parenthood as opposed to married parenthood from the point of view both of a psychiatrist and a practising Christian. The fact is that many ordinary people, men in particular, feel very uneasy about the subject regardless of whether or not they are religious. At some level they are deeply uncomfortable with the idea, and how much this is due to unconsidered prejudice or to an unwillingness to move with the times, and how much they are drawing on some kind of instinctive wisdom, is impossible to say. Dr Raimond Gaita, lecturer in philosophy at King's College, London, whose main interest is moral ethics, expressed to me his own uneasiness: 'One of the things we've learned over the last twenty years, surely, is that the kinds of thoughts that people had which have led to so many broken-down marriages – thoughts like wouldn't it be better for the children if we were divorced rather than going on living together miserably as mum and dad did, etc. – such thoughts haven't led to more happiness, have they?

That's why I think we ought to be sceptical about claims that say, wouldn't it be a happier world if we did such and such. You ask wouldn't it be better to be the child of a single parent than having to go through an ugly divorce and all the miseries of that, wouldn't it be better to grow up free of the possibility of that pain? Of course they'll be free of *that* pain, but it's easy enough to see other things in their life which will cause them just as much pain. We ought to be more cautious about these things; we ought, for God's sake, to learn a bit from experience.' True enough: when you are considering embarking on the amazing adventure of bringing a new life into the world, caution and a great deal of thought are surely the first essentials, whatever your marital status might be.

A taste of the reality
The reality of single parenthood depends almost entirely on whether or not it was voluntary. Where a career is being planned around the possibility that one day one or even two children may have to be supported by it, flexibility of hours as well as the amount of money which will need to be earned have to be considered. Quite a few of the American mothers I met had organized their lives around the intention of eventually becoming pregnant with or without a living-in mate, and they had chosen careers like nursing, psychiatry or the law as being compatible with that idea. Few of the British women had done so, probably because it is only recently that independent-minded (not necessarily feminist) women have accepted the idea that single motherhood can go hand in hand with a worthwhile career. Nevertheless most of them are managing to earn a living and achieve a reasonable standard of life for themselves and their children.

The problems for mothers who are not in this happy position are poignantly illustrated by Pat Verity who was explaining to me how difficult it is to make young trainee assistants in her state-run day nursery appreciate the strains on the women who leave their children with them. 'They don't understand that in the morning these young single mums have to get up sharp on time, though perhaps they've been up half the night with the child, a toddler who's teething, or perhaps an 18-month-old who won't sleep, who keeps coming all night long into her room – she has to get up, give that child some breakfast, get it dressed, then just misses the bus as she gets to the corner. It's raining, they wait and eventually get on the next bus, and when they arrive here the staff cannot understand that they've only got three minutes to get out of here because they're late already, it's not their fault they're late, and they know that they daren't be very late for work because it's their job, so they push the children in through the door sometimes because they're so upset, and the staff say, why are they like this, it's awful! But I say, yes, it seems so, but now they've got to catch another bus, and they're probably going to miss it if they don't hurry, the 311 will have gone, so they rush out and hope. . . . Then in the evening when they arrive to collect the child they've already had to wait for ages for a bus, terrified they won't get here by half past five when officially we close, and then the child's difficult because mum's come late and they're tired and don't want to have their coat put on and they don't want to go, so mum feels totally rejected by this lovely child whom they've got to get home. But then they've got to do everything in reverse, go out and wait for another bus, it's still raining, so what time are they going to get home, and when are they going to get supper. . . ! The strains are tremendous, and I think that applies to any class, but obviously more so to people who may be doing a job that is not so fulfilling to themselves, maybe some menial job somewhere like loading up laundry trolleys in a hospital which is tiring and frustrating, but they haven't any choice because they need the money. And there's all sorts of short-cuts you can't afford to take if you haven't money, like the more expensive sort of nappies, and you can't get a take-away on the way home because you can't afford it. They're caught in this trap, and they're worn out by it.'

The picture that part-time researcher *Charlotte* presents is very different. She deliberately chose to have her child, just manages with part-time editing and a little occasional parental help to run a tiny flat and to pay for baby-sitting so that she can do her work. 'It's all wonderful, it's lovely – I've never regretted it for a moment. To begin with, after she was born, it was very like what I imagine a very very nice love affair must be like. We were absolutely absorbed in each other, and it was totally self-sufficient. Obviously there were mistakes and bad things, but there were always little things I look back on as being markers that it was going to be all right. I don't mean I fell in love with her, I just felt terribly happy and relieved, right from the birth. Breast-feeding was lovely and I went on with it until she was 15 months old. I think I was rather a bore with it, I was always getting out my breast and sticking the baby on it, hoping to impress people, I suppose – I was rather proud how well it was going' (she chuckles warmly all through telling this). 'It was the interaction between us that was so nice – the fact that she was there and I was here and yet we were absolutely together, and that sort of physical joining was an expression of how I felt about her, that she was part of me. And I knew of course it would come to an end, that she'd grow away from me, but what has happened is that the physical closeness has been replaced by a mental closeness. Now already she's learning to run away from me in the park, for instance, and she's not so close to me – sometimes she doesn't even want to be cuddled. But that's fine too: she's becoming a more complicated being and so therefore you can't always rely on the old hug to do the work.'

The dangers of over-closeness in this kind of relationship are obvious, but all the mothers are aware of this and their intention is to be strong-minded enough to let go when the time comes. After all, letting go seems to be just as much a problem for many married mothers, judging by my personal experience both as a daughter and a mother, and from all the recent literature on the mother/daughter relationship.[20] But again, who expects anything really worthwhile in life to come without some effort? The renewed closeness after a necessary break between mother and offspring can be quite as beautiful as that original joy.

Charlotte's happiness is not marred by any bad memories of her relationship with her baby's father. Languages teacher *Sarah*, who unlike most of the mothers I met, had originally hoped to make a permanent relationship with the father of her child, feels less contented. 'No, there was never any point when I actually wanted to be a single mother, I always wanted to share the joy of having a child with a partner. The unhappy side of what is unquestionably a lovely relationship with my daughter is that there is no male here to be the missing link, because there *is* a missing link. I don't regret her, of course I don't, but I do regret meeting *him*. If I hadn't met him I would probably have met somebody else and I would have had a proper family with him, and there would have been another Sophie.' This regret is permanently with Sarah, and it is not difficult to foresee that there are likely to be more emotional difficulties ahead for her than for the great majority of the other mothers I interviewed who had made a positive choice to do it alone.

Finally, returning to the joys of motherhood, I want to end with two irresistible quotations from Ann Oakley's book *Becoming a Mother*. One is from a married mother and one is from a cohabiting mother, but their feelings about their babies were echoed by every single mother by choice I spoke to: 'I didn't think I could feel so *passionately* about something. I'd always assumed that if I had a baby I'd love it, but I never thought I would actually feel like I do about it. If someone said cut your arm off otherwise something would happen to her you'd do it. It's a different sort of love from, say, you feel for your parents or your husband. I didn't realize I could feel so deeply about something. I look at her sometimes and think – I don't know how to describe it really. . . .' 'A few weeks ago I was just feeding her and I suddenly was sort of overwhelmed with love for her and I thought . . . this is what life is about. . . . I've always wanted to be a mother: I wanted a family and I wanted to be a mother to fulfil my life.'[21]

Married, single, with or without a partner, it doesn't make much difference to the way a contented new mother feels if she has wanted the baby she has given birth to. It will be twenty years or more before we can properly evaluate the wisdom of the women who have decided that they do not need a man in their lives to allow them to 'fulfil' their lives, but their seriousness and their good-will towards their children cannot be in any doubt.

2
The women's movement

... so long as every female, simply by virtue of her anatomy, is obliged, even forced, to be the sole or primary caretaker of childhood, she is prevented from being a free human being. (Kate Millet, 1972[1])

The world as we know it has been structured by men, and on the whole they've made a very poor job of it. There are various strategies that people need to engage in, but one very important way to make the world a better place is the creation of separatist communities of women living together and creating forms of social organization without men. I don't take that to mean – though some women probably do – without human beings with Y chromosomes, but rather without those people who have been socialized in the way in which adult men have been socialized. We should try to create communities that are as separated as possible from those sorts of attitudes, from an essentially pornographic construction of the world. I think it would be a splendid thing for children to be born in those communities, to see how they grow up and how the communities flourish. It would be possible for a man to say, I'm sympathetic to this project, and even though I can't directly be a part of it because of its separatist nature, I can give my support through donating my sperm. (Naomi Scheman, professor of philosophy and women's studies, personal communication, 1984)

'I just have a feeling it's a whole lot easier without men around – without men who are worried about power. I've never been a feminist, not at all, this is an emotional realization, not a political one. It's men with their insecurity and their need to have power,

*who make life so awkward for women and children. It's to do with
control. I suppose men have been led to believe they have to
control, it's their way of being in the world and they don't know
what to do without it. We've discovered a great deal about the
female, but the male's been neglected – there's a lot to be done
there yet.'* (Sonia, 1984)

*'I was a typical woman of the 1970s – I'd just begun to read about
women's lib, just begun to ask, who am I? what am I doing? When
I look back it's with . . . wry amusement, and, well, I don't judge
myself as badly as I used to. There's been a lot of changes in these
last years, and there's been a lot of casualties from that time. I
don't consider myself a casualty, but there was a period when I
thought I might be. I'd think, oh my God, what happened to us,
how did we get from there to here, you know?* (Frances, 1984)

*The larger revolution, evolution, liberation that the women's
movement set off, has barely begun. . . . The feminine mystique
was obsolete. That's why our early battles were won so easily, once
we engaged our will. The women's movement has, in the span of a
single generation, changed life, and the accepted image. . . . But to
continue reacting against that [old] structure is still to be defined
and limited by its terms. What's needed now is to transcend those
terms, transform the structure . . . of our institutions on a basis of
real equality for women and men, so we can live a new 'yes' to life
and love, and can choose to have children.* (Betty Friedan, 1982[2])

The growth of the women's movement

Women living in North America and much of Europe are
blessed in comparison to many of their sisters living in other
parts of the world. At a recent international women's
meeting in Copenhagen feminists were appalled when an
Indian sociologist quoted a law-giver who 2,000 years ago
wrote, 'In childhood a woman must be subject to her father,
in youth to her husband, and when her lord is dead, to her
sons. A woman must never be independent,' and then went
on to point out that the situation of most women in India
had scarcely changed over the last two millennia.[3] There are
many other countries, too numerous to mention, where this

statement is also true. But for many of us, especially the new generation coming into maturity, it is difficult to remember that even as recently as the first half of the last century the situation in our own parts of the world was not so very different.

In comparison, the changes in women's situation during this century have been phenomenal. Jessica Curtis, President of the Single Mothers by Choice group, speaking of the present, said to me, 'America's one of the best places to be female. One's demands to take care of oneself are respected because of all this individualism, you know. Nobody's supposed to have to subsume themselves – it's not a societal prescription.' In Britain we haven't travelled so far along the equality path yet, but in working on this chapter I have been continuously aware how fortunate we all are, not only as compared to vast numbers of women across the world at this moment, but also as compared to our great-grandmothers.

Our own century still trails a burdensome hangover, however. My own mother, a young bride at the end of the First World War, was happily enjoying doing war work, not least because it gave her some freedom from the strict watchfulness of her widowed Victorian mother. But the day her young husband was demobilized from the army he insisted that the very next morning she went to her supervisor and gave in her notice. A mild, gentle man, very much in love with his young wife, it nevertheless never occurred to him to behave differently. Nor did it occur to her to refuse him, though – as she told me recently – her resignation was one of the saddest things she ever did.

Catherine, an actress, aged 35 now and brought up in New Zealand, said how conventional expectations still were there, even when I was young. Everything was geared to the man in your life. I was brought up to expect that one day I'd fall in love, one day the right man would come along. My mother, for instance, though she was totally independent of men' (Catherine's father died when she was young), 'she'd get a bit silly and giggly if a man was around, and I used to think how lovely she was being, sort of frivolous and girlish and very sweet, but it was always reserved for a man, that kind of thing. She revered men as though they were always right; her generation had been taught to believe in their man, and their life was half a life if it didn't have a man to complete it. I think I thought then that maybe a man *would* come along and change everything for me, but in the meantime there was quite a lot to be done anyway!'

People sometimes talk nowadays as though it is only the women's movement which has given women permission to work, but this is of course snobbish nonsense. In the chapter on women and work we will look at available statistics on working patterns, but it is as well to remind ourselves that vast numbers of women have always had to work simply in order to feed their families, right from the very beginning when nomadic hominids gathered herbs and roots. As time passed a certain number of aristocratic or wealthy women were able to avoid soiling their hands with hard labour, and the needle flashing in and out of the linen resting on their laps was employed in fashioning decorative embroideries rather than shirts and sheets, but these women were rare exceptions. Almost everyone worked at something: mistresses of country manors went around with bundles of keys at their waists busily organizing much of the complicated self-sufficient existence that was the norm then, and poorer women wore themselves out sharing the farm work, rearing children, spinning, sewing, fetching water and fuel, cooking, all in the most primitive circumstances. No light switches, only tallow candles that had to be made before you could light them, and that not until the animal was killed and the fat melted down; no machines, only your own worn hands and weary back. But at least you knew who you were working for, and there were many shared good times. Later the Industrial Revolution took women and children from farm labour and shut them up in factories or mines with little regard for physical suitability or feminine decency. Now men and women alike were creatures to be exploited for the benefit of a few distant owners, and the old human contacts between master/mistress and worker were mainly lost.

But gradually, as mechanization in factories improved and production became more efficient, men took over the cotton looms and the manufacture of woollens, and women's wages – already low enough – fell even lower. Children were no longer needed to work in the factories and this meant that somebody had to be at home looking after them. In the 1830s discussions on women's work began to occupy parliamentary time, and questions were asked as to what women should be allowed to work at, and how long they should work for, ostensibly for the women's sake but often because men were concerned for their jobs. Oakley reports that in 1841, for instance, 'representatives of male operatives on the Short Time Committees demanded "the gradual withdrawal of all females from the factories".' They claimed that the home was where women belonged, and that for women to work in industry was an 'inversion of the order of nature'.[4] The 1844 Factory Act made women 'protected persons' and John Ruskin idealistically wrote that the home was 'the place of Peace; the shelter, not only from all injury, but from all terror, doubt and division . . . a sacred place, a vestal temple, a temple of the hearth'.[5]

But most working-class women had no choice but to continue to work (as did many unmarried middle-class women whose private income, if any, was insufficient to allow them to stay at home even as unpaid baby-sitters or companions, though the existence of this group of workers – teachers, governesses, clerks, saleswomen, nurses – is often forgotten now).[6] In Britain in 1842 underground work in the mines was closed to boys under 10 and to all women and girls; two years later night work was forbidden to women, and their working hours were reduced first to twelve hours a day then to ten. Limitations on the work women are permitted to do are still a subject for dissension today: some women object to any differences at all between protection for women and for men, and see these restrictions as discriminatory, both in Britain and in the States.[7]

On the whole the US has been ahead of Britain in the fight for equality, and when the struggles of American pioneer women to survive in hostile territory and to settle the land as America was opened up are taken into account, this is hardly to be wondered at. Yet, despite the bravery and tenacity of these pioneer settlers in harshly alien places like Kansas with its floods, storms, fires, droughts, blizzards and hostile Indians,[8] men still had the effrontery to say that women were not the equal of men, and the feminist fight against prejudice was no easier in the US than it was in Britain. But the experiences of these women gave solid backbone and heartfelt vigour to the arguments of the feminist agitators who finally succeeded in disturbing male complacency, and by the end of the nineteenth century much had been achieved.

Until these fights for justice had been won no women had legal rights over herself, her money, her children or her property. The changes came slowly and were reluctantly conceded. In the US, patriarchal law was slowly adapted, state by state, through the 1850s, 60s, 70s and 80s. In England the Married Woman's Property Act, which was first introduced in 1856 and was consolidated in 1882 (various amendments and additions were made to the Act up to 1908), finally gave women the rights they had been demanding.

It is difficult now for us to imagine how such punitive and unfair laws were permitted to remain in force for so long in countries which prided themselves on their 'civilization'. A man could claim any money his wife earned, and could behave as he liked to his family. Kate Millett writes: 'As head of the proprietary family, the husband was the sole "owner" of wife and children, empowered to deprive the mother of her offspring . . . upon divorcing or deserting her. A father, like a slaver, could order the law to reclaim his chattel-property relatives when he liked.' Any wife who wanted to leave her husband could be forcibly restrained by him, and English wives who ran away and refused to come back could face imprisonment.[9] Nowadays I can never read statements like this without an amazed sense of outrage. When I was much younger it all used to seem very far away, neither more nor less shocking than many other ancient acts of human oppression; now I find it inconceivable that such a comparatively short time ago women were so treated. Some film-goers seeing Bergman's marvellous *Fanny and Alexander* might have been puzzled by the legal aspects of the mother's anguish when her second husband, the bishop, forced her to stay in her appalling marriage by threatening to retain hold of her children, even though they were not his own children but were from her first happy marriage – perhaps imagining this was some Scandinavian legal peculiarity. Far from it – in those days the bishop was only one of millions who were given total rights over their wives and children to beat, feed and lock them up as they chose. True, men weren't actually allowed to batter their families to death, but, short of deliberate murder, a woman was supposed to be the passive recipient of whatever was handed out to her or to her children.

In a truly civilized country one ought to be able to rely on the state to put right obvious injustices and irregularities, but alas, countries are run by governments, and governments have other problems on their minds than human justice. Times have changed for the better, yes, but the way women are treated by the state – any state – has never had much to do with moral ethics. The state may now give us protection from our menfolk, but who will protect us from the state? For the state is not concerned with justice but with expediency. Sometimes in the aftermath of a revolution inspired by an ideology of justice and equality, women's lot is improved – in theory at least – but such revolutions are usually followed by periods of harsh economic recession during which individual needs are regarded as an unaffordable luxury. If the state finds it has to improve its output of goods women will be persuaded to work in the factories or in the fields; if it fears or plans a war it will encourage women to breed. When the two apparently contradictory requirements coincide if the state can afford it women will be comparatively well looked after. Crêches, nursery schools, medical attention, state benefits, official recognition (medals, awards) will be the order of the day: to a certain extent the state then takes on the place of the family, so that marriage with its individual support system becomes less important. But more likely the dual requirement means that a woman will find herself working alongside men doing the same job for less pay, parking her children wherever she can, then at the end of the day rushing home (if she is not too heavily pregnant to rush anywhere) to look after house, kids and husband.

In the USSR, for example, one of the first changes to be made after the Revolution was an attempt to radically alter the position of women. In 1917 and 1918 Lenin issued decrees putting women's economic, social and sexual rights into their own hands. In future women would be able to live where they wanted, select their own name, freely marrying or divorcing; contraception and abortion was available on demand and illegitimacy ceased to be recognized. At last the money the women earned belonged to them; they could use it as they thought fit, without permission or interference by their menfolk. Aware that it would take more than a change in the law to make women's emancipation a reality, the state planned to provide nurseries to free the mothers to work, to collectivize housekeeping, and to ensure that equality in work and education became the norm. But sadly, within a few years economic and political pressures caused most of these ideas to be abandoned.

Russian women were not the only ones to lose ground during this period; the 1930s and the 1940s also brought to a halt the impressive advances the women's movement had made in Europe and America during the last half of the nineteenth century and the early years of this. But it was not only increasing militarism and economic problems that were to blame – there was one even more fundamental pressure against the achievement of real equality about which the Soviet authorities were either ignorant or uncaring – that of tradition. As Kate Millett writes in her seminal book, *Sexual Politics* (1970), 'the real test would be in changing attitudes. For Soviet leadership had declared the family defunct in a society composed entirely of family members, whose entire psychic processes were formed in the patriarchal family of Tsarist Russia.'

It was not only Soviet men but many women too who were uneasy with these changes – we see the same conservative objections being raised in every country. Many of these objections were understandable, and are being made just as fervently today, particularly where sexual freedoms are concerned. Abortion, for instance, is an issue that invariably causes intense disagreement. But as far as the state is concerned abortion raises questions of expediency rather than of morality. In Russia in 1936, for instance, Stalin permitted abortion except in first pregnancies. But the devastating manpower losses that the Russians faced during the war years resulted in a total change of attitude, and a return to the family was called for. By 1944 not only was all legal abortion abolished, but anyone found guilty of aiding a woman to secure an abortion was jailed for two years. Russia needed more children, so mothers of seven children or more were awarded honorary titles and decorations, and the importance of the family was stressed. For the time being the revolution was over as far as women's position in society was concerned, and conservative opinion outside the USSR was not slow in pointing out the failure of the Soviet Union as an example of the uselessness of trying to change the position of women.

I have written a brief summary of what happened in the USSR to the position of women because most people are familiar at least with the basic outlines of the background history, but the story of state expediency is virtually universal. In Argentina, for instance, the Peronist magazine *Las Bases* made an unambiguous call for women to settle down to breeding: 'when the year 2000 is at hand, we will have over-populated neighbours with great food problems, and we, on the contrary, will have three million kilometers of land, practically unpopulated. We will not have the arms to work this immense and rich territory, and if we do not do it there will be others who will. . . . We must start from the basis that the principal work of a woman is to have children.'[10]

In Romania recently President Ceausescu made a national appeal (on International Women's Day!) 'urging Romanian women to do their patriotic duty by giving birth to more children. Each family must have at least three to four children, he said.'[11] Liberal abortion laws had been rescinded in 1966, and both abortion and contraception are now illegal. Nevertheless in spite of their illegality abortions more than outnumber live births. In addition, in order to increase the population rate the law has now been changed so that girls may marry at 15, and as a further incentive to breed an extra 5 per cent income tax has been imposed on single men and women, which childless couples also have to pay. Infertile women will be sent to sterility centres whether they wish to go or not to check that no one is cheating, and divorce is to be made more difficult.[12] But the fact is, there is not enough food to feed the population that already exists. A former Romanian journalist writes, 'having a child in Romania is to assume a burden of guilt for the rest of one's life. A lack of vitamins, calcium and proteins can result in mothers bringing physically and mentally handicapped children into the world.' Meat, milk and cheese are rarities, children suffer from malnutrition, and proficiency at school has dropped considerably. But women, he says, are in no position to object to what is being done to them: 'regarded as mere sex objects, sources of procreation, cooks or scapegoats for male lordship' by their menfolk whose 'attitude towards women is still in the tradition of the Ottoman empire', they 'suffer a high degree of male violence, rape and sexual molestation.'[13]

In China female infanticide is making a reappearance, as the Party is insisting that families have one child only and traditionally a boy child is considered infinitely superior to a female. Since two or more children bring heavy penalties on transgressing parents (Chinese newspapers have carried reports of the kidnapping by Party cadres and the forcible aborting of women pregnant without official permission, while 'less spectacular enforced abortion is routine'[14]), unwanted female children are disposed of.

In Britain, fortunately for us, our system of democracy means that the state has to move with greater tact. Currently free contraception and a gross lack of nursery schooling have all played their part in lowering the numbers of births, and some concern is being expressed about this. It will be interesting to see what happens in the near future. It is unlikely that nursery school facilities will suddenly be improved, as they were during the Second World War when an extra three and a quarter million women joined the labour force,[15] because while politicians might argue that we need more babies to keep up the population figures, at the same time the recession with its severe unemployment means that at present we need fewer workers. It is possible we may find that to encourage a higher birth rate contraception will no longer be freely available on the National Health Service, but caution will be exercised, for what the country needs right now is women keeping out of the work force, staying at home and having babies, but not too many – only sufficient to improve on the figures revealed by the last General Household Survey which showed that the average number of dependent children per family was down to 1.83 in 1982 as opposed to 2.01 in 1971.[16]

What would the early feminists have made of these depressing facts which we have just been looking at? I think it would have seemed inconceivable to them that there could have been so little progress in areas that matter so intensely to women after the first goal of women's suffrage had been achieved. It is doubtful if anyone at that time could have realized just how lengthy and arduous a process it would be to make the necessary fundamental changes in people's attitudes. This is not the place to explore why interest in women's rights faded out once the vote had been won (both in America after the passing in 1920 of the Nineteenth Amendment to the Constitution which gave women the vote and in Britain after the passing of the Representation of the People's Act in 1918 which enfranchized propertied women over 30), but when we are considering why it is that the idea of single women having children by choice has suddenly become acceptable, we need to keep at the back of our minds that in spite of emancipation the concept of an independent woman, happy and satisfied to live without a man, continued to be alien to the vast majority of the public, female as well as male. She may have the vote, but she was still a woman, and a woman is incomplete without a man, ran popular folklore. Perhaps for most women it's true, and perhaps for most men a woman is just as necessary. It is certainly very noticeable that recently interest in the importance of intimate relationships is taking over from the 1970s self-discovery search with its burning question of Who Am I?, which took over from the Sex for All obsession of the 1960s.

But important as relationships are, they can only be successful when people have reached a certain stage of maturity. And it was in the early 1970s, when we were thinking about self-fulfilment, personal transformation, going to touch groups and learning how to meditate, that a growing number of women realized that for them self-fulfilment and self-understanding necessitated breaking away from the old conventional female pattern. (This was easier for young women than for people like me who already had a way of life, with children, houses, and husbands who too often had turned out to be more chauvinist than we'd thought possible – though they would deny this furiously – mainly because we had not been aware of how easy it is to slip into traditional patterns of behaviour and had not realized how important it is to guard our hard-won freedoms).

When in the late 1960s the women's movement woke once more out of its long sleep not much was made of it in the media at first. Ann Oakley quotes Sheila Rowbotham as saying that rumours of an emerging revived women's movement reached England in 1968: 'We had only a hazy idea of what was going on. No-one I knew then had actually read anything which had been produced by the women's groups. . . . I can remember odd conversations with women who were friends of mine, and particularly very intense moments when I was hurt and made angry by the attitudes of men on the left.'[17]

By 1969 women's liberation groups were being formed all over Britain, and in March 1970 a national conference met in Ruskin College Oxford and formulated a programme, centred round four points: that there should be equal pay, equal education and opportunity, twenty-four-hour nurseries, and free contraception and abortion on demand. A manifesto was published expressing the sense of oppression felt by the women present, arising not only from economic oppression both at work and at home, but also from anger with what they saw as commercial exploitation by advertisements in the media, the fact that in some respects women still had 'the status' of children, and that they were educated 'to narrower horizons' than men, and were made to feel inadequate.[18]

There was an important difference between the aims of

the earlier suffragettes and the aims of the new women's movement. Whereas the first had set their sights primarily at achieving the vote, without which no advance could be made, the second understood from the beginning that political and economic equality is not sufficient: permission to ape men, to get a certain quota of top jobs, even to become Prime Minister or President, merely makes us pseudo-men. What the women's movement now understands is that women need to bring about a change in society that is akin to revolution; men and women must each be free to develop in their own ways, hand-in-hand where appropriate, separately where not, both sexes fulfilling their own potential and thereby hopefully making a world greatly superior to the one that we have lived with until now. The world needs this change, not just in order to make women happy, but in order to ensure the very continuance of the world itself. Being a woman at the top *on men's terms* won't achieve this – have Mrs Meir, Mrs Nehru and Mrs Thatcher been noticeably more pacific than their male equivalents? It's a great achievement that women have been able to reach those heights of political power: it's pathetic what use they have made of it.

Where we're at now
Betty Friedan, writing of the changes since the publication of her famous book, said, 'it is now twenty years since *The Feminine Mystique* was published. I am still awed by the revolution that book helped to spark off.'[19] She quoted some of these changes, which she saw as 'probably irreversible'. These included the innovation of firewomen, women priests, women rabbis, chairpersons, women Prime Ministers, women's studies, equal pay for work of comparable value, marriage contracts, first babies at 40, the single-parent family and films like *Victor Victoria* and *Tootsie*.

Defending herself from what she described as 'the fury of some of my sister feminists over the position I took in my book *The Second Stage*', she explained she felt we had come as far as we could with the first stage of the women's movement, and that now we must 'come to terms with family and with work.' She argues that people who say the women's movement is finished because the post-feminist generation is 'moving from a different place' don't understand it is inevitable that the new generation is concerned with issues different from their mothers' goals because these have, in part at least, been gained, and their daughters now take them for granted. That they are concerned with more domestic problems like when and if to have children, and how to raise those children while working to finance the purchase of housing – whether sharing with a partner or not – merely shows the difference the revolution has made. She goes on to write that there are now so many issues which need working out that it is useless to expect women to remain fused in a unified front as they were when they were struggling for their constitutional equal rights: that, in fact, so diverse are these issues that they can no longer be considered to be solely women's concern. In the second stage of the fight, she says, 'I think that women's most basic issues now converge on men's – the basic issues of war and peace and economic survival, of quality of life for young and old. But when that different voice, now emerging from women in politics and other fields, also begins to be heard from men, it will become a different politics.'[20]

It is unfortunate that feminists are as divided as they are among themselves, but perhaps this is bound to happen as any successful movement or religion comes to maturity. Once the first struggle which united all has been won, matters of less immediate importance arise, and attention is no longer focused on one issue, resulting in different groups, all equally enthusiastic about their own cause. What is undeniable is that, for the time being at least, there is no risk of the women's movement returning to obscurity as it did earlier this century, though there is perhaps some danger it may become an academic subject rather than a 'live' one. The growth in purely academic women's studies has been phenomenal: by 1981 there were about 275 programmes in the United States and more than 4,000 courses in universities and colleges, ninety granting degrees and three giving doctorates. In Britain thirty universities gave women's studies courses, and others were available extra-murally.[21]

But that this growth is not necessarily as encouraging as it sounds was illustrated by a letter printed in a Feminist Library and Information Centre Newsletter, written by a German feminist who had given one of the lectures during a recent conference on women's history in Berlin, complaining that many of the 300 women at the conference were 'avidly hunting for topics for their final examination paper or master thesis'. She added that she and her colleagues were disturbed by evidence that many young women are doing these courses not so much out of interest in feminism but in order to gain degrees in fields where 'research in the lives of women is novel enough to give you a lead in the race for careers and posts. And many of the young female students taking courses in women's studies find them easier, less strenuous than all the others which they have to attend obligatorily. . . . But if topics of the women's movement are introduced those students turn away bored, uninterested, telling the lecturer that these issues really have nothing whatsoever to do with "Women in Jane Austen's novels".'

What other gains have been made besides those listed by Betty Friedan at the beginning of this section? One is political power in the sense that if women united their vote could dictate the outcome of many elections. In the US women are 53 per cent of the electorate, and recent opinion polls have shown that on issues of peace American women differ considerably from men who were much less concerned about the President's war policies. If women were to act on their beliefs they could ensure that only a President committed to peace would win the next election. However, some feminists consider that to link feminism with peace is to perpetuate the idea that women are gentle, passive creatures (peaceful being seen as a synonym for passive) and that such an image is detrimental to women's progress, while others believe that such objectors want women to turn into imitation men, and that instead of accepting the male structure as it is, they ought to work to change it. It is possible therefore that the power women could have in an election would be dissipated in internecine argument. The opportunity for success is undoubtedly there, because the US has the lowest voting record of any industrialized democracy; many millions of possible voters are not even registered, and of those that are many do not bother to vote. Thirty million of these unregistered voters are women: just think what an effect such numbers could have if even a fraction of these uninvolved women could be helped to see how important they are.[22]

In the UK similar arguments rage in feminist circles over whether or not the women's camps at Greenham Common are useful to the women's movement. Some argue that the very fact that a group of women camping outside USAF bases in Britain have been able to win international sympathy and mass media coverage has to be of benefit to the women's movement as well as to the peace movement – if they distinguish between the two movements at all. Others see Greenham 'as a symptom of the loss of feminist principles and processes – radical analysis, criticism and consciousness raising';[23] for this reason they dislike and distrust its emotive appeal, the use of children's toys and flowers stuck in the wire netting, etc. One of the editors of a pamphlet *Breaching the Peace*, from which the last quote comes, also writes in that pamphlet, 'Greenham Common obviously has enormous appeal. I can see that attraction and am aware of the energy generated by so many women being together. I can also understand the appeal of direct action. What I don't understand is what Greenham Common has to do with women's liberation. Perhaps it is easier to go to Greenham Common than to continue to fight our oppression. It is certainly easier than facing some of the problems in the WLM.' Politically inclined feminists want to see Greenham Common women involved more directly in politics, sitting at the conference table arguing their points and working with men. Others shudder at the thought. I believe that in the end this dichotomy must be overcome – for the present I personally count Greenham Common as one of the most important gains, for I don't think it could have happened had it not been for the 1970s revival.

Another considerable gain is in the field of education. Sexism has been considerably reduced both in the US and the UK: even in naturally conservative Britain many of the ancient colleges have opened themselves up to females as well as to males, and the last Department of Education and Science figures showed a total of 191,500 women undergraduates in the UK. Admittedly there are 255,400 male undergraduates,[24] but this is still a notable advance in a society that traditionally thought it proper to spend money on educating their sons rather than their daughters 'who would be marrying soon anyway'. In America this idea has long been superseded, at least in the more affluent classes: in a country that values material success so highly, the incentive to better yourself applies as powerfully to females as to males.

Nevertheless the path to the top is still much smoother for men than for women, as any comparative list of occupations will show, more so in Britain than in America, and this is a serious drawback for women who want to raise their children on their own. It does not seem that legislation alone can effect the changes women have worked for. In a 'socialist' country like Hungary, for example, where egalitarian laws were supposed to have done away with discrimination, educated women encounter fewer obstacles than their Western counterparts and there are far more of them in the professional jobs usually occupied by men, but even so women's prospects for promotion are increasingly inferior to men's the longer they stay in the job. Nearly 90 per cent of the women work, and the state looks after them well, especially with regard to child-rearing – they are given five month's maternity leave on full pay, with either parent being able to stay at home for three years drawing special allowances and with guaranteed return to the same job, and state kindergartens where 88 per cent of the children go when they are 3 to 6 years old.[25] But it is still mainly the women who shoulder responsibility for running the home and for the well-being of the family, and, when they are working, they still earn only 70 to 80 per cent of the wages men receive. Plus ça change. . .

Unfortunately some legislative reforms have side-effects which can be detrimental to many women. Take divorce, for example. Hard-line feminists approve of legislation which assumes that women can easily be independent of men, and that all a woman will need to put her back on her feet after a divorce is a short period of maintenance while she finds or trains for a job, after which she is supposed to cope on her own. This totally ignores the fact that most women drop out of the work force to have babies, perhaps didn't train in the first place at anything special because they expected to marry, or married before finishing their studies, and that only too often after a divorce it is too late for them to reach the point they would have arrived at had they stayed single and career-minded. This may not apply to many of today's young women, whose attitudes to their own financial independence are different from their mothers', and obviously it will not apply at all to single women who have chosen to have babies alone in the first place, but meanwhile there are millions of women struggling to survive on incomes that are only a fraction of the salaries their husbands, whose careers were never interrupted, continue to draw. For women like this, there are mixed feelings about the blessings the women's movement has brought them.

I think it is difficult for radical feminists to appreciate such women's viewpoints. The split in the women's movement which I have already mentioned seems to be growing stronger as problems of domestic life versus political theory arise. It might be helpful to look a little more closely at this split. Ann Oakley, on whose book *Subject Women* I have already drawn considerably in this chapter, gives a useful table which describes some of the main divisions among contemporary feminists, the two primary ones being 'socialist feminists' and 'radical feminists'. The first see capitalism as the cause of women's oppression, while the second consider men are primarily to blame. 'Socialist feminists' range from those who want equal rights, and are prepared to work alongside men; through to those who feel it is the 'system' that oppresses them and it is the 'system' therefore which must be changed; to those more militant women who demand wages for housework, blame men as ' "bosses" in the family' as much as they blame capitalism's demand for cheap female labour and who, while acknowledging that women's political insights must be used for the socialist revolutionary movement, argue that women need to organize separately from men. 'Radical feminists' have no doubt that it is mainly men we must blame for our oppression, and they range from those who attack marriage and patriarchy in general; through to those who say that 'society is male-supremacist as well as capitalist and imperialist'; to those who consider that 'the lesbian is the only woman who can realize her full potential', and that, lesbian or not, 'women are the only alternative society'; and to 'female supremacists' who consider that, while women are biologically and morally superior, men (phallocrats) hold power 'by force of arms', and who therefore see the struggle as a war with 'no fraternizing with the other side'.[26]

The relevance of all this to our main subject is that although many people assume that women who have babies out of marriage by choice must be men-hating feminists, in fact radical feminists usually intensely disapprove of this new pattern. Sara Maitland, in her contribution to *Why Children?*[27] writes that she has found it difficult as a politically active feminist to accept her own powerful 'romantic love' for her daughter, because as a feminist she dislikes the very idea of romantic love with its passions, its demands, etc. 'Why did I, in the face of being told that marriage and motherhood were the symbols and actualities of women's oppression, choose to have her?' The women's movement, she says, gives her little support in her confusion – they've become better at the practicalities, but they haven't yet 'come to grips with the reality of the painful, wonderful, destructive, liberating love that many of us feel for our children'.

If a mother's love for her children raises difficulties in some feminist circles, love for a man is even more politically suspect, and it is here that the more militant feminists part company from their sisters.

Sexual relationships

Relationships between the sexes were not helped by Freud's contribution of the concept of penis envy. 'Freudian logic', writes Millett pungently,[28] 'has succeeded in converting childbirth, an impressive female accomplishment . . . into nothing more than a hunt for a male organ. It somehow becomes the male prerogative even to give birth, as babies are but surrogate penises . . . were she to deliver an entire orphanage of progeny, they would only be so many dildoes.' Further, women who aspire to equality at work are showing signs of immaturity, incompleteness and arrested development, as they struggle to replace the penis by copying men's accomplishments.

Laughed out of court by women, and outdated as psychological theory except by a few die-hard Freudians, the myth of penis envy has nevertheless sunk into the subconscious of men in general, as their jokes and barbed comments against business women, lesbians, etc. show. It probably played its part in helping produce a drift towards lesbianism among a number of feminists who otherwise would most likely have been straight heterosexuals. Solidarity with women, suspicion of men's motives, and restricted contact with men has caused many young feminist sympathizers to experiment with homosexuality. These 'political lesbians' may or may not stay with lesbianism as time goes by. The mothers I interviewed who had had this kind of experience were ambivalent about their feelings; one or two had never actually had sex with a woman at all, but still felt closer to women than they did to men. Child psychologist *Anna*, for instance, said, 'The feminist movement in Holland was telling us all the time you have to choose for your own needs. In the beginning of the 1970s you couldn't be a feminist *and* have children or live with a man. You had to be a lesbian or at least you have to be free and sitting in women's groups and talking – I found I was getting more interested in women than in men and didn't want to sleep any more with the man I was living with, though I didn't really want to have sex with a woman either. But I liked very much to be with women and had very strong feelings for them.'

Part-time researcher *Charlotte* had had some lesbian experiences at school and went through a period of being bisexual: 'I'm not a lesbian single mother because I was never terribly whole-heartedly lesbian, and I think that has something to do with my feeling that I'm perfectly all right on my own with my baby, and that I've never had a terribly strong desire to live with a man. Lesbian affairs tended for me to be more in the head than physical, and I was sleeping with men as well as women until I got pregnant. But I've had much closer, more intense affairs with women than I've ever had with men, though at the same time I've never felt very happy in bed with them, it's never really worked as a long-term thing. So I sort of accepted that, and I've given up practising, as one might say, although I'm still very close to one person I see sometimes.'

Naomi Scheman, professor of philosophy and women's studies, told me that she did not think there was anything biological about sexual *preference*: 'Sexuality is enormously malleable. Biologically we have sexual desire, biologically we are equipped to derive sexual pleasure in a whole range of ways. But there's an enormous amount of pressure to channel that sexuality in one particular direction. In Adrienne Rich's terms, it's "compulsive heterosexuality". When there's so much social pressure I don't think we are in a position to know what influence biology has here. In terms of evolutionary argument, if one says, well, we have the sexual organs we do have because they fit us for sexual intercourse, of course that's true, but that carries no more weight than saying that we have the hands and fingers that we do have because they enable us to gather food from the ground and to hold tools. It doesn't follow from that there is anything less natural about violin playing than food gathering!'

'If there is anything characteristic of us as a species it is that we're inventive about what we do with our bodies. We all do get hungry, that's biological. Sexual desire may be similarly biological, but the kind of food our hunger expresses a desire for is cultural, and so similarly I would think the kinds of physical stimulation and relationships and so on that our sexual desires express a need for is similarly cultural. All of us start out with an intimate physical sensual connection to a woman's body, namely our mothers, and looked at that way it can be seen as amazing that most women turn out heterosexual. How is it we learn to make this transfer to a distant, harder, colder, more judgmental sort of person? I think the social processes that coerce women to make that change of object choice are very powerful and very interesting to examine because the maintenance of patriarchy requires that switch, and the vast majority of us do make it. I'm impressed by the malleability of desire because, for instance, I know what it was like to acquire a taste for single malt Scotch (there was nothing like the pressure there is to be heterosexual!) I remember the first time I tasted it, I thought – yuck! At first I couldn't stand the taste of Scotch at all, but now I love Glenfiddich and can tell it from Glenlivet and so on. I'm not fooling myself about this. It isn't that I manage not to grimace when drinking it so I can get through the social situation – I do very much like the taste of it, and it feels biological. I mean, there it is in my mouth, stimulating my taste buds and causing me very direct immediate pleasure, and yet I know I used to hate the stuff. In the face of that experience, I'm not prepared to go with the "it's biological" argument.'

I have quoted Naomi Scheman at length because several of the mothers I interviewed and will be quoting are exclusively homosexual and it might seem from the total number of women with lesbian experiences quoted in the book that I have chosen a biased sample. This is not so. As I have just written, a side-effect of the women's movement has been to increase the number of young women who are ready to experiment sexually, and if men are disturbed by this then it seems to me it is very much up to them to ask themselves why this is so. Of the women I have quoted from three were of the 'political' kind I discussed at the beginning of this section, two had had bi-sexual experiences but are now fully lesbian, and there were also two pairs of lesbians living together as established couples. Strictly speaking this book is about single women living alone, but since lesbian couples face many of the problems of women living singly I wanted to include them. Also, to be absolutely honest, both these couples were such a joy to talk to, especially *Stella* and *Jan*, that I thought it important to use their personal experiences as couples because of the light they throw on the difficulties many of the other mothers have faced in the past in attempting to make permanent relationships with men.

Perhaps the major difficulty in forming relationships is

that the kind of woman who is likely to coolly and calmly make the decision to have a child on her own is probably an independent woman, intelligent and not easily dominated. Most men have problems in coping with this kind of female. *Lynn*, a nurse, had hoped for some years to find a permanent partner, but finally gave in and has had two children by artificial insemination: 'I'm very independent, and I've been told I can be very aggressive – one boyfriend said he was put off by me because I was so independent and I wasn't dependent on him – well, I'm sorry, but I don't want to be dependent on somebody. It's nice to have somebody there, to have the love coming back, but not so much I can't function independently, have my own friends, my own likes and dislikes.' Psychologist Hendrika Vande Kemp who is a devout Christian: 'By being a successful professional woman in a Christian community I've already broken too many of the rules for me to easily find a meaningful relationship with a man. That's a personal pain I have to deal with, and I can't separate my responses into professional and personal. Being this successful a woman in an evangelical Christian community is something the men can't cope with. I'm sure this was the reason the last serious relationship I had with a man broke down – you aren't supposed to be that competent. I think I haven't had a date in a year.'

Obviously there are always many reasons why a relationship doesn't 'take', but as I talked to mothers and other people, I soon came to see that there was a common thread running through these discussions. Lillian Rubin, who has had a long and happy marriage, writes nevertheless in her book *Intimate Strangers* of a stressful period she and her husband went through when they decided that, since she was making enough money from her private practice as a psychotherapist and her teaching and writing to support her family in the style they were accustomed to, it was time she took on that burden herself in order to allow her husband, who wanted to write, to do so untrammelled by the need to earn a good living. It was a decision mutually arrived at over a period of two years, with high expectations, even 'eagerness'. But within a couple of months both these mature, well-adjusted people were appalled to find their emotions were considerably different to what they had expected. He fell into a six-month long depression, while she went through a period of great anger. 'Suddenly,' she writes, 'we had to confront the realization that we were still dominated by the stereotypic images of male and female roles – images we would have sworn we had, by then, routed from our consciousness.' She says that he feared his manhood had been damaged and that he had failed, while she felt 'outraged and enraged' that he wasn't looking after her any longer. Eventually they were able to leave behind these unexpected feelings, but not before they had both worked very hard, individually and together.[29]

This was a couple who already had a good marriage. For most of the mothers I interviewed marriage had never been tried, mainly because the kind of problems centring around society's expectations of suitable role-playing out-lined above had never been solved in any of their relationships. It doesn't take much imagination, for instance, to see how men would react to the proud strength of the women who talked to me frankly – *Laura*, who 'earmarked' an old friend as a possible father when she was 16: 'As far as responsibility is concerned, no, I don't want him around, he's not going down on the birth certificate, why should he? He's done his job; if he wants to come and visit, fine – if he wants to be an uncle, godfather – he can choose his role, but I'm not giving him any rights. I think if you're married already and you're prepared to take an outside lover, you've got to be aware of the risks you're taking. And if you come up against a tough nut like me, too bad!' *Rosa*, Dutch specialist in child psychology: 'When I decided to get pregnant I stopped taking the pill, I refused to take anything or do anything, so when I slept with someone then *he* had to use condoms if he wanted me not to get pregnant. I told them I would do nothing, that *they* had to take care of it.' Hardly unfair, but it staggered her boyfriends! *Catherine*, actress, who had been very much in love with her married lover, found her feelings for him changed by her pregnancy: 'I felt slightly guilty about going ahead with having the baby when he wanted me to abort it – I thought, I'm disrupting somebody else's life. But then I decided it was nothing to do with him. I remember saying to him, I cannot abort my body for *your* life. Once my belly was swelling and my breasts were enormous (which was unusual for me) I discovered it was to do with me and nothing to do with him, that he could bugger off! I felt wonderful, I felt so healthy; I had nowhere to live and I stayed with a girlfriend, but I was just really happy, really content.' Later, talking about current boyfriends, she said, 'Tommy's 5 now, and yes, I do have boyfriends again. But I find men's attitudes very odd. You go through your teens realizing that sex is all men ever want from you, but when *you* get like that – and I don't want much more than that right now – they hate it. They can't stand that you want to be the way they are, to treat sex as a casual thing, have fun, have a laugh, sleep together and then leave it at that – they hate it. They say, well, where can I fit into your life? You drive your own car, you have your own career, you have a child, you have your own home, where do I fit in? I say, where do you want to fit? You have your own life, and I have mine. That's all there is to it.'

Jenny, on the other hand, the only mother in this book who became pregnant entirely unintentionally and certainly would not have chosen to become a mother at 20, insists on sharing the care of her son with his father. 'It never occurred to me Ben's father wouldn't share the care of him half and half – he's as much *his* child as he's mine, he has equal responsibility for him, and yes, he's gone along fully with that, but he had to, in any case. Why not?' At the moment they find it possible to share successfully because the father is mainly at home working on his PhD thesis, but later on problems may arise when he gets a job, marries, or has to move a long distance away. What particularly interested me was the total assumption by Jenny that he *would* share: certainly this new generation just coming to maturity has very different expectations from mine. Dr Elphis Christopher tells how at a recent conference on sexuality she was touched by a comment made by one of the attenders, a counsellor: 'There was a guy there who said very sweetly – he was a young man about 30 – "I've just got a new girlfriend and I can put my arm around her and she doesn't shout at me and tell me that I'm invading her space!" He'd obviously had all these feminist girlfriends who'd scared the life out of him, and yet he was the most gentle, sweet, calming sort of person!'

Pride in themselves, in their capabilities, makes these young women strong: it seems to me that young men are going to need a great deal of help and understanding to get them through what might turn out to be a period of the most radical change in sexual relationships ever. But who is going to help these men? Certainly not their fathers, unless they are extremely fortunate and have a father who himself had been an unusually sensitive man. I foresee a spate of books within the next few years addressed to this problem, advising men how to build up their self-esteem, how to cope with their uncertainty in the face of an increasingly independent opposite sex, and how to redefine for themselves what their own sexuality means. There are already a few men's groups – will they, if they haven't already – turn into consciousness-raising groups? Why not? And will they be able to avoid the pitfalls of many of the early feminist groups, which women like myself found off-putting because – much as we felt ourselves in sympathy with feminism – faced with virulent attacks on men by the one or two violently angry women who always seemed to be present at any meeting, we often found ourselves forced into the unwanted position of defending men! Unfortunately there are always people who have been so badly hurt that it is impossible for them to be rational about their aggressors: some incest victims I have met, for instance, could scarcely endure to be near a man, let alone consider men's problems sympathetically.[30] As far as men are concerned, I suspect the anger will be most likely to come from those who have been through a divorce and who consider themselves scarred victims of legal and personal injustice. It would be a great pity if this kind of division between the rational and the bitterly angry were to arise: will men allow themselves to learn from the experience of the women's groups?

One thing is for certain, marriage will never be the same again. Marion Fabe, author of *Up Against the Clock*, discussing with me whether having a child as a single mother was threatening to the family, said, 'The family was cracking apart – there was all that resentment and hatred that grew up from the categorizing and isolating of the woman in the suburbs. I think the heterosexual impulse to have a child with someone you love is very powerful, but when those kinds of urges become institutionalized, sometimes the institutionalization makes them so awful you can almost say the original impulse is not being expressed any more, and then the institutions start to crumble and change. In other words I don't see the single woman having a child as something that is threatening. I think it is a healthy variation; part of a women's ability to determine her own life, to make her own choices. To make the one thing that you can do, the one thing no man can do, to make *that* dependent on a man is just laughable.'

The final words are art gallery owner *Frances*'s, who had a child after her divorce, and has had several good relationships with men since. 'No, marriage basically has no interest for me any more. I think women give up a lot in marriage. I feel like I struggled like hell to get to the point where I had a life that I could live on my own that felt all right to me. I was socialized in a very traditional kind of way, and I think I would fall right back into all the things about marriage that are taken for granted, with the roles all set, and I think I'd feel trapped and I don't want to be trapped. I can see myself living with somebody for a long time, but not getting married – though I don't know, maybe when my daughter's grown up and gone. . . .'

Women's changing view of themselves

There is no question that women today see themselves differently from the way their mothers did. This is in spite of social conditioning which in many ways continues almost unchanged. As a mother I was appalled some years ago to find my small daughter being told by a contemporaneous 5-year old male neighbour that girls can't do this, that, or the other, in tones of confident superiority. His parents were and are 'liberated', intelligent people, his mother a writer and teacher, his father a well-known TV journalist and presenter. He cannot possibly have got that viewpoint from home – did he pick it up at his liberated nursery school? Or from other local children, equally coming from liberated, intelligent, etc. etc.? I felt a kind of despair that it was all taking so long, and perhaps also (though I didn't see it then) because I too was succumbing to early indoctrination of what marriage meant more thoroughly than I then realized.

My daughter is now a supremely independent, bright 22-year-old given to charging around the world as though she doesn't know what fear means, but it will be some time before the serenity she is also searching for is achieved. Growing up she not only had to fight against the social conditioning which I had been surprised to find was still alive and kicking (like others of my generation I thought all that was over and done with – how could we have been so blind in the 1960s?) but also, later, she had to cope with the marital struggles of parents who were unable to solve the kind of problems that I quoted a few pages back from Lillian Rubin's book.

Today's indoctrination is not much reduced as far as small children are concerned. Ann Oakley quotes a 1976 study by Glenys Lobban which examined six much-used British reading schemes: *Janet and John, Happy Venture, Ready to Read, Ladybird, Nipper* and *Breakthrough to Literacy*. I summarize below the table of findings she gives which 'shows the same definition of girls and women as relatively passive, indoor creatures, the same glorification of masculine adventurousness, as the American research'. Girls are given dolls, skipping ropes and prams to play with, while boys have cars, trains, aeroplanes, boats and footballs. For activities, girls prepare tea, play with dolls and take care of younger siblings. Boys play with cars, trains, play football, lift and pull heavy objects, play cricket, watch adult males in occupational roles, and do heavy gardening. If they're together, girls take the lead in hopping, skipping, shopping with parents, while boys take the lead in going exploring alone without parents, climbing trees, building things, taking care of pets, flying kites and washing and polishing dad's car. The only new skill girls are shown is how to take care of younger siblings, while boys learn how to take care of pets, making/building, saving/rescuing people or pets, and playing sports. The adult roles the children are presented with to copy from are: for girls – mother, aunt, grandmother; for boys the male roles are much more varied – father, uncle, grandfather, postman, farmer, fisherman, shop or business owner, policeman, builder, bus driver, bus conductor, train driver, railway porter. The only role shared by both sexes are teachers and shop assistants.[31]

This situation is beginning to improve. For instance, there is a Children's Books Co-operative which runs what it claims to be 'the only bookclub to specialize in non-sexist books for children', and they select books 'which show both boys and girls as independent, resourceful, caring and emotional'.[32] Many teachers attempt to make their own unbiased selection, as do public librarians. But it is going to be some time before the old role expectations are even partially discarded throughout society as a whole.

It is very difficult to clear one's head of what is learned and to distinguish what actually *is*. Women have been traditionally blamed for almost everything from the beginning; in the Pandora myth when Pandora opened the box (Millett suggests that the 'box' is a metaphor for her cunt)[33] and in the Judeo-Christian myth when Eve persuaded Adam to eat the apple, knowledge about evil, especially sexuality, was let out on to a golden world innocent of such wickedness until women got up to their tricks.

We must be careful not to let such ancient prejudice persuade us that our correct goal is to change ourselves and become as like men as we can. If we try to become exactly as men are, we can only become second-class men, because we will be merely copies, and a copy, however faithful, can never be as 'first-class' as the original. Very few feminists would want this anyway, but – because jobs which women have been traditionally good at such as caring, nursing and teaching; activities such as the Greenham Common women's demand for peace, and certain qualities, such as gentleness, have been devalued (men who do these jobs or have these qualities are also devalued in other men's eyes) – many ambitious women want to prove themselves by achieving a triumphant success in traditionally male professions and beating men at their own game. But this is rarely possible: man's need to be at the top makes his rules endlessly adaptable. In Russia, for example, where there are now more women doctors than male ones, it is not so special any longer to be a doctor. In Britain the old male mystique of the god-like doctor is also fading – is this partly because of the rising number of female doctors? Ordinary GPs are becoming merely a superior sort of nurse (themselves shamefully downgraded), while men still manage to keep the top consultancy jobs mainly to themselves. You can't win, sisters, if that kind of equality is your game. Betty Friedan in her latest book writes of women executives becoming pseudo-men, workaholics, trying to make it to the top with the same blinded push as men, and succumbing to the same diseases. On a larger national scale, an ominous increase of lung cancer and heart attacks recently reported among younger women is also being blamed on the women's movement.[34] Who wants this kind of 'progress'?

Fortunately most women are more sensible. Millions are pursuing their own goals without one eye over their shoulder to see where they might have been at if they had been born men. Equal but different is their motto. Above all they have learned to like each other much more than they used to, and to trust each other. Remember how women were supposed to be catty, bitchy about each other? Now there is an openness, a warmth among women, especially among youngsters, that I find really heart-warming. Nowhere is this more obvious than among the single mothers by choice whom I met – almost without exception they all relied on their friends to back them up and to supply the emotional warmth they had not been able to find in relationships with men. As I pointed out earlier, mutual support among women is a very ancient pattern, and a return to it is to be applauded. This has to be one of the biggest gains of the women's movement.

Motherhood
It changes you. Theories are one thing, motherhood is another. *Anna*, Dutch child psychologist: 'Before I was

pregnant I thought I could make my life with my ideas alone, but when my child was about 2 years old I found out my emotions were going into a different direction than my rational ideas were telling me. And it is really a big fight with yourself, because I know as a feminist woman I don't want to accept this; I approve of feminist ideas, but there's another part in me, an emotional part that makes me want something else again.'

Oakley, on the other hand, reports in her book that half the sample of sixty-six mothers she interviewed before and after the births of their children found that becoming a mother had considerably changed their attitudes to the position of women.[35] They felt differently towards men, towards society, towards their position in society, which they said treated them as second-class citizens. They found the hours they worked exhausting and quite unexpected. Their experiences made many of them sympathize with the women's movement, and question things about society they hadn't noticed before, such as why it is that our society is not geared to children, in spite of the fact that nearly everyone has them.

Laura, who had picked out an old family friend as the future father of her child when she was 16, now 26 years old and heavily pregnant with her first child when I interviewed her, talked about how her desire to have a child had emerged over the past few years. 'I was beginning to feel, what am I here for, what is my role in life? and being very fond of children I thought, well, my role in life is to be a mother. Which is something I would never have admitted to five years ago. I think there's something very strong in nature, and I think this is why you're getting a lot of women going this way. With the women's movement generation there was this – oh, we're as good as men, as strong, we don't want children. The maternal instinct was shoved underground, but now, as you say, they're in their middle to late thirties and it's beginning to come through again. They think, yes, I've proved myself in a career, and yes, I've been as strong as a man, and now I want to be a mother.'

'*What about the women's movement emphasis on a woman being an individual in her own right?*'

'I've always felt the importance of that and still do. I'm me first, and a mother second, and other roles third and fourth. But part of me is being a mother, yes, and my major fear is becoming very dependent on the child, and of giving it smother love instead of mother love. I know that when it's born I'm going to have to make very conscious efforts to keep up outside interests, and to keep part of myself to myself. The child can have three-quarters of me, but the other quarter is going to be for *me*. Whether it'll work out like that I don't know, we'll have to wait and see!'

3
Man as stud

There is much to suggest that the male mind has always been haunted by the force of the idea of dependence on a woman for life itself, *the son's constant effort to assimilate, compensate for, or deny the fact that he is 'of woman born'.* (Adrienne Rich[1])

Research reports that women tend to view morality in terms of responsibility in personal relationships, while men's moral concerns address the rights of individuals to non-interference. (Carol Bruch[2])

'I *was living with a man, but I thought I don't want to have a child dependent on a love relationship with a man, because love doesn't last for ever. . . . Already at 16 or 18 I said to my mother I'm not going to marry at all, I just want to have a child. By the time I was 19 the men that I met were saying to me but you want to have children so you need me as a father. I would say, no, I don't need you, I need your sperm, and that's something else.'* (Anna)

'No, *if a woman asked me to do that for her, I wouldn't accept that I'd have no rights over the child, because I think it would be unrealistic. I mean, she could enforce it legally, but the fact is you'd go on living in the same world along with those people, and there would be a relationship, whether the mother says there is or there isn't. In other words, I would be the father, that would be the child, I would have a special feeling for that child, so I think it would be quite artificial to say, go ahead, I don't want to see it again.'* (David)

Man as stud

When I started researching this book it didn't occur to me that women would have a problem finding men to impregnate them. As one of the mothers commented in the previous chapter, when you're young, the general problem is keeping men out of your bed rather than getting them into it. But men seem to have a greater sense of responsibility than most women think. Or is it more complicated than that?

The experience of some of the women I interviewed is that men will agree if you ask them when you're together in bed and they haven't had time to think about it, but once they have thought about it in the cold light of day they have second thoughts. If you conceive first time off, fine – if not, you are going to have problems. Jessica Curtis talked about this. 'Some time after the divorce I decided I wanted to have another kid, so I tried with various friends – they weren't lovers necessarily, they were people who wanted to help me out. But I found they'd say yes one week and no the next. What happened? Well, one guy went off and got married, and others – well, they'd say different things and I'd respect that. For instance, they'd say, no, I'd want to raise the kid myself; or, listen, I really don't like children, let me not make one. It all ended with my not getting any help.'

'*What do men say if you ask them when you're not about to make love?*'

'They say no. If you ask them they say no, almost universally. The other women at the group [Single Mothers by Choice] say they found the same thing. And that makes it very difficult, because it's virtually impossible for a woman of my age to get married – I'm 38 now. It's not totally impossible, but it's very very difficult. So you can't find a man to marry you and you can't find a man willing to make a child.'

'*But if 50 per cent of American married women end up divorced, where are the 50 per cent of divorced marriageable men?*'

'Most of them marry younger women; they marry someone who's ten years younger, and so I'd have to look for someone ten, fifteen years older than me. And if I find someone who's 48 he's at death's door in lots of cases! And he's had all the kids he wants to have; he wants to have a fling, not to settle again straight away. Then a lot of guys are gay, about three or four times as many as gay women. And one of the main traps is this, traditionally men marry down and women marry up in terms of status. And that can make for problems if you're used to a certain lifestyle. So the age thing especially leaves a lot of women out in the cold. Yes, it's true that more older women are marrying younger men nowadays, because they're the only people left. It's to men of lower status usually – that's fine, I'd do it myself. But men of my age who've never married are single for a reason – they're professional bachelors if they're not gay. So in the end I gave in trying to find a guy to do it for me, and went to a fertility clinic for artificial insemination.'

I asked *David*, an Englishman who spends a lot of time in the States, what he would do if someone asked him the question. 'I *was* asked once, at a dinner party in Santa Barbara. The husband had had his tubes tied not meaning to have any more children, then he'd remarried and his wife wanted a baby. At first it seemed a kind of sexy question, but then I went home and thought about it seriously. As I said just now [see the last quote at the beginning of this chapter] I thought about – would I accept that, because it would be my child. I decided that for me the most important thing would be the woman herself. In that particular case the woman didn't particularly interest me in any sense, so I wouldn't have done it anyway, but I can think of two or three women that I think the world of, and I'd be happy – if the child grew up in their world, it would be a good world. It's not a sexual thing, it's just that I feel that as human beings those two or three people are very special.'

This attitude I found to be typical of the men I interviewed. I admit that I spoke mostly to the kind of men who were the sort of person the women I was meeting might well have chosen for themselves – it is true they were a mixed lot, but I didn't try stopping total strangers in the street, for instance. It is also true that the women I was meeting, as I wrote earlier, might seem to have been from a fairly limited range – mostly intelligent, self-aware types – but at present this is precisely the kind of woman who is daring to go ahead and become pregnant on her own. But I suspect that the responses I elicited from men would be fairly universal: first reaction (with a pleased grin) – wow, that's a sexy question; second reaction – on the other hand, I don't know; third reaction – well, no, not unless the circumstances were very special.

I talked to a child psychiatrist about this and his reaction followed the usual pattern. At first he said that if he really liked and trusted the woman, and was absolutely certain she would be a good mother, then he might well do it, but it would be essential he found her physically attractive also. But, he then added, he'd insist on keeping in touch with the new family, and that he supposed, would make for all kinds of complications. His wife, he said finally, would hardly care for that – he was so busy he saw little enough of his own kids as it was – so, on further thought, he supposed the answer was no, it wouldn't be on. He was, I felt, a bit reluctant to arrive at that conclusion; the prospect of doing such a kindness had obviously set off a pleasant train of thoughts in his head.

Rosa in Holland had the same experience as Jessica in New York. 'No one wanted to have a child the way I wanted it. One wanted to live together with me, not to marry but to be close. Another one didn't want children at all, he didn't want the responsibility, and when I told him I would take all the responsibility he didn't want that either. The third one – it is always the same, men don't believe what I say; they say, oh well, when we live together she will be changing and we will get married and so on. He wanted that, but I didn't.'

Part-time researcher *Charlotte*, like several of the other mothers, chose a gay friend, who was rather pleased, though very cautious, about the idea. *Sharon*, an assistant professor of women's studies, would be happy to have a child by an ex-lover who, since their four-year-long relationship, has become gay and is in a long-term relationship with another man, but, she says, 'he thinks it's a little too weird. His attitude is, there would be this child in the world, and what would his relationship to it be? It doesn't feel right to him.'

Joanna, a graduate student of Third World studies, who had selected a father with immense and remarkable precision, even down to the shape of his skull, and who had intended the relationship to be purely one of sperm donation, found herself 'growing a little dependent on him; it's very hard not to, I think – when you're pregnant your body makes certain demands, and there's a definite physical response. We had gone on making love, but after a month he pulled out – he was frightened of getting too involved. He'd really wanted to please me, it was one of the most charming things that ever happened to me, that he wanted so much to make me happy, but he pulled out after a month because he was frightened I'd swallow him up – all my lovers had felt that way.'

Who can blame men if they are growing frightened of this confident army of women who know so clearly what they want? It *is* difficult for them to accept that the women mean what they say, that they don't want domesticity and marriage, and perhaps they are right to be cautious, because for every Rosa who means precisely what she says, and has proved it, there is her opposite, who means what she says at the time, but who, like Joanna, finds pregnancy and motherhood make surprising changes to her, both physically and emotionally. Dr Cohen, a Californian obstetrician, says, 'Fifteen or twenty years ago, at least in California, it might have been easier in some ways for a woman to get pregnant by a casual male friend, but because of all the recent litigation and court cases here in paternity suits a man now will be much more careful. He'd say, hey, I'm not going to be involved with you, you're likely to end up suing me for everything I've got to raise this kid that I didn't want in the first place.'

Psychologist Hendrika Vande Kemp has no doubts about her feelings. 'I must say that in spite of all the pessimism and cynicism I sometimes feel about men, I think that to use men as studs is the most insulting, degrading, dehumanizing thing that anyone could do to someone.'

'*But isn't that what they've always done to women.*'

'They may have, but that's not an excuse. To come back

with the same thing is not a solution. I find it very upsetting to contemplate that.'

Is man 'haunted' because 'he is "of woman born"?'

The first identification a baby makes is with the person closest to it, which almost invariably is its mother. It is her image that the child internalizes as part of himself, she to whom he feels similar because his sense of self at this stage owes almost everything to her, and it is she whom he wishes to emulate. Lillian Rubin points out that boys as much as girls have their earliest experiences of attachment and identification with a woman, so that boys of 3 or 4 will often say that when they grow up they are going to have a baby. When the mother explains that only girls can have babies the boy child may burst into tears, feeling anger and disappointment because he cannot understand why – since he has learned to identify with his mother – he cannot copy her and have children of his own.[3]

Dr Elphis Christopher, after talking about how many girls have babies at an early age partly in order to feel grown-up because society makes them feel that that is a sure path to maturity, added, 'the fact that women can carry a child within them gives them this fantastic power that a man can never have. A woman has her role but a man doesn't, he's always defining it, he's always trying to find what the heck he's there for.' The very existence of sperm banks must threaten men too. Until recently there was no way a woman could have a child without being impregnated by a man; now not only do sperm banks make all except a tiny number of men unnecessary from a reproductive point of view, but science is moving to the stage when it may soon be possible to produce a human foetus from an egg that has never been fertilized by sperm at all.

Discussing male sensibilities about fertility Elaine May, who writes on the history of the family, said, 'At my father's infertility clinic, the women found it fairly easy to deal with problems such as blocked fallopian tubes, but men learning they had a low sperm count, for example – which is just another physiological accident and has nothing to do with virility – frequently were terribly upset and had a much more difficult time coping with that than did the women. There is a cultural tradition of a man's machoness being wrapped up in how many children he can father, or his sexuality as manifested through paternity.'

Rubin, writing of the necessity for boys to finally make a total separation from their mothers because of the need to develop an independent, effective self of a different gender, points out that this is something girls never had to do. It is true that at one level it is harder for girls because the break is more complicated as they share the same gender as their mother and some of the same expectations; working out just how far the separation has to go is a difficult task both for daughter and for mother. A few years ago Nancy Friday's popular *My Mother My Self* set out the age-old struggles with candour and painful accuracy.[4] For boys the task is more brutal, for the break has to be complete if acceptance of a different gender is to be achieved. He must destroy this identification within himself with his mother and instead identify with his father or whatever male figure is dominant in his life, but this may be very difficult since males are usually so peripheral to a small child's existence. Tearing himself away from his mother leaves him vulnerable, and to 'protect himself against the pain wrought by this radical shift in his internal world, he builds a set of defences that, in many important ways, will serve him, for good or ill, for the rest of his life.'[5] This, she says, is the beginning of the formation of the rigid barriers that men set up around themselves, making it so difficult for them to stay in touch with their inner emotional life. Betrayed, hurt, no longer able to trust women, men come to believe that women are weak, contemptible creatures who can never be anything but subordinate to men.

This is a very simplified version of a theory that sounds highly plausible to me. Certainly huge numbers of men fit the picture outlined above, and it seems to me that one of the surest ways of changing this entire unsatisfactory scenario would be for men to share equally in the raising of their children right from the beginning. This is obviously not possible for women who are having their children alone, but hopefully the kind of men whom these women consciously bring into their families because they recognize the need for male models will, at the very least, give the children warmer, less aggressive and more communicative models to copy than the average Western father.

Man face to face with the New Woman

'I don't need you, I need your sperm!' It made my flesh crawl thinking about the effect this comment must have had on the man Anna had said this to. But have men in the past been more sensitive about our feelings? I could give endless numbers of quotes from things said to me over the years by boyfriends, husband, and general male acquaintances, not to count all the chauvinist assumptions in over two thousand years of male-dominated literature. It's hardly surprising if some women get a bit abrasive in their new-found confidence.

But leaving aside attacks from the more extreme radical feminists who dislike and distrust all men and make no pretence about it, how often are men faced with the kind of mental knock-down they have so cheerfully handed out to women over the years? In my interviews with the mothers I came across little straightforward female chauvinism – it was mainly a question of fairly gentle gibes or saddened disillusionment; behind it there was nearly always a remote hope that in the end they could find a man with whom they could have a good relationship. There were only two instances of a cold calculating approach in woman's search for a stud of the type which I had originally envisaged, and one of those was at second hand, reported to me by *Catherine*. An actress, she had been interviewed a few years back by someone who during the course of the interview happened to drop that she had had a child by choice outside of marriage. Catherine, thinking of doing this herself, had been curious about it. 'She went out and found this man, and it was just like going out for a loaf of bread. I asked her if she had anything to do with him now, and her face had an expression of horror – "Certainly not!" she said, "I wouldn't have anything to do with him at all." I asked her what it was

like, and was she happy, and she said, "Oh, it's a bit of a
nuisance, really, the child's 8 months now and I don't see
that much of her, but I get tired of being woken up in the
night," and her whole attitude was really cold, towards the
child as well as the father. She did it the way you were
expecting to find in your researches, completely calculating,
but she didn't seem at all happy. I think if it's all as casual as
that the child won't mean much to you, it's more like
buying a new car.'

The other extreme is *Janice*, who had had an 'open'
living-together relationship with Jack, her child's father, for
five years before she got pregnant. Although she has total
responsibility for her daughter, who is in her name, Jack
shares her care completely. 'One of the reasons I took this
job of research assistant,' Janice said, 'was that it's part-time.
It gives me enough money to live on, and I'm able to see my
daughter more than at the weekends only. I came back to
work when she was 7 weeks old and Jack looked after her
then – at that time he wasn't working, so that was fine. Now
both of us work three or four days a week and can spend
time with her. On days when we can't avoid both being out
she goes to a child-minder. It works very well.'

Not many men are so ready to accept genuine sharing.
In modern marriage the typical attitude of men towards their
partners seem to be that yes, working women have a tough
time doing two jobs at once, and that even women who stay
at home need relief from a twenty-four hour day but, as Mary
Ingham, investigating male attitudes in her book *Men*,
found, very few of them actually do anything about it.
Curiously, some of the men she interviewed whose wives
didn't go out to work gave their wives more domestic help
than some of those whose wives worked full-time outside
the house. 'Only a handful came anywhere near shouldering
half the burden of the housework and cooking.'[6] American
men seem to do a little better, especially on the West Coast
and among academia in general, but reports from more
conservative areas like the Mid-West show progress is slow.

How and why is it that men can acknowledge that
women ought to be helped, but continue to avoid doing so if
they possibly can? In marriage I suspect they get away with

it because most women find it easier to get on with the chores than to be perpetually asking for help from reluctant or 'busy' husbands. Women deciding to have children on their own know this perfectly well – they have many married friends, after all, and see what the reality of marriage is like – and a reluctance to care for not only a genuine child but also an adult 'child', as many of them have put it, is one of the main reasons they are still alone.

This problem of men lagging behind in what I see as the inevitable metamorphosis of female/male relationships is almost universal in the Western world. This is not the place to explore modern man and his place in marriage, but it is worth recording a few comments made about this subject by some of the people I spoke to when we were discussing the possible effects of an increase in deliberate single parenthood on men and on the family. I have just reported Mary Ingham's findings on British men. Child psychologist *Anna* (Dutch), found much the same thing in Holland: 'I know a lot of men who with their words feel a lot of solidarity with women, but in the things they are doing they don't change at all. They don't want to give up their careers, they want their status, because what is looking after children? It doesn't give you a lot of status. It *is* happening, it *is* changing, I know couples, but not a lot, where they really share. I think it's coming, but so slow – the men say the words but they don't want to be responsible for children.'

Marilyn Fabe (American, author of *Up Against the Clock*[7]) in a personal communication: 'From my sample and looking around at friends, I think that nowadays most middle-class men who are married to women who take their careers seriously – and the marriage isn't being ruined by that – are very committed to their children and are very conscious of what they need to do. If the wife can let go, the man is often all too happy to take on that role. But for so many years women haven't had anything else to define themselves around, and children have been inordinately important for their identity, and they've shut the male out, so he doesn't participate. It's a sort of spiral downwards. But boy, you just leave a space for it, and I think they find the same sort of pleasure and fulfilment that women have found.' (I comment that it is probably far more common in the celebrated University of California at Berkeley than elsewhere.) 'That's probably true, I think you always have to put in a grain of salt when you're talking to someone from Berkeley. On the other hand, when we went to the Mid-West in '79 to talk about our book on radio talk shows, people would be shocked about our subject [career women considering whether or not to have children] and say I was a sort of devil for even suggesting that women should work *and* have children too. But when a trend starts such as men wanting equal participation in child care and cutting back on work in order to be more with the children, the idea trickles down. I do think it's a genuine desire that men have to relate to their children in a very significant and intimate way, but it has culturally been squelched. Antagonism came through strongly on certain talk shows, but then I'd notice there'd be sympathetic articles from that same part of the country that suggested there was a new trend starting. It may be minor, but it's there. Also watching people at my Lamaze group [preparation for birth classes] you get people from all sorts of different backgrounds, not just middle-class college teachers, etc., but a whole group of people of different races, social classes – the way men were dealing with holding the children and diapering them – I think that is significantly different.'

Sharon (American), assistant professor of women's studies: 'I want a child but it's not something I would choose to do alone, not without another adult who was committed to co-parenting with me – it could be a woman, it could be a man who might have no biological connection with the child. It has to be another adult who takes living with and caring for this child seriously, so that means it can't be a man who is going to do it the way men have traditionally done it. I don't mean *helping* me, I mean spending as much time as me with the child, changing as many diapers, getting up for as many broken nights. There simply aren't many men who would be willing to do that, whatever they said in advance.'

Rosa (Dutch), specialist in child psychology, who chose

a Greek whom she met on holiday to be the father of her child: 'He loved children very much, he cared about them: I think he was an honest man, he was a sailor and had been all over the world, but he is not an educated man, and that is one of the problems. We have a different culture, different thinking about how men and women should live. He came here to Amsterdam to see us, but it was not possible for him to work here – he cannot speak the language for one thing, only some English but he can't write it. I went at Easter to visit him in Greece, but I decided it was not possible to be with him: it was good in many ways, yes, but he wouldn't take any responsibility: he would put the baby in the bath, give him food, change his clothes, but only if *he* wanted it. If he was sitting in the sunshine and the baby needed something, I was the one to go. In the night-time I was sitting in the house alone, he was going to have coffee with his friends – that's the way of life there.'

Obviously change *is* in the air, but there aren't going to be enough New Men around in the near future to provide enough husbands, legal or otherwise, for the infinitely larger number of New Women. So they are going to go it alone, because what other choice do they have?

Will men change? Recently a new book called *The Redundant Male*, written by two men, came out, its thesis being that men's 'role as hunters and providers has been made redundant by our modern way of life; their sexual role is much reduced – indeed, even non-existent'.[8] There will be many other books of this kind in the future. As I said earlier, men are going to need help if, in the face of all these threats to their self-esteem, they are not going to close hatches and cut themselves off even more from their own emotions and real communication with the other sex. Ed Cohen, an American gynaecologist, feels this strongly: 'There's been so much attention paid to women's libber type people and their putting down of men as a group as being amoral and non-caring, insensitive – but interview some men about their experiences with women and you may hear the same thing in reverse. There is no monopoly on feeling or sensitivity by the gender one happens to be born with, and to see all this attention and publicity being focused on women's needs is very frustrating to men. Ones I have spoken to, the husbands of my patients, have been very sensitive and caring, but they've felt very left out, that *their* emotional needs are not being considered whatsoever these days. Interestingly enough, I had one husband recently tell me that he felt very much like this, left out, unconsidered, during his wife's pregnancy. He happens to be a clinical psychologist, and since that time he has started a group for men, and I told him this was a beautiful idea, because for the past ten years so much attention has been focused on women's needs but nobody has thought that men even have feelings about these situations.'

Of course men do – the only problem, in Britain if not in California, is getting them to admit it.

Men wanting children without women

As yet there aren't many of them, but the number may be growing. One kind is the divorced man who is missing his children. I met recently an architect whose marriage had broken up and who, because of the distance involved, rarely saw his small daughter. I have never seen a man more 'broody'. We were with a group of friends having tea in a sunny tea-garden, and all the time his eyes were on the small children running around, playing, crying, laughing, chasing the resident cat. 'You look as though you can't wait to get married again,' I said. He shook his head vehemently. 'Absolutely not,' he said, 'Never again. Once should be enough for any man. But I want children so badly I feel trapped. It's not just that I miss my own kid, it's that I always wanted a proper family, several kids, a real family. But after what my wife did to me, and the money she ripped off me, I've learned my lesson. Why should I have to get married and support another human being just so that I can have a child? Women don't have to do that!'

Another kind is the gay man who will never set up a permanent relationship with a woman but who would love to have a child of his own. One gay couple I know recently had a visit from the son of one of them by an early marriage. 'It was lovely, we all get along very well,' the other man said. 'But it brought home to both of us a lack that I, at least, wasn't particularly conscious of before. We are very close, it's a very good relationship, but it's our one sadness, this, that we can't make a child together.'

Male gays may not be able to make a child *together*, but at least they can father a child if they want. Quite a few of the mothers I met had considered having their children by gay friends. *Catherine*, actress, who had had a baby by her married lover, said she wouldn't have another by him because of the problems centred around him being married, but she added, 'If I was really stuck now and wanted to have a child, I'd find my dearest gay friend who also would have liked a child in his life. It would be lovely to have a man who really loved the child and who came and visited it regularly, and yet who gave the woman total independence. I think it would be almost ideal, really.'

The Gay Men's Press has published a book called *Jenny lives with Eric and Martin*,[9] which is a book for young children and is about little Jenny who lives with her father and his friend Eric. The publishers tell me that the book has done very well and sells not only to gays but also to libraries and to parents who want their children to grow up with a knowledge of various lifestyles. There are, they tell me, quite a few gay men, single or in couples, who are bringing up their own children – numbers are impossible to check because tact has to be exercised in divorce courts when care of the child is being settled, and no doubt there are other cases where a woman unintentionally becomes pregnant by a gay (many of whom occasionally sleep with girlfriends) and who doesn't want to bring up the child herself.

Gays are also exploring the question of surrogate mothers. Currently there is much argument about how surrogate motherhood will be treated from a legal point of view: the British 1984 Warnock Report will almost certainly ensure that if surrogate mothering is allowed at all it will be stringently controlled, but it is difficult to see how unofficial arrangements can be ruled out. One doctor commented she was afraid it would go underground, like abortion, if it were made illegal, and that it would be preferable to control it under some kind of licence. Some of the possible problems have already been highlighted in cases reaching the courts in America; what happens if the child is born handicapped and the 'purchasing' parents reject it? What happens if the supposed father on seeing the child decides it is not his, and insists that the surrogate mother cheated on him and was impregnated by her husband or someone else? What happens if the mother decides she doesn't want to part with the child after all, especially if she has been paid a large sum of money in advance to ensure her well-being during pregnancy, a sum she is unable to pay back? Having a child can't be treated like going out and buying a new carpet for the bedroom, and only the most naive could suppose it is. But the need to reproduce oneself can be so powerful that sometimes the very real problems involved can be blindly overlooked.

I asked Ted Nagle, gynaecologist and fertility expert, what he would do if a gay couple asked him to arrange for a surrogate mother to be impregnated by the sperm of one of them through artificial insemination. 'I would be opposed to it because of the fact of their being so far from the social norm.'

'*Supposing a "normal", straight man, divorced but wanting a child of his own, came with a woman prepared to be a surrogate mother?*'

'Well, I would suggest they go rent a motel. My concern here – and I can sympathize with both these cases – is that for a child the optimal situation is one that's normative for that society. I often have a lot of sympathy for the man because he doesn't even have the option that the single women you're writing about have: you know, he's in a worse bind, the guy who wants to become a father but who is single and who doesn't want to be in a relationship with a woman, etc.; there's no way he can carry that child. At least the woman has that option.'

Another gynaecologist, Ed Cohen, said he probably wouldn't help someone who wanted to have a child through a surrogate mother either, but his objection was mainly that there were too many legal cases already on record, and doctors had learned to be cautious. 'On the other hand if a woman brought in a semen specimen and said she wanted to be impregnated with it – I might question the conditions under which she had obtained the specimen and so on – but, as I think I'd be perfectly safe as far as the legal aspects go, then I would be happy to do it.'

Yet another way out for men who don't want a relationship with a woman is to adopt, but the problem here is the difficulty of finding a child to adopt. Ed Cohen sums up the general position which is the same in America as in Britain: 'The relative liberalization of the abortion laws in the past fifteen years has meant that the number of children available for adoption is far less than it used to be, and most adoption agencies are less likely to place a child with a single male parent than they are with a couple or even a single female parent. You have to wait several years if you want to choose the age, the sex and the race of the child even if you are a "perfect" couple, though if you are prepared to accept *any* child you can probably have one next week. If you wanted to adopt a 15-year-old male black child with a juvenile delinquency record you can probably have him tomorrow. A working single man wanting to adopt a small child therefore would have tremendous difficulty.'

Dr Nagle wasn't entirely right, because there are a few avenues open, but these are complicated and require a fair amount of initiative. *Nora* and *Adina*, an American lesbian couple, are awaiting the birth of a child they have arranged to adopt in one of the Central American countries. *Jane*, a lawyer friend whose house they share, already has a daughter of 7 months through the same agency. They told me that single men also have adopted children through the same agency, but in the time available to me I was not able to track them down and interview them personally. This is not an easy route, but it can be done, though the problems of making regular contact with other families who have adopted children of a similar race would be considerable for a man not living in an area where there are large numbers of immigrants originally coming from his child's country of birth.

A further way for a man to be involved with a child is to share the care of an infant with a single mother, but even if he agreed to share equally this would most probably mean that he would not be given any rights over the child, and would risk losing contact with it if the mother moved away or chose to refuse him access. Quite a few of the mothers I interviewed hope to meet a man who would be prepared to do this – a few pages back I quoted Sharon, for example – but I must admit I find it difficult to see why a man would be prepared to share child care equally with a mother without some sort of reassurance that it was a lifelong commitment if that was what he wanted.

Rosa, Dutch specialist in child psychology, is one mother who succeeded in finding such a man. Like herself he is a mature student, and they became good friends at the university in Amsterdam which they both attend. 'What happened was, Dirk was talking with some jealousy to me because I had decided to have a child and had had it just like that. How can a man get a baby? he said. So I said to him, you can talk about it a lot, but if you want you can have my baby for one day a week to practise. Then I heard nothing about it for one month, so I thought it was bluff. Then he came here to my house and he said, well, I have a bed, I have a pram, I have a chair, when can I have the baby? I was surprised! So I said, you can mind him one day a week, but you are responsible for that day, and if you are ill or you have a meeting, *you* have to arrange about that. So for one and a half years he has cared for him one or two days, sometimes three days a week. For example, today I will bring my son to the children's playground where the staff will look after him until he collects him, and tomorrow he will take him again to the playground and in the afternoon I collect him. Yes, he has the child all night too. It's a struggle a lot of the time, because he wants to have him *this* day and I want *that* day, but . . .

'I can talk properly with Dirk about education [they are both studying child psychology] which is good, about what we think is right and wrong, and we can discuss easily if he thinks I am wrong because we are not lovers. He is very like me – he was married for some time, and then divorced, and then he goes to university. He thinks a man can raise a child as well as a woman, and that a family is not necessary. If you give a child safety and good feelings and so on, that is enough. He started looking after Alex when he was just over a year old – he was walking then, so it was easier than looking after a small baby. But there is a problem now, because he has got a girlfriend he is living with, and she has to accept Alex too. I can hear that she feels jealous about his relationship with Alex – when Alex is there with him he is number one; and also, she wants to be pregnant. So I don't know what happens now.'

'*What happens if Dirk moves away?*'

'That's a risk you always have – sometimes people close to me when I was a child moved away. Dirk and Alex have a very strong relationship, and though there might be trouble, especially if his girlfriend has a baby, I think it is such a good relationship it will be all right. I think Dirk is more important to him than his own father because he hasn't seen him for so long.

'There are other little problems we have – sometimes Dirk has him for a weekend when I want him, if it is a special day of celebration, for instance, like yesterday, but I had him last year, so this year it is Dirk's turn. Christmas time, Easter, we have to share it, and holidays too. This year at Christmas Dirk came to my place with his girlfriend, and others too, and it was really good. But this can be difficult for Alex when Dirk and I are together, because Alex doesn't know what to do. Most of the time he comes to me, especially when we are here in my flat, but last week we were in the park together, and when Dirk said he was going to look after him Alex says no, I want my mother; but sometimes he says no, I want Dirk. But he is a happy boy – I think it is a good arrangement for him.'

Men's rights over their children

Adrienne Rich writes, 'Through control of his children [man] insures the disposition of his patrimony and the safe passage of his soul after death.'[10] Now that few of us have our souls prayed for when we are dead it is even more important for those of us who care about such things that our children carry the memory of our existence forward into new generations. But what if our children don't know who we are? What if a man doesn't even know that he has fathered a child, or, suspecting it, cannot find out for sure?

First of all, let us look at the legal position on men's rights over their illegitimate children. In Britain these are still being debated, following the 1982 Law Commission's recommendations published three years after the law reform group had put forward proposals to entirely abolish the official status of illegitimacy. These earlier proposals, which suggested that distinctions between legitimate and illegitimate children should no longer exist (thereby giving *all* fathers rights over the children, not just married ones), caused a great outcry, not only from people concerned about 'morality' and the family, but also from women's groups. The Rights of Women organization 'was indignant: "The proposals . . . are a direct attack on women who have chosen to have children independent from men." '[11] It might be fine for the children to lose the stigma of illegitimacy, but for unmarried women it meant losing sole control over the future of their children. In the face of such combined opposition the Commission decided to recommend only certain changes which would increase the rights of fathers but would not make them total.

So far there have been no such changes in the law, and at present fathers have no automatic rights over their illegitimate children; if they want rights of access or custody they must apply to the courts. If they have kept up regular contact with the child they might be given rights of access, but if they want custody they would have to prove the unsuitability of the mother to raise the child (obviously lesbian women are in danger here from a prejudiced judge). If the father has had no contact with the child then he is unlikely to be given access, though if the mother has refused to permit him to see the baby and he could prove that he had made repeated attempts to do so then he might stand a chance of being given an access order provided he made his application within a reasonable time. But the primary concern of the courts is to do what they consider to be best for the child, and I was told by a solicitor specializing in divorce and custody cases that in this last instance the courts would in fact probably refuse access because the inevitable tension and stress that would arise between the two parents would almost certainly be harmful to the child.

Another consequence of the present law can be that if an unmarried mother were to die, the father of their child – even if he had been living with the mother as though they were legally married – could find the child being taken away from him by the social services and placed for adoption: as an unmarried father he has no automatic rights unless the couple has foreseen such a possibility and made the father a legal guardian.[12] It can help if when the child is born the father's name is put on the birth certificate, but he cannot insist that this is done, nor does he have any right to insist that the child carry his surname, nor any right to choose its school or to have any say in its upbringing.

Men's pressure groups, such as one called Fathers Need Families, have been formed to fight this situation, while equally concerned women's groups are arguing that these men's primary desire is to achieve control over mother and child. There is no space here to go into the rights and wrongs of the case – I can only suggest that a woman deciding to have a child on her own should bear in mind the possibility of a change in the law and act accordingly (this is a major reason why many mothers choose artificial insemination) and that a man should remember that at present if the woman he is making love to gets pregnant, unless they marry he has no legal rights at all over the resultant child.

As men see it one of the unfairnesses of the present situation is that while a man has no rights he does have responsibilities, and can find himself faced with an affiliation order making him pay towards the upkeep of the child. In the USA, where the situation is very similar to that outlined above, there has been much legal argument over cases where the man wanted the woman to have an abortion and she has refused. Under current law even if the man has offered to pay for the abortion he will be liable to be ordered to support the child, and the justice of this is being challenged. The opposite situation is that if a man wishes a woman to bear his illegitimate child but she chooses to abort he has no legal say in the matter – the decision is entirely in her hands. 'A number of court cases have decided that the man is not party to the woman's decision and, should she choose to abort, has no further recourse. Thus, even if the man offers to take custody and completely support the child, he cannot legally influence the mother's decision.'[13]

In another well-publicized case in New York, however, a woman who decided without his knowledge to have a child by a particular man and then sued him for upkeep found the courts unsympathetic. The man claimed that he was 'deceived into being an unwilling sperm donor' and that the woman 'was known to have told others that she was not using birth-control pills' in order to have his child. 'Intercourse occurred . . . under false pretenses that the woman had taken precautions against conception. Based on scientific evidence . . . the man was adjudged to be the biological father of the child, and the mother sued for support. The court ruled in favor of the father, and while his obligation to support was not completely voided, placed severe limitations on the extent of that liability.'[14] The author of the passage from which I have been quoting comments that it is very difficult for a court to decide what actually happened between two people (in this particular case the woman had told others what she was doing), but he points out that if a man wants to be really sure he will not impregnate a woman then he should take his own precautions – after all, everyone knows that no contraceptive is one hundred per cent perfect, and that if he is prepared to take such a risk then he should be responsible for the consequences.

So how does this work out in practice with mothers I have interviewed? *Rosa* faces possible problems with the father of her child, who is a Greek. Greek law is different from Dutch law, and although her son is safe in Holland there is the possibility that if she should take him to visit his father then Greek law would permit his father to refuse to let her take him home again. 'I have not registered him here in Holland as Alex's father, but in Greece you don't have to have a mother's signature to acknowledge who the baby is and I know that Alex is registered there as his son – he's already bought a small piece of land for him. He can put Alex on his passport and I can do nothing about it.'

Angela, an American PhD graduate student, had an affair with a lover who wanted a child – it was actually he who suggested they should have a baby together. They took Lamaze birth classes together, and he assisted at the birth. He insisted that they had joint custody of the child, which seemed right at the time, but she feels that since she doesn't want to marry, this arrangement might cause problems later.

That women need to be cautious is exemplified by two cases told me by *Pat*, a midwife. The first was about a woman who had several children in a marriage which eventually broke up. She was awarded custody of the children, but when a lesbian friend moved in with her the husband decided to fight this. The judge ruled that unless the lesbian friend moved out the children should be given to the father. The women had no choice but to agree, and the couple were forced to pay for separate accommodation for the friend, which they could ill afford. The second case was also about a lesbian couple who chose to have the non-biological mother's brother as their baby's father 'so that the child would be some part of both of them. But during the pregnancy they broke up. It just blew my mind – they'd planned so long to have this child together! Then this brother got married, and sued for his child. The judge first awarded the brother the child – she was taken away for several months – and the mother was going crazy, she's a real natural mother, still nurses the baby now, and in the end the child was returned to her – I don't know why exactly. I certainly learned the lesson – if *I* do it I'll do it through a sperm bank, it's much safer.'

Stella and *Jan*, themselves a lesbian couple, had the same arrangement with Stella's brother, who is gay, but they were aware of the possible danger. 'If my brother had been straight we'd never have considered him, because you don't know what's going to happen in the future. If he'd been straight and got married his wife might have convinced him he should have custody of the child, and in a custody battle a court would be more likely to give custody to a straight married couple than a lesbian couple. . . . We have very good relations with him, and he has an option to be considered the father – right now we call him the donor and he considers himself an uncle. We've written up a contract which says that in the future if he wishes to become known as the father he will also have to accept all the commitments and responsibilities that go with that role, including financial and emotional commitments – also that later on down the line if our son really presses to know who his father is then we shall tell him. What we tried to do was to protect everybody's rights, and we all sighted it.'

Janice, who continues to live in a good relationship with the father of her child, discussed all of this with her lover before they had the child. 'I can't imagine a situation where we'd split up and not have some kind of agreement about our daughter seeing her father, but that's because he's always been very involved in caring for her since she was born – he was there at the birth. His name isn't on the birth certificate, no, but if we *did* split and when she was older she said, right, I'd rather go with him, then I wouldn't stop her. He's got such a good relationship with her, he's cared for her, he's put almost as much into that as I have, and at the moment anyway I can't see any reason even if we did split up why he shouldn't have access to her.'

What finally seems to matter is the amount of caring the father puts into his relationship with his child. A father who has little or no contact cannot expect the mother, nor for that matter the child, to take his claims seriously. *David* told me about a friend of his whose father had been a well-known figure and who had had lots of affairs in his youth. The mother married someone else and brought the son up as the child of the marriage. One day 'this man rang him and said he was passing through the town. This often seems to happen – daddy, who's been a great lover in his youth, gets old and begins to want his security, and thinks, God, I have a son! I should go and see him and be friends. So my friend was nervous because he was going to have lunch with his father whom he'd never seen, and afterwards when I saw him I said, how was it? and he said, "Nothing happened. He was like a stranger." He was saying to me, this friend, "Look – when I needed him when I was a kid he wasn't around, and now that he needs *me* he's suddenly trying to be friendly. But I'm just not interested. Why should I be?" '

If a man wants a personal relationship with his child that means something important to both of them, then – as in any other relationship – he has to earn it. Meaningful paternity is not just a matter of sperm, nor even a matter of cohabitation. Children *take* continuously – they demand care, attention, love: the rewards are subtle and enduring, but a man has to move into a different mode of understanding than that of the average bachelor if he is to experience them.

4
Why women make the choice

'I felt that I could go through life without being married, I could be fulfilled without having a man in my life, but I knew I couldn't be fulfilled without at least having experienced a pregnancy and raising a child.' (Mary)

'I've always wanted a baby, I must admit, very much so – not quite to the stage of taking somebody else's baby out of a pram or anything, but I must admit it was a very strong urge.' (Felicity)

'I want the sense of connection, I want my life to feel less transient than it does. I love my job, my friends, but nevertheless I want that connection. . . . When I think about it I think about the Marlboro man – the American brand of cigarettes where the advertisements consist of the quintessential cowboy who has some sort of unspecified relationship with his horse, but aside from the people he shoots and occasionally the women he'll fuck when he goes to a whorehouse, he has no essential relationship to other people, he's just sort of out there on the prairie by himself smoking his cigarette, and I mean, surely I can't have that as an ego ideal! . . . I want there to be somebody I can't walk away from. And yet on the other hand I value my ability to walk away, and I've become very attached to it!' (Sharon)

'Reason? There's no logical reason to have a child! I just wanted one. I can tell you reasons that people have. One of them is to reparent yourself through somebody else; another one is investment in the future, to participate in life after you die; a third one is to have something better to spend your time, money on than titillating experiences like Club Med!' (Jessica Curtis, President of Single Mothers by Choice)

The difficulty of finding Mr Right

As we will see in Chapter 6, most of the mothers I interviewed would very happily settle down with Mr Right if they ever met him, and even after they have had their babies they are still hoping to find him. But they never have met him, or, if they have, either they haven't recognized him or at that stage in their lives they were not yet ready to cope with the strains of a permanent relationship. I mention this now because it is obviously an important, if not the most important, reason why most of these women are having children on their own. For them there has been no compromise – they aren't the sort to marry a man in order to have a baby, and they are too bright to fool themselves.

Psychologist Afton Blake said, 'I was never determined *not* to get married, but I would never have married anyone unless we were really compatible in a companionship way, and that hasn't entered my life yet. I still have hopes that it will. I've had three relationships when I lived with men, and they didn't work out – these were men I might have married if I hadn't lived with them, but, you know, after three years of living together it was clear we weren't that compatible. And as I get older I get more picky, so it's going to get harder.'

Julia who lived with the father of her child for three years after it was born: 'We didn't live together until after the baby was born, but it became clear after a while it just wasn't working. He wouldn't compromise at all. We only had one room, for instance, so the baby slept there of course, but he liked to have music on at night and I'd say, I really do want her to get to bed earlier, can't you get headphones? – oh no, I don't want to get headphones. That sort of thing. I think he was just being very stubborn about compromising his lifestyle, he didn't want to put himself out. He wouldn't carry her when we were outside, he hadn't come to terms with being a father and owning a child.' They had been good friends before the child was born, but marriage takes a lot more than simple friendship, and in the end she decided to move out with the baby.

Mary, a children's nurse, whose quote starts this chapter, had given herself until 30 to find the right man, and had decided very young that if she hadn't met him by then she would go ahead and have a child by artificial insemination, which is exactly what she did. As her mother had been just under 20 when she had Mary, 30 had seemed to her quite long enough to wait. 'I suppose the problem was I wanted a special sort of man, and my expectations got more demanding as I got older. Now, of course, any man I might eventually meet and want to settle down with will have to be even more of an exceptional type of person if he's going to be willing to take a child on as well as me – there aren't many men who'd want to do that. To take on someone else's child, let alone not knowing who that someone else is, you know? Anyway, I'm with the baby during the day and I work in the evenings, so my social calender's not all that great.'

Language teacher *Sarah* is the only mother I interviewed who never planned to have a child outside a permanent relationship, apart from 20-year-old Jenny. It took Sarah a lot of pain and emotional trauma before she finally accepted that her lover would never be the man she had hoped. 'I knew Peter probably wouldn't marry me because he didn't want to risk his close relationship with his children, but he'd left his wife some time previously and what I wanted was that we would set up a home together and be a family. I wanted nothing else. I wanted commitment, I wanted a family set-up, I wanted a man, and I wanted a child. And I wanted it so strongly that I didn't see the writing on the wall. Physically I loved him enormously, with a great passion, and I admired him, he was such an interesting man, did such interesting things. But he was a child in his emotions, in his understanding of other people, a young child!

'We'd known each other for about four years before I got pregnant – we were trying for a year – we weren't living together but we spent a lot of time together. By the time I had the baby I already knew that he wasn't the type to settle anywhere with anybody – emotionally he just isn't capable of making that sort of relationship with anybody, not for a long period. I didn't see it for a long time, or rather I supposed it would be different with me. And he can be cruel, very mentally cruel, you know? He doesn't care how much he hurts.' (Their first child died at birth, and by the time she was ready to try again their relationship was almost at an end: she had been refusing him sex after one particular quarrel.) 'But I was desperate, because I knew I wouldn't have a child without him. Then gradually he started being more friendly again, kinder, and yes, he has such charm when he wants! I knew it would be disastrous, but I was exhausted and so unhappy. So we came together again, and made love, just twice, that's all. Immediately all the old troubles began again, and this time I told him to go. I couldn't take any more from him.' (But in fact that episode had made her pregnant again: she had intended not to tell him, but her mother rang him about the pregnancy and the evening Sophie was born he came to see her.) 'Yes, I wanted to see him very much, yes I did. He was very loving, that first time – he was stroking my face, telling me I was beautiful, and what a wonderful thing I'd done – I couldn't believe how gentle he could be, he'd never been like that before. We were holding hands, and. . . . But as the days went by I could feel that things had not really changed.'

When Sarah left the hospital Peter came to visit her regularly and she longed to tell him to stay on, which he seemed to want to do, but by then she knew finally that he would never commit himself in the way that she wanted. Eventually, after a breakdown, she refused to let him come to see them any more but, after a year or so of insistent persuasion from him through the intermediation of her mother, for her child's sake she finally let him visit them again. By that time he was deeply involved in another relationship: 'Even now, when I see Peter – and God knows I dislike him, even hate him at times – I can't stand the pain of seeing him. Sophie is part of me, she is part of him: he comes here, but he is not mine. He is not with me, I'm not his. It seems outrageous, it seems a contradiction of physical terms. She looks so like him, she looks at me with his eyes, but now he's marrying himself to someone else. I find it an extraordinary insult, that life hasn't kept its biological promise of togetherness, wholeness.' Sophie is now 4, and although Sarah would very much like to meet another man she is still not sufficiently free of her feelings for Peter (which are at present a profound anger) to be able to start a fresh relationship with much chance of success.

I have included this outline of Sarah's story because it illustrates how much many of us will put up with from a man because we are in love with him or because he has qualities we admire and which make us love him, and also because we want to be settled and begin a family. Often it is impossible to untangle which desire is the strongest. The difference between Sarah and the other mothers in this book is that the latter knew exactly from day one what they were doing, and even though a few of them found the actuality of bearing and giving birth to a man's child much more complicated, more emotionally involving than they had anticipated, their original intention of independence saved them from the depth of misery and bitterness that Sarah still undoubtedly feels.

Is she a special kind of woman?

Planning this section from the appropriate index card I made a brief list of the important characteristics I had especially noted in my interviews of the mothers which seemed directly relevant to their choice to be a single parent. They may have been marvellous needlewomen or excellent car mechanics also, but such qualities were a bonus, not a basic. I ended up with twenty 'qualities' which I had noted typified individual mothers and found that certain of these had come up again and again among the women I was talking to. Making another list in the order of frequency of recurrence of these 'qualities' I found that 'independent', closely followed by 'likes solitude', scored heavily; then came – each recurring several times – 'determined', 'mature/ reflective', 'aware of sexual politics', 'had always wanted a baby', and 'wanted baby to have a known father'. Other characteristics, in no special order, were 'intelligent', 'cool', 'adventurous', 'planned career with eventual baby in mind', 'organized', 'dominant', 'does cross-gender activities'.

Statistically speaking this list is valueless, being nothing but the results of brief notes made roughly as I skimmed through the parts of the transcribed tapes relevant to the index card head 'character', but I felt them worth setting out here since they confirm the picture I had received during my researches, that virtually without exception *the mothers who had chosen their conception deliberately* were independent, intelligent, determined women who liked their own company, relished solitude and were not going to give it up for anything less than a first-class marriage. When you think of what these women have chosen to take on, their independence, etc., is hardly surprising. But what may surprise is their liking for solitude, considering they have, after all, chosen to have babies.

Children's nurse *Mary*, for instance, answered me when I commented that many of the mothers I had been speaking to seemed in essence to be solitaries: 'I think I'm like that myself. I enjoy being alone. Before I had the baby I worked every day except Sundays, and if I didn't go to church Sunday was a nice quiet day when I just kind of sat around with the paper, watched something on TV, and I always thought that was so nice. Now I live with my sister I don't have so many solitary days, but every once in a while I will, and before the baby came it was just nice, to have the place completely to myself, to do what I wanted, just sit around and relax.'

'*But what about now you have the baby?*'

'It's the same type of thing – there've been a few days when there's been just the two of us alone here, and it's nice, because on your own it gets to the point where you get tired of talking to yourself. Now there's someone else at home I can talk to, and that's not taking away from my solitude, somehow. It's hard to explain, but it doesn't seem to make that much difference – I mean, I'm still by myself, and yet I'm not! I don't know whether it's just now when he's little. Right now he's dependent, so he pretty much does what I do, but when he's older, I don't know.'

Mary's son was 21 months old when I met her. Afton Blake's son was a month younger, and although for her also solitude is important – 'I'm very much of a loner person, and many of my peak experiences have been when I've been alone with music, nature . . .' – she believes in 'symbiotic' mothering (we will look more closely at this later), and spends 'one hundred per cent' of her time with Doron when she is not working. But she *is* working for two and a half days a week away from home, and another half day at home, during which time her housekeeper cares for Doron, to the great pleasure of both of them. Perhaps without these breaks she would not be able to cope with the intensely involved kind of mothering she believes in, which gives her no time at all to herself when she is not working.

Psychoanalyst and therapist *Stephanie*, whose son is now 3½ said, 'When he was about 6 to 8 months I caught on to the fact I needed to be alone part of each day. There are moments when I think I must have been out of my mind, omnipotent grandiose of me to think I could do all this alone. But those are my lowest moments and they don't last long. Once I get out of the house they're gone. I aim at four hours a day, almost every day, away from him. That's my goal. If I've had a blissful day with him, I feel sad that I have those four hours away, but I make myself do it because it gives me a new perspective.'

'*Even at weekends?*'

'Yes. Something happens when you get physically away – you get yourself back in a way that you lose when you're alone with this primitive, demanding, little thing, as cute as they are. I don't always enjoy the hours off, and sometimes, before he went to nursery school, if I couldn't get away then I'd import a child for him to play with and a mother for me to talk to. That wasn't so freeing, of course – the latest in child development says outright that up to 3 or 4 years old they don't understand that *you* have needs at all, it's terrifying to them in some ways that you're not able to be there for them, and the more you say, go play, the more grabby and clingy they are.'

Rosa, Dutch specialist in child psychology, as we saw in the previous chapter shares the care of her 2½-year-old son with Dirk, a fellow student: 'I am a very dominant type, and he's a very strong child – so I think it is very good for him to notice other people caring about him. In the group at the playground the same girls look after him during the day, and there are twelve children in his group. For me also, I need this. I have this problem with myself, being at the same time a mother but also being an independent woman. If I had him all the time without a break I would have to stop doing my own things, but now I can do them. Sometimes I don't see him for three days while Dirk has him.'

Elizabeth, museum curator, whose son is now 10, found 'lack of my own space – and I need a lot of it – the most difficult thing I've had to cope with in having a child. You lose an awful lot of freedom, which I didn't realize – what do you do when you've got to work overtime, or when the boss wants to see you at ten to five and you've got to get back to the kid? There were the most ghastly problems when he was smaller – what do you do when he's ill, what do you do when *you're* ill! But the last two or three years I've begun to feel an ever-increasing sense of relief, I feel at last I'm beginning to have a little bit of life of my own again. And he's a really nice companion to have around – his friends too – I have a jolly good giggle with them, I think they're hilarious, small boys at that age. But also he's much more independent, which I really enjoy – a lot of the time now he's off on his bike, and I don't see him for hours on end.'

Obviously the desire to have their own space, the need for solitude, means these women are likely to find marriage very difficult, especially as independence is another major characteristic. *Sharon*, assistant professor of women's studies who has not yet worked out how to have a baby of her own, was married at 20: 'I was going to do everything exactly according to this plan – not even my own plan, my parents dreamed it up before I was born. *Of course* I was going to get married, *of course* I was going to have a child – I even knew when I was going to do it. But after a couple of years of marriage I realized I was not cut out to be a wife. I didn't actually want to leave the man I was married to, but essentially he gave me no choice – he said you're either going to stay and be a wife and do it properly, or this marriage isn't going on. Since I felt I had no aptitude at being a wife, since I wasn't doing it very well and didn't expect to get any better at it, I left.'

This acceptance of the kind of independent people they are rings out through all the tapes. Jane Mattes, founder of the Single Mothers by Choice group, discovered this for herself during the group's early meetings: 'We are very different in many ways, but the one thing we found we had in common as women – we discovered it quite accidentally just by talking informally – was that we all had a lot of trouble asking other people to help us, that we were do-it-yourself types, very independent, which is a plus and a minus in certain ways. Taking on the responsibility of a child was the first thing many of us had faced that we really couldn't do alone. We found we needed some sort of extended family support network to really do it well, and during all this talking together we found we'd given each other permission to ask for help. Here we were doing it alone, and at the same time admitting we couldn't do it alone. It was real interesting. It was emotional support we needed primarily from each other, yes. If the child cried with colic and didn't stop screaming for six hours, we were entitled to ring each other and say, ouch! We gave each other permission to ventilate and complain, to admit it wasn't easy and that there were terrible moments, frightening moments.'

I have already quoted the remarks *Lynn*, a nurse, made on her need for independence: 'One boyfriend said he was put off by me because I was so independent and I wasn't dependent on him . . . well, I'm sorry, I don't want to be dependent on somebody. It's nice to have somebody there, to have the love coming back, but not so much I can't function independently.' *Catherine*, actress: 'There were men in my life, of course, but looking back on it now I think I assumed they were just a stepping stone to something better. I remember having a relationship with a fellow who was absolutely wonderful. He really adored me, and I took it for granted, like it was my right – I wouldn't do that now, I'd feel very pleased if somebody adored me! But no way did he feature in my life, he was just somebody to keep me company for a while – I was very arrogant, I think, and very independent. I didn't want to share a flat at all, not with other girls either as some girls do when they are young – I thought it would be a nightmare. I always lived on my own – I went through terrible loneliness, but at that time I preferred that.' Dr Catherine Peckham, during a conversation we were having with several women including research assistant *Janice*, expressed a fear I also have, perhaps unnecessarily. She said to Janice, 'But you have a high IQ, you are independent, you thought it all through very thoroughly before you did it, and what worries me is that a lot of women won't think it through as clearly as you did.'

In Part 2 the reader will see how these qualities of independence and mature reflection shine out as the mothers explain how they coped with motherhood. For the present, let us look at an article appearing in the first issue of the newsletter which the American Single Mothers by Choice group put out (July/August 1983 issue) in which they asked, 'Who are we?' (SMC hold regular group meetings for women who are trying to decide whether or not they want to have a child alone. Most eventually decide they do not.) First they pointed out that 'barring severe physical, mental or emotional disability, any woman who really wants to marry can find a husband. He may fall far from the "image" we grew up with, but at some point in our lives we have met a man who would have married us if we had been willing. This being the case, our single status is then by choice.' The article goes on to explore the issue of selfishness which many unmarried career women are accused of: 'being selfish is not necessarily a negative trait. To satisfy oneself without harming others intentionally is surely a good thing, for only those who know how to love self can truly give to others. There are too many angry, dissatisfied women out there who resent the constant giving to men and children without having any time to meet their own needs. By the time we have reached our stage in life we have built up our "self" image through experiences which have added to our sense of security about who we are.' The 'child issue' is then examined. The article, stating that some women decide they do not need to reproduce themselves in order to be 'a complete woman', says there are 'many factors to be taken into account, including financial stability, physical condition and emotional stability. Many of us come to realize that we're not parent material, not ready yet, don't want to do it alone. . . . We do not think less of ourselves . . . rather we respect our right to make an informed choice.

'Opting for deliberate single parenthood is a commitment to oneself and child alone. No one else can be depended upon to support this lifestyle . . . these women realize . . . they are breaking the tradition which carries the high risk of alienating themselves from everyone. So, the answer to our question 'who are we?' is that we are mature, independent, strong women who are making our lives what we want them to be. Most of us will decide that we only want children as a result of a loving relationship between husband and wife and wait for that special man to come along. Others will conclude they do not want children at all and go on with their lives secure in the knowledge that they are doing what is right for them. Those scant few who choose to become single mothers will never be in the majority. They accept that, and make the best possible life for themselves and their children.'

As long as women are encouraged to make their decision in a rational, well-informed way I have no fear for the future, and my concern expressed a few sentences back, echoing Dr Peckham's, would prove unfounded. It seems that strong, independent-minded women can in general be relied on to arrive at a viable conclusion. Exactly what has made these women so independent-minded, why they value solitude to the extent that, unlike most women, they eschew marriage, is too interesting and important a subject for me to attempt to deal with in a few words. Is it that they are too uncertain of themselves to risk their boundaries being violated by another person? Is it that they are products of the 1960s and 1970s, when do to your own thing, to explore life untrammelled by conventional expectations, was what bright young people were doing; when one-night stands, sexual experimentation and being 'cool' was in, and romantic dreams of commitment for life, was out? Can we therefore – now that relationships suddenly seem to be the new 'in' thing of the 1980s – expect that the phenomenon of single parenting by choice will decrease rather than increase, or has the women's movement brought such a fundamental change to women that they will continue, regardless of contemporary pressures, to have high expectations of male/female relationships which for the most part will not be fulfilled until men themselves also change? Traditionally women value relationships, men value independence: modern psychology continues to bear this out, but with reservations – ask a man if he will remarry if his wife dies and he usually says yes: ask a woman and she says, not yet, or no, or maybe eventually.[1] There are no simple answers, and there never have been. So the answer to the question raised at the beginning of this section, 'Is she a special kind of woman?', is, yes, she is – but what woman isn't?

'It never occurred to me I wouldn't have a child one day'

For the majority of women the social expectation all their lives is that sooner or later they will have children. The pressure to do so is probably less than it was, but, whatever parents or friends say, almost every book or magazine they read and every film they see, right from infancy, take it for granted that women have babies; it is a rare woman who avoids drawing the inference that one day, she too. . . .

Lynn, a nurse, states straightforwardly, 'I was raised in a culture where woman grew up, got married, settled down, had a family. And I wanted kids anyway. I've always liked children.' *Mary*, children's nurse in the opening quote at the beginning of this chapter, said bluntly that while she could go through life without being married, she 'wouldn't be fulfilled without at least having experienced a pregnancy and raising a child.' Her assumptions were formed even in high school; she wanted to be married and have children by the time she was 18 – though in the event she decided to train herself for a career first.

It was clear as I interviewed more and more women that for most of them the maternal urge went far deeper than could be accounted for solely by the pressure of society's expectations. *Felicity*, medical researcher: 'I've always wanted a baby, I must admit, very much so – not quite to the stage of taking somebody else's baby out of a pram or anything, but I must admit it was a very strong urge. It was emotional rather than biological, I think – I was always fairly lonely. I'd always assumed I was going to get married, as people do, and have a large family, but it wasn't meant to be. I didn't have my son until I was 37, but that was only because I expected all along I'd get married. I had a lot of men friends, but none of that came to anything. I was engaged once, but it didn't last very long. As I said, I was always conscious of wanting babies, and I think I used to tell people and they might have had the impression that I wanted them as a stud – that I wanted a baby more badly than I wanted a husband.'

The reader might remember from earlier in the book child psychologist *Anna*'s very similar comment: 'I would say [to men], no, I don't need you, I need your sperm'; the difference between Anna and Felicity being that Anna was perfectly happy not to have a man tied to her as a life time partner. On the other hand Dutch specialist in child psychology *Rosa*, like Felicity, had expected to be married first. In fact she did marry, but eventually the marriage collapsed. 'I always imagined my life with children – from the beginning I was working with them, and I married somebody who worked with children too. We wanted to foster children – it seemed a good idea – but the marriage didn't work out and we divorced. But I couldn't imagine myself not living with children. It is not possible [in Holland at the time of the interview] to adopt children if you are not married, don't have a house and all that, but I think I would have adopted them if I could have.'

Having a child isn't always as physically straightforward as people often expect, and sometimes plans misfire. Psychologist Afton Blake said, 'I was always going to have children, but I just wasn't in a relationship situation to have them. I had tried in my early thirties, in fact, and miscarried – I was in a relationship then. When that happened I devoted myself to my profession, still knowing I would eventually have children, but not feeling the time was right, after all.'

Frances, art gallery owner, was divorced after trying unsuccessfully for some time to have a baby. 'I don't think I'd ever stopped to think about the possibility of *not* having a child. I mean, I'd always liked children, I had a degree in early childhood studies, I liked to teach children, I'd baby-sat. I wasn't brought up to be something separate from a wife and a mother. When I grew up in the fifties I assumed I'd get married and fall into that extraordinary American model of togetherness, and was in fact married and did go off the pill which I had been on for years and years like the good middle-class girl I was, and I waited to get pregnant and didn't and didn't and ultimately I began to go through that miserable business of trying to figure out why normal things weren't working. My husband's sperm count was down and my mucus was hostile and my cervix was this and . . . you know, when you start to analyse all the factors that make pregnancy possible it really is a miracle that *anybody* ever gets pregnant at all. There was even a point where they were spinning his sperm down to concentrate it, inject it – it does cause dissension in a marriage to be so intent on wanting a child. I was at the point where I wanted one so badly that if I saw a woman with a baby I would just want to weep with longing. We were even thinking of adopting – but then the marriage, for a bunch of other reasons as well as that, ended. But I didn't stop wanting children.'

But of course this urge to procreate is by no means universal. BBC 'Woman's Hour' editor Wyn Knowles is one woman who never found the idea particularly attractive. 'I was never hit as many people are in their thirties by this great feeling that time's running out – I ought to be having a child! I liked the idea of the relationship of being married eventually, but I was not in any hurry, I wasn't very eager for it. I didn't see myself much as a homemaker and helpmate – I didn't really want to do that, though I felt that sooner or later one would have to and ought to. The thought of children rather worried me when I was young because I was a Roman Catholic with a very devoted mother, and I knew you weren't allowed contraception; I visualized endless pregnancies and like a lot of my RC friends we just rather hoped we'd marry non-Catholics which would solve that problem. Yes, it's true, I assumed I would have kids, but not yet. Somewhere in the dim distant future

I'd have them.'

'*Was that cultural more than anything else?*'

'Oh yes. Yes. Definitely.'

Elizabeth, museum curator, was another woman who had not wanted children, though later she changed her mind. 'When I first met John he was having a relationship with a very good friend of mine, and we just became friends. At that time I had this theory that kids were absolutely ghastly and should be kept in glass bottles until they were 6 years old or something! This was all considered a huge joke among my friends, so that when a few years later I actually had a child all my contemporaries fell about with laughter. I think I felt that way because my father was headmaster of a boys' preparatory school, and I'd been brought up with hundreds of small boys around. By the time I was doing that course, at 21, I'd *had* kids! What changed me? Well, I don't think it was that I suddenly wanted a child, exactly, no. I think the thing is that we'd been sleeping together, John and I, for about four years, and I came very much to want *his* child. I think that that was really why I did it, but it's a long time ago – David's 10 now – and it's muddled up, really. Anyway, I stopped using the pill and I became pregnant immediately.'

Nearly all the mothers I met, though, had always expected to have a child, and for them the question of whether to have one or not was never really at issue. For some it was only a matter of waiting to see whether or not they got married, for others they wanted to organize their career first. For others again there was yet another issue to work out first, the question of their sexual orientation.

Lesbian mothers

Lesbians have had to put up with a lot of mud-slinging. People didn't worry overmuch about possible lesbianism in the past: girls walking hand-in-hand caused no one to turn a hair, and women living together were mostly thought of as two 'old maids' who hadn't 'caught' a man, people to be sorry for rather than castigated. Certain rather obvious couples like the two old ladies of Llangollen, or Radclyffe

Hall (author of *The Well of Loneliness*) and her friend Una, Lady Troubridge, enjoyed a certain amount of notoriety in their time, it's true, but on the whole no one bothered too much about what women on their own got up to. We are all more sophisticated today, and know what's what, or can guess at it. But our so-called liberalization has been two-edged: in Victorian days young men or young women could stroll along arm in arm without anyone assuming anything – how often do you see couples like that today? Physically expressed affection has come to have such sexual overtones in Western countries that hardly anyone dare touch anyone outside the house any more.

As for lesbians daring to live openly together as a united couple and having children! Stephanie Dowrick's and Sibyl Grundberg's introduction to their excellent book *Why Children?* makes such lesbians' position clear: 'To choose to have a child as a single woman or a lesbian is still to invite all the Furies that society can loose upon us. A woman whose identity does not include alliance with a male figure is labelled "unfit". The lesbian who wants a child is seen as contemplating an impracticality at best; at worst, a double perversion, a threat to the child.'[2] Psychiatrists cast their doubts on even the happiest of unions. I was discussing with Hendrika Vande Kemp a lesbian couple I had interviewed, *Stella* and *Jan*, whose example as a happy sharing pair I had been praising, and she said, 'The problem with their relationship is that, yes, they are close, but they have not learned to live with differentness, and this is one of the major issues in relationships. The biggest test for a heterosexual relationship is that two people who are very different in all sorts of ways can still love each other and not be threatened by the differences. And in any marriage it's differentness that so often isn't tolerated. You can't really love me if you think differently than I do. You can't really love me if you do differently than I do.'

'*But these two women are very different from each other, they're very different kinds of people in all sorts of ways. Isn't that sufficient?*'

'In terms of the ideal, no.'

But isn't it immature to demand the ideal? And can

there ever be such a thing as 'the ideal' reality? And what 'test' are people supposed to pass in their relationships? *Stella* and *Jan* have had their difficulties, yes, but what couple hasn't? Their serenity as a pair, their joy in their child, is something that many married people would envy if they were to regard the couple with an unprejudiced eye. We will be looking at these two women in other chapters of this book, but various comments they made might be of interest here. First, on how other people received their decision. Jan, the non-biological mother; 'I felt out what people thought about it – I'd say, I'm thinking about having a kid, and I'd talk about having artificial insemination. I work in one of the caring professions and people there are a little more liberal. I got positive feedback about that. Later on I'd say that I was going to share parenting with Stella, my roommate – that's how I'd present it to people at work.'

'*Had you made up your mind at that stage who was going to be the biological mother?*'

'Pretty much – it took us two years of talking about it first before we made the decision to actually have a child, and we wanted to be sure we were pretty stable in our relationship too. We've been together now five years. People were very supportive – they knew it was going to be an artificially conceived baby, that Stella was going to carry the baby, and knew I was going to share the parenting as a parent, and the more I talked about it and acted as though it was normal and everybody does that, people just accepted it. I get so much support from work it's really neat. No, not everybody at work knows we're a lesbian couple – some do, some don't – it really hasn't been a major thing to bring out.'

Lesbian mothers usually know others like themselves and consciously learn from each other. Stella: 'I belong to a support group of lesbian mothers, and some of these have kids who are older and who've gone through the problems at school, so we are hearing about it and know what they're going to be like. Problems like teachers not wanting the parents to mention anything about their lifestyle to other parents. Or like a 7-year-old talked about "my mommy and her lover", and the teacher called home and said no, no, she mustn't do that", and the mother having to say to the teacher, "yes, I am a lesbian and I'll speak to my daughter and tell her that it's inappropriate behaviour to talk like that." So you have to talk about your "roommate" and use terms like that.'

Most of the problems seem to be perfectly soluble with good will and a fair amount of common sense. I asked Dr Catherine Peckham what she felt about the children she knew from lesbian relationships. She said, 'I've been very struck by children who are brought up in these situations, how much support they have, and how very secure they are. They do meet men, they're not totally isolated from men. We look for problems because we expect them. Men *have* to be involved, after all; you can't conceive if a man isn't involved, and I don't see that how much he is involved – from the conception point of view – makes all that much difference. Yes, it's true there are some lesbians who use artificial insemination because they couldn't stand a man touching them: if they're very strongly anti-male and they happen to have a boy child then they might decide to have the child adopted.' But among the lesbians I met this was a non-problem: none of them admitted to really minding which sex child they had, although some marginally preferred a girl child simply because they understood women better and they thought it would be easier. None of them made an issue of it.

Charlotte, part-time researcher, who doesn't call herself a lesbian mother because she was never fully lesbian, said she hadn't minded which sex her baby was, but she added, 'I do remember when she was tiny feeling pleased she was a girl because she was sort of one of *us*, and sometimes I feel rather against men and I think, oh, they're too complicated, why do we have to have them in our lives, they're so pathetic, they're so childish, so immature – you know! Not all men are like this, needless to say, but the fact is I felt a feeling of solidarity with her, pleased she was like me, and sorry, though, that she would grow up to the same sort of problems I've had, but also that made me feel closer to her. I think that feeling of feminine solidarity is something that lesbian feminists especially get out of the women's move-

ment. But if I had another baby I would positively like it to
be a boy. I think that the fact of my first baby being a girl
has helped give me confidence, and now I more or less know
the ropes I'd be prepared to tackle a boy.'

As I wrote at the end of the last section, for some of the
mothers making up their minds whether they were hetero-
or homosexual was an issue they wanted to settle before
having a child. Elsewhere I have discussed how the women's
movement has influenced some women sexually. Some, like
Charlotte, have remained ambivalent about where their true
feelings lie. As one young mother said to me, 'We feel
differently about sex from the way you were probably
brought up – we accept now we're not monogamous
animals, and that we're not strictly one-way. Our generation
is beginning to accept lesbianism much more: we don't
necessarily feel we have to come down one way or the other.
Whether it'll backfire on us later on goodness knows.' But
other women consider it important to know exactly who
they are; for *Jane*, a lawyer, lesbianism was an issue she
settled with herself in her early twenties and 'by the time I
was 25 I had decided for sure I wanted to have a child. By
then I knew I was going to do it as a lesbian, so it was never
an issue whether or not to get married and do it in the
traditional way, though I did think about doing it with a
man who had been a lover in the past.'

I also talked to Jane (who in the end had adopted her
baby) about the worries some people express that children
brought up by lesbians might be taught that all men are
shits. 'It won't happen among my circle of friends, not
among the people who are going to spend any time around
the child. There are certainly those kinds of attitudes among
some lesbians, although there are fewer women with
attitudes like that than there are men who have horrible
attitudes about women. It's more likely that my daughter
will come across men who essentially hate women, who
don't think of women as whole human beings, than she'll
come across women who feel that way about men. And no,
when I was finding out about adoption I didn't ask for a
girl, I'd have been just as happy with a boy – in the event I
waited for the mother to give birth and so had a newborn

baby without choice of sex just the way you do when you give birth yourself.'

Finally, finishing as we began with a psychotherapist, Lillian Rubin has a different viewpoint to Hendrike Vande Kemp. In her chapter in *Intimate Strangers* discussing 'The sexual dilemma', she writes that one of the 'seductive' aspects of heterosexual sex is that because two sexes with all their differences are involved there is a natural limit to the amount the boundary between them can be crossed, so that the sense of self is left safely intact. With lesbian sex this difference does not exist, and though lesbians will often say with pleasure that loving another woman is like loving oneself, this very fact of similarity raises all the old conflicts that the women had to face in breaking away from their early fusion with their mothers. These conflicts, she says, must be faced and overcome if the relationship is to become a lasting one. If, however, the couple succeed in coping with these problems of 'boundary issues' while still maintaining the remarkable depth of intimacy that such relationships are capable of, then the resultant 'relationship may be most instructive for the heterosexual world.'[3]

Is it selfish to choose to have a child as a single mother?
Prospective single mothers shouldn't worry too much about this, because whatever they do they will probably be accused of being selfish. They will be told by some people it is selfish to bring up a child who will not have the benefits of conventional family life, but if they decide not to have children they will be told they are behaving selfishly because they are only living for themselves. Equally women who marry and make the decision not to have a family because they prefer a lifestyle unencumbered by children are likely to be accused of selfishness – Wyn Knowles told me that in her *Woman's Hour* afternoon slot for the BBC they had 'broadcast some programmes on married working women who had decided to remain childless and listeners wrote in to us to complain how selfish it was of them to go out to work instead of staying at home to have children. They complained they were taking jobs away from men, and all

that. But when there's a war and you're needed, then you're told it's selfish to stay at home!'

Accusations of all kinds are thrown at single mothers by choice: *New York* magazine published an article on the subject which attracted a pile of readers' letters, most of which were strongly against such parents. The letter-writers used words like 'irresponsible', 'selfish', 'inhuman', 'perverted' and 'narcissistic'.[4] Elphis Christopher, psychosexual counsellor and doctor, a warm, sympathetic person, nevertheless had strong doubts about the wisdom of mothers having children alone: 'It strikes me that in many ways it's a very narcissistic kind of choice. It's part of the me-too generation that's got to have everything – careers, travelling, and also, to cap it all, a baby.'

But Rubin sees a woman's need for attachment as being as much a part of her as her need to breathe: without someone to connect herself to in genuine intimacy she cannot help but feel ultimately deprived and alone.[5] It is this need (which terrifies many men who see this as dependency and are frightened of the responsibility this entails, although they themselves have similar if unadmitted needs), rather than the classic penis-compensation theory of motherhood, which is behind a woman's urge to have a child. Ordinary people who haven't .had the benefit of a knowledge of Freudian theory understand this need perfectly well, and this partly accounts for the tremendous pressure on women to have children. More than one mother commented to me that one of the reasons behind her decision to have a child was to feel 'normal', 'like other women'. *Tam*, a clinical social worker and therapist: 'I've always felt different, not normal, and I felt like that because I wasn't in a relationship. Then when I did have a long relationship I realized that that doesn't change anything, that it was my own inner feelings I needed to work out. So then it sort of shifted to, well, if I had a *child* I'd feel like everybody else. At least I'd be normal, you know? I've spent a lot of time these last couple of years, clearing that last out of me, because that's not a good reason to have a child! And of course it wouldn't really accomplish that need to be normal, either.'

As I have said again and again, these women are very

conscious of their responsibilities to any children they might have, and they ruthlessly examine their motivations. *Charlotte*, part-time researcher: 'I'm very glad you've brought up the question of selfishness. Of course I've thought a lot about this – is it simply to give me a love object, is it just that now I've got somebody I can take to bed with me, somebody to love so that I'm not alone? I think in fact it partly *is* that, but I also think that you can be aware of the obvious danger that you might not respect the child's own being and needs, and so you can do something about it. I try to make sure my daughter is secure enough in herself not to always need me, and so far that seems to have come out right.'

Stephanie Dowrick makes no bones about her own feelings: 'I don't need to have a child to give my life a purpose. It is already filled with purposeful activity: work, politics, friends . . . I want to be filled to the limits with pregnancy. I want to stretch myself with motherhood. . . . I do not want to choose between work, lovers, a child. I want everything.' And why not, if she can manage it so successfully?[6]

Sharon, assistant professor of women's studies and a philosopher by training, has given a lot of thought to the disruptions a child would cause to her life. She is already a fulfilled, secure woman, enjoying her life and her friends. I will quote her at length, because I think she draws a very clear picture of how satisfying her life is now, and why, in spite of her enjoyment of it, she wants a child. 'I'm not responsible for anyone else. I travel without very much advance planning, I'm essentially free to come and go as I please, and I'm involved with a very large number of different people and communities – my life is extremely varied. All of that would change very fundamentally if I had a child – my time wouldn't be my own any more. But I'm not certain I want my time to be my own – there's a kind of loneliness that is the other side. That I don't have to go home if I don't want to is correlated with there's nobody there waiting for me, and if I do go home for dinner it's home for dinner alone. I love my solitude. I mean it's a treat to spend enormous amounts of time alone. I think about five o'clock, and I think about getting home and pouring myself a glass of sherry and turning on the radio and going through the mail and doing some reading, and think about what I'm going to have for supper, and the sense that all day long I've been running around doing different things and meeting with students and teaching classes and going to meetings with colleagues, and then I get to go home and there's no one there, and I get to just unwind. But that would be the time my child would need me most. Presumably the child would have been in day care, and I'd pick him up and bring him home, and all my friends with children say that's the time when they most want, crave, need, desire your attention. So a lot of my feelings centre around that time, because there *is* a kind of loneliness, there *is* no one there when I go home. On the other hand there's a luxuriant sense of self-indulgence – do I want to be most intensely needed by somebody at the end of my day and have to wait for several hours until the child goes to bed to have some time of my own?'

'*Do you feel sort of empty when you open your front door?*'

'No, my loneliness is very rarely a focused thing, it's more when I think about the future. I want somebody with whom I share the – you know – the indefinite first person plural future tense. It's very rarely that it's a sadness there's nobody on the other side of the door when I come home. I do very deeply love being alone. It's that I want the sense of connection, I want my life to feel less transient than it does. I love my job, my friends, but nevertheless I want that connection, not just to the future but to the past too, in some way. When I think about it I think about the Marlboro man – the American brand of cigarettes where the advertisements consist of the quintessential cowboy who has some sort of unspecified relationship with his horse, but aside from the people he shoots and occasionally the women he'll fuck when he goes to a whorehouse, he has no essential relationships to other people, he's just sort of out there on the prairie by himself smoking his cigarette, and I mean, surely I can't have *that* as an ego ideal! And why am I so defensive of this sharply individuated well-bounded self when as a feminist theorist I don't believe in it. I believe in a self that exists in connection, in intimacy and the importance of nurturance, to nurture and to be nurtured. Theoretically my sense of the self is not this autonomous well-bounded separate self who can walk off freely at any time.'

'*That last sounds like a male ideal.*'

'Yes, extremely male. The ability to say no to anybody about anything without feeling guilty is not a human ideal as far as I can see, it is a very specifically male ideal. No, I want somebody who has a right to make a claim on me, and say, you've taken on something, you don't get to walk away from me. So part of my fantasy of a child is that a child would be the one person in the world I couldn't walk away from. I *want* there to be somebody I can't walk away from. And yet on the other hand I value my ability to walk away, and I've become very attached to it!'

Having a stake in the future, and the need for a blood tie

One important function of the family is to act as a clearing house through which physical and spiritual 'possessions' are passed on to the next generation and so on unto infinity, not only possessions such as money, furniture, houses, genes, habits, noses, chins, whatever, but also that more indefinable thing that is not exactly 'soul', not exactly 'essence', but some part of us which we shrink from imagining being totally exterminated at death. Even those who believe in Heaven like to imagine that in some way they will 'continue' on earth through the following generations. The 'blood tie' is one aspect of this metaphysical concept, for when we talk about blood being thicker than water we mean more than the literal sharing of the same forebears. We also include that rather sticky sense of connection that we have with relatives we were brought up with or amongst, who have become part of ourselves in a way too diffuse to define. So that brothers and sisters who couldn't stand each other in childhood, meeting again late in life, will find themselves unexpectedly stirred by shared early memories no one else could completely understand. And the emotion felt then goes beyond the facts that are being recalled, the mere sharing of some remembered incident; it is as though one is drawing on some almost mythical fund of common experience, achieving a communication which touches a depth of meaning so profound we shall not easily forget the experience.

These two needs – for continuing into the future through our progeny, and for a connection with others beyond ordinary intimacy – are shared by men and women alike. Though they may not acknowledge it, the first lies heavily behind the refusal of so many men to act as unacknowledged stud to women who requested this. And both needs spur women on to undertake the immensely difficult task of rearing a child on their own.

I asked Karin Meiselman why she had wanted to have children, and she said, 'I can only give you a very diffuse answer to that. It just felt like, that's part of life; also, I like the feeling of making a long-term commitment personally, of something of me carrying on into future generations, both biologically and from my efforts. I had something of the same feelings writing a book, that I will carry on, affect people in the future – I guess it's a form of immortality, though of course I didn't think about it like that at the time.'

For some, there is considerable pressure from family to continue 'the family name', as it is sometimes expressed. In the book *Why Children?*, one of the contributors writes of her Jewish grandmother's desire for her line to be continued, her close family having been wiped out by Nazi persecution.[7] Where a daughter is the sole link with the future there can be strong pressure on her to become pregnant; the unspoken criticism and obvious disappointment not only of parents but also of grandparents has been felt by millions of young people who are resisting marriage or pregnancy.

The need for blood ties was occasionally talked about by some of the mothers I interviewed. *Jan*, the non-biological lesbian mother referred to earlier, explained why they had decided it should be her lover, *Stella*, who would physically bear their child. 'It was nothing to do with roles. It had to do with family background. I come from a very large family, both my parents are living, and I have tons and tons of relatives, so my situation is very different from

Stella's. She's an only child, neither of her parents are alive, she has no close connection with any relatives, and we felt that her having a child would give her a close blood tie which she doesn't have with anybody else. I didn't need that. I felt I'd be able to love our son without any reservation that, gee, I'd had to get pregnant in order to feel that kind of tie.'

When I asked graduate student *Angela* why she had had a child, she said it was for the sense of security of having a family of her own. 'My mother had died when I was 6 and an aunt had come to live with us to look after us, but she died when I was 14 and the whole family broke apart. In that one year *she* died, my brother went into the army, one sister entered a convent and the other sister was taken away because she was mentally retarded. After that I had basically no home, and no discipline at all – my father was a steelworker and he worked different shifts; he didn't much like the way I started living but he kind of respected me and thought I wouldn't do anything too way out. I was very liberated, I did whatever I wanted, slept out, took a lot of drugs and so on. At 18 I moved to Boston, so I'd had no real family life since I was 14.' Security, the need for close family, blood ties, personal growth: many of the mothers have spoken of this kind of reason.

Tam, clinical social worker and therapist, whom I reported in the previous section on selfishness as wanting a child so she would feel 'normal', like other people, added, 'I love babies, I'm very good with them. I also feel I have something worthwhile to offer a child that I'm real happy about, and I would like to share what I've learned with another human being. I recognize that in some ways my desire to have a child does have a lot of selfishness in it at this point – this whole business of craving for a sense of peace and oneness and belongingness and yes, I admit I do feel I must have a child in order to attain this state – this feeling is selfish, totally selfish. But at the same time I think there is a selfishness in nearly everyone's craving for a child, in the sense that having one is serving one's own needs – if that's a definition of selfishness. I don't know that it's necessarily negative, though. No one has a child totally selflessly and says, this is purely a spiritual experience and I'm offering myself to be a channel for this soul to enter the world.'

It is often almost impossible to distinguish many of the needs we have been looking at, especially this need to have a stake in the future and the need for blood ties, from a straightforward biological urge to reproduce ourself. Is there even such a thing as a 'straightforward' biological urge for humans?

The biological urge

From a species point of view as long as enough women still have a physical urge to replace themselves or to start the cycle of replacing the human race if a catastrophe happened, that is sufficient. For the rest of us the decision to have children is so tied up with other issues that to isolate the biological urge from other factors is not really feasible. Stephanie Dowrick expresses some of this uncertainty: 'It is not my mission, my destiny to be a mother. . . I am not, I hope, a victim of biological determinism. I would prefer to see it as a conscious act of gainful adventure. But I don't know. As we begin to throw over aeons of male control, there are so many more questions than answers.'[8]

The mothers I raised this subject with varied tremendously in their replies. Languages teacher *Sarah* has no doubt about *her* feelings. For some mothers the problem of increasing age obscures the issue, but for Sarah this was not so: 'I didn't start thinking, oh God, I'm 39, I must have a child now or else it's never – I started having the biological pull of wanting to be pregnant before I met Peter. As I got more and more engrossed in this relationship with him it built up until the pull of wanting to be pregnant became just immense. On the other hand I'm sure I would have felt that way even if I hadn't been with anybody because the feeling had been building up inside me for some time anyway. I mean I couldn't see kittens on television, let alone a child, without bursting into tears; the gorgeous lucky mother cat was blessed with so many kittens and I wanted so badly to have my own kittens!'

I will not give the source of the next quotation because while the mother was extremely open about most things concerning her story she did not want the following facts to become general knowledge. She said, 'I think the biological urge thing is quite strong. From the way I went about getting pregnant you can see I rather left it to my body to make the decision, and I think that was because I couldn't have justified doing it on rational grounds. If I'd been asked beforehand if I was going to do it, I would have said it seemed a silly thing to do, and yet, once I became pregnant I was very pleased, I realized it was what I'd been wanting all along. I never for one moment wanted to get rid of it, though with my first pregnancy when I was much younger I wanted to get rid of it from the word go, and did. What happened was that I behaved quite differently from what was normal for me in several ways. For a start, though I didn't exactly decide to get pregnant, the fact is if you sleep with someone without contraception at a time of the month when you're *likely* to get pregnant then you're taking a chance, in effect you're saying "I'm quite happy if I do get pregnant." The man I slept with was a very old friend but neither of us had ever had the slightest desire to sleep together before, and yet for some reason we did it that night. Then, to cap it all, as if I wasn't certain enough, the next night I slept with another man with whom I'd never slept before either. We then went on to have an affair that lasted several months. When I look back on it I think what I was doing without being conscious of it was saying, right, it's time I had a baby, I'm going to make sure I get pregnant. But of course I didn't think of it in those terms at the time. I don't usually behave like that, I'm usually quite restrained – I've hardly ever slept with two different men on subsequent nights. In fact, as blood tests showed later, it was the first man anyway who made me pregnant, that first night. I think it makes you different somehow when you're very newly pregnant. I don't think I would have slept with the second man if I hadn't been in a terribly good mood – perhaps he was affected by it and that's why it happened.'

Other mothers were less certain of exactly what lay behind their desire to conceive. An example of how difficult it is to isolate the 'straightforward' biological urge to reproduce oneself from other desires is shown by the second part of Karin Meiselman's reply to my question as to why she wanted to have a child: 'I didn't think about it a lot at the time, I just very much wanted to mother somebody. I remember some of our childless friends who would bring up in conversation things like – "parenthood is a long-term commitment". They'd say it in a negative way, as a reason why you shouldn't do it, and I would think to myself, if you can seriously subscribe to that position, that that's a negative thing about being a parent, then there's no way you should be a parent. If it sounds attractive to you, as it did to me, then that's when you're ready to be a parent.' Is wanting to 'mother somebody' simply a part of the biological urge, or is it mainly psychological, or something else again?

Is the need for a *family* biological or cultural? What do we mean by those terms? Can you satisfy the biological urge to have children by creating a family by adoption? *Nora*, who together with her lover *Adina*, is adopting a child, thinks you can. They had originally considered the possibility of one of them physically bearing a child, but when *Jane* (whose house they share) adopted a child 'we both found we felt really good about that idea. I felt real strongly about there already being lots of children who couldn't live with their biological families, and it seemed to me a tragedy that so many of them were growing up . . . ' (she shrugs, but she is referring to the poverty and other problems of the Central American state from where their adoptive child is coming). 'Even when I was heterosexual I wanted to adopt, so the desire to have my own child is minimal – I feel I could bond with any child that's put in my arms just like that. The whole philosophy that a lot of people use to bear children, which is that it's to reproduce part of themselves, and how exciting it would be to watch a part of yourself grow up, is something I personally don't put much stock in. I do have some of that physiological urge to bear a child and birth a child and hold a child in my arms that is mine, yes, but larger than that I have this incredible psychological desire to be part of a family, to have a family, and I know that once the child is here, there's not going to be any difference in how that family need is met, so I would rather put aside this physiological desire and go the adoption road.'

Family was also important to *Stella* and *Jan*. Jan, asked whether she had felt a biological urge to have a child, replied, 'No, I personally don't have any biological need to carry a child myself. I think it's a societal, cultural thing rather than a biological one. With Stella and me, it wasn't like, in order to be a woman we had to have children. Well, it hadn't even occurred to me to have children, being a lesbian, but then four years ago I realized it was an option for us, to have a kid through artificial insemination. And for me, family has always been important, ethnically and culturally, and it seems real natural to be a family, to have a kid, so it was that that initiated it for me. I guess the biological time clock was important too, that if we were going to do it we had to get on with it. But it wasn't that we felt we *needed* to do it.'

But Dr Vande Kemp, whom the reader might remember refuses to have a child outside of marriage for religious and psychological reasons, answers the same question unhesitatingly in the affirmative: 'Yes, I do feel a biological urge. As I said, I have to struggle with this. But I know, however I feel personally, that my biological need is not a justifiable reason for me to make the decision to have a child. As an adult, I have to consider what the child would need more than my own need.'

Finally, *Tam*, therapist, on the biological urge: 'I do feel that's a part of what has been driving me in the last few years. I don't know if it's physiological/biological or if it's mental/biological – it's like I know that time is winding down and I feel like, oh my God, I've got to do this. But the fact is I felt that way three months ago and now I don't, though I'm three months older and I've disseminated three more eggs out of the storehouse in there. No, I don't feel that urge at the moment, so I don't know if you *could* call it biological.'

Biological or not, whatever the reason was that was driving Tam towards wanting a child, she also voiced the one ineluctable reason for making a decision now rather than at some vague time in the future, the reason that has forced so many mothers to face up to whether or not they are going to take the plunge – the unavoidable fact that women, unlike men, run out of time.

The biological clock, or, The age factor

Bio-panic, it's called in Hollywood, where it was intensified by the locally made film *The Big Chill* (which is partly about an unmarried lawyer who wants a child and is looking for a prospective father among her old college mates), for Hollywood itself has a large contingent of actresses, married or unmarried, who have put aside maternity while consolidating their careers and who are now succumbing to the maternal urge. 'Panic', though suitable for hyped-up Hollywood, is a rather strong word, but it is not so far from what many women feel as they reach another birthday and have not yet found the man/had the baby.

Myths about late motherhood abound: children born of 'elderly' parents are weakly things, pallid flowers growing in the shade of age ('I've not noticed that at all,' says obstetrician/gynaecologist Ed Cohen, 'nor heard of it, medically speaking – it's an old wives' tale as far as I'm concerned'); it's almost impossible to get pregnant after the age of 35, 40, 43 – the age varies according to the locality; it's terribly dangerous for the women/the baby if the mother is an older woman; most probably the child will have Down's syndrome if you leave it late.

Myths, all of them. I will open this section with a necessarily superficial summary of the facts as given me by various doctors, and by dipping into Marilyn Fabe and Norma Wilker's book *Up Against the Clock*. Certain facts are universally agreed, but others vary slightly by a percentage point here, a certain emphasis there. I don't think there can be much doubt that any woman over 33 or 34 who is seriously thinking of having a child should consult a gynaecologist if she is considering putting off her decision to a later date. A few women have certain physical problems that make conception difficult for them, and it is as well to check that you are probably not one of these. If you've cleared this possibility, relax – you're in good company.

More and more women are putting off having children until they feel ready for it – the 1984 Census Bureau study reported that while 70 per cent of women born between 1935 and 1939 had had a first child by the time they were aged 25, this figure fell to 60 per cent for women born between 1945 and 1949, and to 53 per cent for those born between 1950 and and 1954.[9]

Marilyn Fabe, talking to me about her own pregnancy, said, 'I was 38 when I finally had my baby, and in my exercise class which had maybe twenty women in it, there were only two or three who were under 30 and having their first child, and they felt very peculiar!' She added, 'I think the point is that women aged 45 today are maybe like women of 35 fifty years ago – nutrition, health, amount of exercise, etc., just turns back the biological clock for everybody, and the only determining factor, given that you're healthy, is how late you stop ovulating. It's harder when you're older because your periods aren't so regular and an increasing proportion of the eggs are not good eggs – it took me two years and it just terrified me that I had waited too long.'

Figures on how long it takes most women to conceive do not seem to be available, presumably because ordinarily women conceive without the aid or intervention of doctors and do not enter the statistics. The decreasing rate of fertility which is accepted as being connected with ageing could also be partly caused by the decreasing incidence of intercourse common amongst married couples who have been living together for many years. However, Bridget Mason, a gynaecologist who runs a fertility clinic which normally uses only fresh sperm and an ultra-sound scanner to ensure that a patient is inseminated only on the days when she is ovulating, finds that between 20 and 25 per cent of her patients conceive the first time they are treated. 'How long it takes them to get pregnant on average is entirely age-related: at 18 the average is 2 months, at 21 3 months, 26 4 months, 29 5 months, 30. 6.6 months, 32 8 months and 34 10 months. Pregnancy after the age of 45 is very rare, and after the age of 40 probably only slightly over half the ladies are going to conceive however long they persevere. Fertility falls off tremendously fast after the age of 36, with any method. So it's very unwise to wait until you're 40, I'm afraid.' (It is as well for mothers choosing a father for their babies to also remember that men's fertility declines too: a man in his forties will not be as fertile as a young man of 20.)

Another important reason why it is unwise to wait too long is that time will make it still less easy to conceive again should the first conception result in a miscarriage. Again, if a second or third child is likely to be wanted, then the problem of steadily decreasing fertility should be borne in mind.

While it is true you can get pregnant so long as you are ovulating, it is not so easy to determine whether or not this is happening. Dr Cohen: 'Physically a woman is capable of having a baby up to the time she stops having periods. The fertility rate decreases as age progresses, but there is no problem with conceiving and carrying a pregnancy up to the time the menses actually cease. But as age progresses an increasing number of menstrual cycles go by and are anovulatory, but ovulation still does go on – so it's relative infertility, not absolute infertility as age progresses.' However, other gynaecologists have told me that apparent menstruation can continue for some time after ovulation has ceased – some women are now having 'periods' well into their fifties, but the likelihood of them conceiving at this age is so negligible as not to be taken seriously into account.

Dr Cohen says he would hesitate to give artificial insemination to a women over 40 'because of the increased chances of foetal problems and the chances that the mother is going to have more of a problem during pregnancy. But if she felt strongly she wanted to go ahead, depending on the situation, I would probably help her out.' When I asked him how old one could be before giving up hope, he said, 'I've delivered a woman in her late forties, she was 49, I think. It turned out well, as it happened, but statistically if you take a group of 49-year-old women versus a group of 22-year-old women you're going to find a lot more problems.

'Down's syndrome is the most common one – as far as I know it's the only genetic problem that has been specifically age-related. But the risk is less than most people realize, and

I think that if someone wants a child then it's a risk worth taking. What I advise my patients is that they should consider what would happen if a pregnancy did result in a Down's syndrome child, would they be amenable to abortion, and, if they would not, that they had better consider very seriously whether or not to go ahead with the pregnancy attempt.'

The statistics that Dr Cohen gave me regarding the severity of the risks were similar to those given in Fabe and Wilker;[10] for women under 20 the risk of having a Down's syndrome child is about 1 in 2,500. Up to 30 it remains low, increasing only to 1 in about 1,500. Between 30 and 34 it increases again to 1 in 750 and then rises beteween 35 and 39 to 1 in 280. After 40 it is 1 in 100 and after 45 1 in 40. So even at this late age the risk is small, and since the syndrome can now be detected by amniocentesis most women will not be deterred by the possibility.

It is true that amniocentesis itself (a little amniotic fluid is withdrawn from the womb between the thirteenth and sixteenth week of gestation and the foetal cells checked for abnormalities) carries a slight risk – Dr Cohen says, 'Most people are quoting a risk of about 1 per cent approximately.' Since this is about the same chance as that of having a Down's syndrome baby if the mother is between 40 and 45, not everyone will consider the risk worth taking at that age. Afton Blake, who miscarried three times before she finally had a child, did have amniocentesis when she was carrying Doron, but she says, 'I'm not sure I'd do it again, though, as I had to stay on my back for three or four days because I started leaking amniotic fluid as a result of the amniocentesis. On the other hand, if I had another child I probably would, because I'm 42 now. Would I recommend it to other women? Yes, I suppose so, but it's important they don't feel pressed into doing it, because the risk of having an abnormal child is minute.'

About 98 per cent of women having amniocentesis find that their child has no defect: however, since seventy inherited biochemical disorders not related to maternal age can also be detected (plus the sex of the baby) some mothers will find this an additional reason to have the test.[11] Cohen also points out, 'There are several studies that show the chances of a miscarriage after amniocentesis are not any higher than they would be normally. The overall chances of a miscarriage is approximately 20 per cent in pregnancies up to approximately sixteen to seventeen weeks of gestation. By that time the chances would be less, because most miscarriages that were going to occur would have happened by that point, but there is still a small percentage chance of a miscarriage even at that age, probably as high as 1 per cent anyway.

'Then there are other problems that go along with increasing maternal age, such as an increased chance of high blood pressure, more chance of toxaemia, and other things too. A woman's physical resilience is such that the ideal age for having children is probably between 19 and 24, and the little things of pregnancy – sore back, problems with discomfort during pregnancy, problems with their legs or digestion or other minor discomforts – often seem to affect the older mothers, they don't seem quite as resilient to it, or at least that's what I've noticed. But it's not inevitable, not at all. And in some ways older women are psychologically more accepting of the discomforts because to them the pregnancy is a premium event, whereas younger women, while they have fewer of these problems, when they do have them, they seem to complain about them more because they're unwilling to accept any sort of debilitation whatsoever, however mild.'

Dr Maida Taylor is quoted in *Up Against the Clock* as saying, 'Psychological stability, as we know, has a profound effect on physical well-being. Personally I would rather take care of a mature, well-nourished 35-year-old woman who has deferred until such time that pregnancy really fits into her life than a 22-year-old who is ambivalent about the pregnancy.'[12] Other doctors agree that, provided the woman goes into her pregnancy healthy and with the right attitude, as long as she is able to conceive there is no reason why she should not have a successful pregnancy.

Generally speaking, being an older mother seems a clear plus. One or two of the younger mothers I spoke to had not wanted to wait because they thought mothers shouldn't be too much older than their children, that the relationship between them would be better if the age gap was not too large. Personally, I feel that the actual number of years' difference doesn't matter; what counts is more a matter of personality and attitude. Some people seem elderly at 30, others stay young until they die.

Jenny, who got pregnant unintentionally at 19, has no doubt at all about her mistake in having a child so young. 'We were using the rhythm method but it didn't work. My reason for not going on the pill was that I was worried about what it would do to me physically. It's a valid reason but it doesn't stand up to the reasons *for* going on to the pill – it's much worse for you physically and emotionally to have a baby if you're not ready for it. I didn't enjoy the pregnancy or giving birth – I felt really good towards him when I had him, but during the pregnancy I felt sick most of the time and it was very, very tiring; after about four months I couldn't walk, my ankles ached very badly, and I had blood sugar problems. I felt faint all morning, I couldn't stand up, and I had to keep eating biscuits all the time. I felt really grotty and tired, and I got bigger and bigger and bigger. . . .'

Later, after the baby was born, 'It was deadly at home counting the hours until his father got back, with nowhere to go, nothing to do, because Ben wouldn't let me do anything when he was awake. When he was asleep I could do the things I really wanted to do – reading, making things, drawing, even decorating the house – but I couldn't do anything once he woke up. He's always been a happy baby but he needs attention, he won't just play quietly in a corner, he has to be interacted with. If I give him some bricks to play with and then try to do a bit of crochet or something he'll come up and start pulling the crochet to bits, clambering up my legs or something. At that early stage he couldn't even crawl, so he'd lie in his cot and get fretful because he'd be bored. I'd have to amuse him, pick him up, walk him about, give him good vibes all the time, but you couldn't actually communicate or do anything together – he couldn't even pick up rattles at that stage. I loved Ben very much and I still do, but I don't enjoy looking after him at all – I'd have a nanny if I could afford it. It's a bit like looking after an aged relative who's senile: you may love this person very, very much, it's your dear old grandma, but to have to actually clean up after they've been incontinent and all that: – people do it, but they hate it.'

Compare this tale of woe with comments from other older mothers who had deliberately chosen to have their children: psychoanalyst *Stephanie*: 'I think at 25 I would have been a terrible mother. I certainly don't think I could have done it alone then – I had too many of my own needs, I wasn't ready to put them aside. It's still a struggle to do that, but now at least I feel ready to do it. I *want* to do it. Then I was really into myself, you know, the old prolonged adolescence that we seem to be experiencing now. There's a certain kind of energy I have now I certainly didn't have then, the persistence to stick with things, whereas then I had more *flippin' around* energy, which wasn't particularly useful! If anything I've got more energy in straight physical terms now at the age of 40 than I had then. And I think Danny gains the benefit of my maturity, and my having suffered through life's changes and a certain kind of wisdom which you get as you mature, hopefully! I think it's a trade-off!

Jessica Curtis, too, says, 'I think I'm a much, much better mother at my age now than I was with Peter, my son from my marriage. I was a very immature 24-year-old when I had him, and I can say from experience that a number of things are better when you're doing it on your own. First of all, you don't have to take care of another baby, your husband, somebody who's immature too and makes constant demands.' *Charlotte* part-time researcher: 'You have to be sensible. You can't stay up to one o'clock every night and expect to get up at six and feel all right. I've not been out properly for a year and a half – every couple of months or so I get myself together and go out to something and have an ordinary *adult* evening, and usually I pay for it the next day. But I don't begrudge it. I'm lucky in that I'm now at the age of 34 and I feel privileged to be doing what I'm doing, so I don't regret the change in my life having a child has brought me.'

Of course mothers who hadn't intended to have a child

find the care of it stressful, particularly so if their lifestyle is dramatically changed. Pat Verity, who runs a day nursery, said, 'I find older mothers are often quite resentful because they are used to having a lot of time, money, quite a nice life, and you do have to make concessions; if your child is ill you have to stay home, you have to be there, and they find that quite difficult. They find it more stressful than they imagined, and sometimes they can be over-protective, too. I've got this baby at long last, they think, and they're watching it every minute. I think in most of the cases here they really did want to have a child, but they don't ever really understand what it's about until it happens. No one does.' I think Pat Verity finds reactions from the mothers using her nursery so different from the mothers I spoke to because – it being a state-run nursery and therefore very inexpensive – there is a great demand for its services, and only mothers who have fairly severe problems of one kind or another are lucky enough to find a place there. But her experience certainly means that any mother contemplating single parenthood should search herself deeply and also do her best to find out about the reality of parenting small children as opposed to the idealized dream of it.

Finally, let us look at what the two psychologists, Karin Meiselman and Hendrika Vande Kemp, have to say. Elsewhere I have occasionally used these two women to contrast different attitudes, but on this point they are in agreement. First, Vande Kemp: 'I think older women do just fine. I have two older sisters, neither of whom started their families till after 35, and they're not having small families, so they're having kids right into their forties and they do fine. They're less uptight about a lot of the things that younger mothers get uptight about, both in terms of worrying about the kids, but also in terms of things like housework. I think older women are much more able to be relaxed, so I don't consider the age of the mother is a problem at all. There is a difference, yes, with older and younger mothers, but I think the difference is very balanced in terms of the advantages and disadvantages.'

And Meiselman, with two children close in age: 'I think it's wonderful to be an older mother. From my own point of view as one, I just wouldn't have been ready for motherhood in my twenties, and would have felt that my children had deprived me of my career and so on. When you're in your thirties, or even forties, you don't have the same urgency about life, you're not frightened that life will pass you by because of your children. You don't worry about not being able to go out on Saturday night with other people. For me, also, I think an older parent has a longer time perspective – I knew from being relatively more experienced in life that nothing stays the same and that even though I may go through a year of horribly hard work having to change two sets of diapers at once, that that'll be over with and I don't have to feel like that for the rest of my life. I have a certain time frame that I don't think I had when I was younger. I was 21 when I married and my husband was 23, and I was 35 when I had my first child. We didn't want to have children for quite a long period of time because first he was in graduate school, then I was. When we did try, we had difficulty in conceiving – but we finally succeeded and of course that added to the appreciation for me, I didn't take it for granted any more.'

'*Did you find it difficult to adapt to such a different life?*'

'No, I don't think I did, really, because again I can see that time moves on, whatever frustration I may have this year won't be the same next year, and so forth. That's not to say I haven't had to make any adjustments, but I just started out motherhood feeling so enthusiastic about it that that carried me through most of the difficult parts. And there are certainly plenty of those!'

The message, then, of this section seems to me pretty clear. Try not to leave having a baby too late, or you might have trouble conceiving, but don't panic – it is possible to do it much later than you probably thought. And once you are a mother, take heart – all the experiences, good and bad, that you have gone through in life will stand you in good stead now. Wiser than when you were younger, grateful to be a mother at last, you will be undertaking something that – when you look back at it in later years – you really will see is an extraordinary privilege.

5
Family

'What law says there has to be a man in a family? We're a family, me and my son. Who says there has to be a man around to make it a proper family?' (Mary)

I suppose I see a family as being any group of people of more than one whose lives are bound together by reasons of economy, finances, accommodation, sharing of resources, sharing of space – you don't need a marriage to make a family, you don't need two parents to make a family – you need a common interest of space and money and resources to share. A commune can become a family. (child psychiatrist Tony Baker, personal communication)

Because one in two marriages are ending in divorce 'half the children born in the United States today can expect to be eligible for an order of support for their benefit during their childhood. Half can later expect, as adults, to be either the payer or payee of an order of support for their own children. The child-support system will reach two-thirds of all Americans born this year either as children or as adults.' (David Chambers)[1]

When you think about 'the family' in relation to the subject of this book, certain questions come immediately to mind, such as – what is the future of the family? can single parents make a family? what kind of family life did single parents have themselves as children? Before we can even consider these questions we need to look first at just how successful marriage as an institution is at the present moment.

The state of marriage today

Very shaky, is the only possible description. It is true it continues to be popular, but rather in the same way that Mark Twain is supposed to have joked how he had no problem giving up smoking: it was, he said, his favourite hobby. Divorced people rush into second marriages, but chances of success are even lower than for first-time marriages. The concept of marriage as a life-time commitment is seen more as a hope than an expectation by most people undertaking it. Making divorce easier to obtain inevitably meant that divorce figures shot up as a backlog of couples previously unable to legally part took advantage of the new laws, and although recent trends show that the annual increase has slowed right down numbers have remained considerably higher than they used to be: in 1961 in England and Wales there were 25,000 divorces, in 1971 74,000 divorces and in 1981 146,000 divorces (source, National Children's Bureau Library).

Compared to the number of divorces before the Second World War – never higher than 10,000 a year – these figures assume an even more startling appearance: current divorce rates are fifteen times as great. At a recent government enquiry John Haskey of the Office of Population Censuses and Surveys (CPCS) gave the following projected figures for divorce (assuming current rates of divorce continue unchanged at their present levels, neither increasing nor decreasing): (a) One in three marriages would end in divorce (b) One in two marriages in which the wife married in her teens would end in divorce. Almost six in every ten marriages in which the husband married in his teens would end in divorce. (c) The chance that the marriage of a divorced man would also end in divorce would be 1½ times that of a bachelor who marries at the same age. Similarly a divorced woman who married would be twice as likely to divorce as a spinster who marries at the same age. If, in addition, it is assumed that fertility rates within marriages were to continue unchanged at their present levels (d) One in five children would, before reaching their sixteenth birthday, experience the divorce of their parents.[2]

Incidentally, I found the following 'IMPORTANT

NOTE' heading the paper giving the above information extremely interesting, because it shows an official acceptance of current mores with regard to people living together outside of marriage: 'The statistics on marriage and divorce contained . . . in this memorandum refer only to *legal* marriages and *legal* dissolutions. The marriage statistics do not, therefore, include unmarried couples who live together. Similarly, the statistics on divorce take no account of, for example, informal separations. The divorce statistics should not, therefore, be interpreted as measuring the full extent of marital breakdown.'[3] Even a decade ago I am sure the writers of a memorandum about divorce submitted to a parliamentary committee would never have thought the final sentence necessary, considering as it obviously does 'informal separations' to be part of the picture of 'marital breakdown'.

The number of children involved in such figures is frightening: OPCS figures for 1982 show 146,698 couples receiving their decree absolute; the number of children under 16 years of age in these families was 158,268, with a further 68,455 aged 16 or over. At any given moment one in eight children are being brought up by a single parent.

American figures are even more startling: with one marriage in two ending in divorce the result projected by David Chambers (quoted on the opening page of this chapter) will be that half the children born today will become eligible for a support order some time during their childhood, and that when they become adults half of them can expect either to pay out or to receive support orders for their own children. An expected total of two-thirds of Americans born this year will sooner or later be involved in the child-support system.[4]

In Australia the story is similar, in 1973 there were 16,196 divorces, in 1976 the figures peaked to 63,230 divorces, fell to 40,608 in 1978, fell even lower to 37,854 in 1979, but rose again to 41,312 in 1981. The numbers of children affected by divorce for the same years were respectively, 23,078, 73,645, 51,599, 46,130, and 49,616. Since 1976 a total of 7.3 per cent of all Australian children under 18 have been affected by divorce.[5]

A recent EEC study shows that Europeans are three times as likely to get divorced and twice as likely to have children outside marriage as they were a generation ago. In the ten EEC countries, for every divorce in 1960 there were fifteen marriages. By 1981 for every divorce there were only 3.8 marriages. Illegitimate births rose from 46 in every thousand in 1960, to 78 per thousand in 1980, and new statistics suggest that the figure of over 100 per thousand has now been reached. For Denmark, where it is commonplace for couples to live together without being legally married, the latest count shows 382 illegitimate births per thousand, while Britain, coming second in the EEC listing, has 141 births per thousand.[6]

How do these figures relate when you are personally involved? Jessica Curtis, divorced with one son from her marriage and a daughter as a single mother, said, 'I don't think my daughter will feel very different not having a father around. I guess well over half the public school kids here [American state school] live with one parent. Most of those divorced fathers don't support and don't visit, or visit sporadically, and some of the mothers are single mothers by *no* choice.' *Marion*, a mother I met at a Gingerbread group (an English organization for single parents, usually single by *no* choice) whose husband left her: 'If you do it by choice it's different, but when your kid's dumped on you because someone's walked out on you it's a horrible feeling, you feel rejected and despondent and everything. It's really hell trying to manage on social security. I get £33 a week, and that's got to cover everything – clothes, food – except for heating and rent; they pay that for you. I've got two children, one boy of 10 and one of 7½; they've got tremendous appetites and I just can't fill them up. You get the money on a Monday and by the Friday you're nearly skint and you've got nothing for the weekend shopping. So it is very hard. The food I have to buy is the most fattening food, like bread and potatoes because they're filling. I've looked at healthfood stuff in a healthfood shop, but it's such a lot more expensive and I can't afford to buy it.'

'*Could you get together with friends and buy it in bulk?*

It's a lot cheaper then.'

'The thing is where to put it? Most of us are living in small flats – I only know one person who has a fridge freezer – we just wouldn't have any space to store the stuff. I haven't even got a handbasin in my bathroom, it's so small, and when you open the door you hit the bath. In the kitchen you can just get one chair in it and that's it.'

'With the stress you must be under I don't suppose you can find the energy to bake your own brown bread or anything like that?'

'That's right. I seem to have plenty of time, but I've never got the motivation to go and do it, if you know what I mean. It's a horrible feeling, you think you must go and do this or that, but there's never any motivation to get up and do it.'

Sonia, who initiated the break with her Israeli artist husband and moved to a flat nearby, was reasonably happy at first until her husband decided to refuse to let her keep her children with her. Shortly afterwards he spirited them away to Israel, and although she tried endlessly to get them back she was eventually defeated by Israeli law, which she decribes as totally patriarchal. Her son seems to have been the one who suffered most of all: 'My daughter appeared much more equable, she just gets on with whatever there is at the time, but *he* was terribly disturbed for about four or five years, he refused to accept that he had to live in Israel. He was very unhappy. His father couldn't cope with him and he took him into therapy – it was awful, he wanted to kill himself at the age of 10, he had all these awful dreams about swimming under the sea and struggling through walls of ice. He had a very difficult time, but his father wouldn't let him come back to England. Eventually I realized it was tearing him apart – I was writing and saying how I wished we were together, those kind of messages, and he was going along with that. So I stopped writing that kind of thing, though I still went to see them as often as I could. I think he was able then to accept that he was an Israeli – now he's 19 and he's in the army.'

I discussed with art gallery owner *Frances* the differences between children whose parents were divorced and the children of deliberately single parents: 'My daughter benefits from something that I think is only possible for people who've done it alone by choice, which is that there haven't been battles about her. I've raised her according to what *I* thought I should do. I don't ask Heather's father, though we're very good friends, his opinion of where she should go to school, what she should wear, what her habits should be – we don't discuss that stuff, we don't have any conflicts around her. She has never been caught in the middle between a father and a mother who want to kill each other and focus only on that. I see it around me, women whose marriages have finished, and there have been miserable break-ups and terrible anger and pain all around, with the kids caught in the middle. My sister has a child my daughter's age, and he is wise beyond his years as a result of having to deal with the terrible anger his parents have for each other. When Heather goes to stay with her father and his wife she has two people there who love her, and her daddy is *the* perfect father figure. I think if she ever lives with him she'll probably find some of the reasons why I couldn't live with him, but he's a great figure, and *in absentia* he's perfect. I know that kids of divorce have this illusion that maybe they can get their parents back together again, but she knows differently without any pain on her part.'

'*Perhaps it's better for a child to be part of a stable relationship of two – mother and child – than an unstable relationship of three.*'

'I don't think there's any doubt about that, *any* doubt about that. Heather's a marvellous girl, as I said. She gets on well at school, has lots of friends – sure, she has trouble with math, but so had I!'

Money is nearly always a problem with single mothers who did not plan to raise their children on their own. Chambers writes, that 'Without substantial prodding, most fathers who have never lived with their children never pay support at all, and even divorced fathers who have lived with their children typically pay regularly for only a short time, then pay less, and then pay nothing.'[7]

So many wives give up careers when they marry or start

producing children, and divorce leaves them in a much worse financial state than their husbands, especially if he avoids paying them maintenance. *Marion*, the Gingerbread member whose story we have just read, said, 'Most of the people who choose to have children alone have got careers, but I cut mine short to get married. I was a hairdresser – I could go back but it's such long hours it's ridiculous with children to look after. I do it sometimes for friends, but they can't afford much, so they buy me cigarettes or sweets for the kids. I couldn't have people here in my flat to do it and get more money that way – like I said I haven't got any room at all for that sort of thing.'

Arranging the combination of work and child care is the worst problem for most women, especially for those whose jobs are non-professional and who are unable to arrange the hours they work according to their needs. Yet women seem to take it for granted that it is *their* responsibility to look after their children after divorce, however difficult it makes it for them to earn money. Carol Bruch writes that a 1977 study made in Los Angeles showed that few men actually claimed custody of their children: asked before the divorce came through 57 per cent of the fathers said they wanted custody, but only 38 per cent asked their lawyers about the likelihood of their getting it, and in the end only 13 per cent asked for custody on the divorce petition. Those who asked for custody usually wanted the older, teenage children only. Of the divorcing mothers, however, 96 per cent said they wanted custody of their children, and 88 to 90 per cent of the final decrees granted them it.[8]

In Britain research shows a similar situation. Approximately 90 per cent of British mothers are awarded custody with care and control of their children after divorce, and only 10 per cent of the fathers are given custody. At present there are very few joint custody cases. Where there is a dispute, courts nearly always keep the status quo: since most children stay with their mothers after a separation and since the courts will almost automatically order the situation to continue except in exceptional cases, it is mothers who nearly always end up with the custody of the children.[9]

So why then do people – like lemmings on a death

plunge – go on marrying when the odds against success seem so high? Could there be some biological urge to make a family unit, I asked family historian Elaine May. 'No, if it were so then why do so many units break apart, even after having children? I believe much more in cultural determinism than in biological determinism. I think the high rate of divorce indicates that if it were not for cultural expectations people would either mate and stay together for ever, or they wouldn't marry at all, just mate and go their separate ways. I think political, social and institutional realities put such pressure on people they try to create their personal happiness in the family, because our society makes it very difficult for them to find satisfaction elsewhere. Certainly there is *some* definite mating urge that keeps people forming and reforming unions – they marry again after divorce, still looking for happiness – but I just can't endorse the analysis it's a biological urge, because so much of our biology is culturally determined.'

Should couples try harder to stay together, especially if there are children? *Lynn*, the nurse with two daughters, talking about her own decision to be a single mother: 'Sometimes I feel like I have the best of two worlds. I don't have that significant relationship in the home but my kids are mine, nobody can come and take them away, and I don't have that threat that the marriage isn't going to last, as is so common nowadays. It didn't happen that way in New York when I was brought up, though it might be happening now. My parents, and my friends' parents, they all stuck together for the sake of the children, that generation did.'

Not everyone has lost that sense of duty, for better or worse. Psychologist Hendrika Vande Kemp says, 'You can't turn your back on a relationship like marriage. It's there whether you like it or not. So even if you have turned your back on it, the relationship is still there, you've just made a different kind of relationship, that's all, and you've made it a worse kind of relationship. There *are* marriages where there is just nothing that can be done, but I think there are too many divorces that happen because people are too lazy, too uncaring to make their marriage work. I think there is something wrong with society itself – the institutions are not giving people the support they need, especially where children are concerned.'

But Tony Baker, child psychiatrist at London's St George's Hospital, considering the position of children of single parents by choice, compared it favourably with those involved in acrimonious divorce. 'Children are much more likely to run into psychological and emotional problems where the divorce was one of enmity and where the parents continued to remain in some kind of struggle, so that even though they were divorced in name they were actually bound together by the enormous struggle, particularly where a child is triangled into that because of custody or access issues. There the potential for the child developing stressful symptoms is quite high. It's not the divorce itself that's so much the problem. There's evidence to show that children who live in unhappy homes actually suffer more emotional and behavioural conduct disturbance and educational problems than children living in families where there has been an amicable separation and where there is reasonable contact and access to both parents, and that *those* children in divorced families actually do better than children who live in disharmonious homes.'

No one is suggesting that to have a child alone without a sharing partner is necessarily best for a child, but neither should it be taken for granted that any marriage is better than no marriage. We have seen some of the damage that divorce can do, and today's women are right to bear this in mind when they come to make one of the most important choices of their lives.

Women's relationships with their own families
A finding I was not anticipating but which makes sense is that many of the mothers I interviewed had had very uneasy relationships with their own fathers. Relationships with their mothers varied, and were not noticeably different from any ordinary cross-section of women, but time and time again the single mothers reported that they hardly knew their fathers because they were so uncommunicative, or that they were authoritarian, unsupporting, or sometimes drank to

excess. Most of their mothers stood by them in their pregnancies, but in most cases their fathers had to actually see and hold the baby before they were able to accept their daughters' unconventional choice.

Frances, the gallery owner: 'I wasn't brilliant, but I had an enormous amount of pressure from my father so I was a good student, yes. Of course I'd like it if my daughter were too, but I'm not going to give her that kind of pressure – I'm not comfortable with being authoritarian. I was afraid of my father, he was this impossible, demanding authority figure. I grew up very ambivalent about him, he was a difficult person. I think my relationship with Heather's father, who is a strong, really remarkable man, has had a lot to do with putting to rest my anger at my father. The way that women are socialized makes it really hard to relate to strong men and to figure out what an equal relationship is.'

Pat, midwife, talking about how her son Josh gets on with his grandfather: 'But my dad isn't very child-oriented – he's just a very autocratic narcissistic man, he's always been that way, even in my childhood – so I started realizing I'd better not create an imaginary relationship for Josh. You know, I used to say, "grandpa's coming over today, we'll have real fun", but then it just never happened. It either wouldn't be fun or he'd say, can Josh stay here and I'll take you out to. . . . He just didn't want to fool with the kid.'

Felicity, a medical researcher, had never got on well with her father and he was totally unable to accept her pregnancy. Unusually for the mothers I interviewed, she had hoped to marry the father of her child, and when he broke off all relationship with her she was very upset: 'I went through quite a bit of depression – my father was also not speaking to me. He had leukemia, and he was completely devastated by what I had done. He didn't speak to me all the time I was pregnant. I'd go back home for Sunday lunch but he'd leave the room or just completely ignore me. Oh, he'd give me a drink, but that would be it. It's a very conventional family and my mother was born Catholic, whereas he was only a convert, but it was she who was supportive of me, quietly. It was very hard, especially knowing he was getting worse and worse – his doctor told me he'd be lucky to live a year. We just didn't talk at all – in fact he was in hospital having a blood transfusion when I was in myself, and I rang him up and said I'd come and see him, and he told me not to, so I didn't. Four weeks after the birth I put my baby in his arms, and that was it – he adored him straight away. It was his first grandson and he was smitten with him. But he died without really making it up with me. We were both very stubborn people, very alike – he couldn't ever say he was sorry, and I think we both found it very difficult to approach the subject. Yes, it was very hurtful.'

For others the father figure was virtually absent, either factually or because he was not involved in the family in any meaningful sense. *Tam*, a clinical social worker and therapist, who is thinking about having a baby alone: 'It was a friend who made me see that by planning to have a baby on my own I was repeating what my mother did to me, bringing me up in what was a basically mother/daughter family because my father just wasn't emotionally there, ever. For a start he wasn't even physically in my life until I was about $2\frac{1}{2}$ as he was in the army then he was hospitalized for a while. But his character is that he is intellectual and removed, sort of in his own world. I have a lot of recollection as a child of trying to tune in on his wavelength and having difficulty doing that, feeling like he just wasn't there. That was very difficult for me as a child, and made me feel very isolated and removed from any sense of being in a real family.'

Actress *Catherine*'s father died shortly after she was born: 'I think this is a very important factor in my not feeling I need a man around. For me the norm was for a woman to bring up a family on her own, which my mother did very well.' *Sarah*, a languages teacher, had a mother who was very dominant, while her father, though physically present, drifted further and further away from any sense of communication with his own family. She remembers him as a very impotent, almost non-existent member of the family.

However, whether or not the family relationship had been satisfactory, keeping in touch was very important to many of the mothers, though distance often made regular contact difficult. Women occasionally mentioned how they found certain particular family members supportive – siblings sometimes assumed an important supportive role when they lived nearby, even if it was only to be at the other end of the telephone when the mothers needed someone close by to talk to. I have written earlier how a couple of lesbian pairs had such good relationships with their brothers that the latter donated their sperm so their sisters' partners could become pregnant through artificial insemination.

Even where fathers had done their best to play their role constructively circumstances sometimes meant that a satisfactory background could not be achieved for their children. We have already heard how *Angela*'s father brought her up with the help of her aunt after her mother died when she was 6, then on his own after the aunt's death, until Angela (a PhD student when I interviewed her) was 18. As an adult she wanted to have a child 'for the security of living in a family': 'My family life disintegrated when I was 14, so by the time I was 25 I felt a real need to have a person who was related to me who would live with me. No, I didn't see that in terms of marrying, because my mother died when I was 6 and my father didn't remarry until after I was grown up, so I never actually saw or lived in a family with a married relationship.'

The urge to have and to live in one's own family can become intensely important where that need was not satisfied in childhood. *Mary*'s parents separated when she was very young, and it was her grandmother who brought her and her siblings up because the mother was often ill. *Angela*'s father brought *her* up. As children some single mothers lived in reconstructed families resulting from divorce. It is inevitable that fewer and fewer of the new generation will take it for granted that a family means mum, dad and two kids. But the urge to be an integral part of *some* kind of family persists, and, for women, having a baby is one obvious answer.

The death of their own mother leaves an emptiness it is particularly difficult for a girl to fill. Stephanie Dowrick writes movingly of her mother's death when she was 8, and talks of the empty space left behind which is partly filled by her love for other women, but the image of her mother stays with her. She sees her in her dreams, has danced with her, together with her as yet unconceived child. When she *does* conceive, she writes, she knows her relationship with her dead mother will change, that she will increase her knowledge of her.[10]

For others the actual mother has been so unsatisfactory that the single mother may find herself wanting to 'reparent' herself through her interaction with her own child, though most women know the dangers of this. Irene Klebfisz writes with devastating honesty of her awareness of that desire in herself, and that by becoming the warm supportive mother she had so often imagined, she had hoped 'to annihilate the impatient critical voice within myself, the voice that has kept me insecure and dissatisfied'. But the fantasy of being the perfect mother has in fact more to do with her need to experience something she herself had never had than with the reality of having a child. 'It is not a child I wish to mother, it is myself. . . . This is clearly a wrong reason for having a child – one which can be ultimately disastrous.'[11]

For most women, though, relationships with their mothers have not been a particular problem, though there were occasional reports of difficulties. *Tam*, the social worker and therapist: 'I told you how isolated I felt from my father, so my mother was very important to me. I was very close to her, and she loved me, there was no question about that. She was a very good person in a moral, ethical sense, but she had a lot of difficulties in her life, and a very poor self-concept. She was 38 when she married, and she became so intertwined with me it was hard for her to see me as a separate person. Her low self-concept carried right over to me, so that I could never quite do anything right for her. She always found what I left out, or what I didn't do quite right, so I didn't get a lot of positive feedback in my life. I realized later when I was thinking about this really powerful need I had for a family that what I was lacking was a sense of real emotional connectedness between everyone. I think with my mother it was that she couldn't really connect properly with me because she was trying to meet her *own* needs out of her relationship with me. She was such an unhappy person I don't feel she was free to love me as a human being separate from her or to really know me for who I was. I think, though, that that sense of separateness in the family was typical of the 1950s. It's changing now, people my age are determined to make it different, and men's roles especially are changing enormously. My father was typical in many ways of his generation: to this day he doesn't really have any concept of other people's needs.'

I was talking to *Stephanie*, psychoanalyst and psycho-therapist, about how some children in abusive families try desperately to make their mothers happy, with 4-year olds giving instead of receiving comfort. 'That's the story of my life,' she said. 'I was my mother's mother. So my friends have accused me of bending over backwards the other way with my own child, which can be equally dangerous – you know, you're not here, honey, to make mummy happy. I went through a break-up of a relationship a few months ago, and I was very depressed and crying a lot, and Danny was going around saying, are you happy, mummy? are you happy? So I got very nervous; I said, honey, you're not here to make me happy, it's not your job to make me happy. And he said, why mummy, you make *me* happy. And I thought, oh, my God, maybe I should shut my mouth and let him make me happy, because what he was doing wasn't coming out of him being *forced* to make me happy, it was out of a feeling that I had done it for him and he was identifying with that. So I let him cheer me up when he wanted to.' Even psychotherapists don't always get it right first time!

The ideal marriage
Does it ever happen? I doubt it, but it's nice to imagine it might. I remember being very moved by the showing on television some time ago of a documentary programme showing Dr Michel Odent – the obstetrician who believes that women should respond to their own deep primitive instincts and give birth in the way most natural to them – helping in the labour of some of 'his' mothers. Watching the births was extraordinary enough, but what stays in my

memory is the tenderness between the spouses (for at that time in Odent's practice the husband was nearly always present at the birth), and the love and warmth expressed between them as a father would kiss his wife again and again with amazed joy. The intimate sensuality only possible between mates, the tenderness, the deep love – who could have seen this and not been overcome by it? I thought at the time how sad it was for single mothers that they should not be able to experience this deepest of unions and for the babies too, that they should be denied such a blissful entrance into life. The reader may remember how in an earlier chapter *Sarah*, the languages teacher, expressed this very sadness. I imagined marriages of such profound and daily happiness that comparison with my own more earthbound union was a chastening experience.

But alas, it seems that even for Dr Odent's couples their actual marriages were not necessarily so out of the ordinary, because recently he has stated that he no longer automatically asks fathers to be present at births. Mothers, he says, in fact do not always want them – apart from anything else he has found that an attending father delays the birth because the woman does not relax as much as she does when alone with women midwives to help her, and that given a free choice without any psychological pressure, she will mostly opt not to have her husband present. All the same, whatever becomes of the new orthodoxy of having fathers present in the labour room (and I must say I was certainly very happy to have my husband present at the birth of my own two children), I still think there are bound to be sad moments for single mothers as they observe other mothers in the ward being embraced by visiting husbands. But let us not romanticize: even if a father is overcome by joy at the first sight of his newborn, how long does that joy last?

Dr Elphis Christopher, who is herself happily married, answered me firmly when I accused her of comparing single motherhood with an impossibly ideal marriage: 'Perhaps I am, but when things are going well and you're actually looking at the person that you love, and you know that you've created these children together, there's something very deep about that, something very . . . animal isn't the right word, but it's very, very deep.'

Karin Meiselman, also happily married, said, 'Since I'm involved in a two-parent family I see the benefits of that. When you have the right two parents and the right relationship going, then it's wonderful that children can learn to relate intimately to both a male and a female in the parent role – because I really think there are important differences between the two sexes – and that they can see at first hand how two adults relate to each other. I think that's a very desirable part of the traditional nuclear family if you can get it. But the ideal is not always possible; and many times people have to accept something that's a little less ideal and try to make up for it in various ways. I guess it's why we're starting to use the term "single-parent family".'

So let us stop dreaming about the ideal, and compare the actuality of most marriages with the situation of single mothers by choice.

A comparison between married and single parenthood

Anthropologist Janet Proctor: 'First of all you mustn't confuse marriage with the family. If you look cross-culturally, non-Western, if you look at the broadest range of what family might mean, it doesn't necessarily mean the nuclear family as we conceive it. Speaking of the species I don't think a monogamous male, female, children is at all the norm of the family.'

The fact that babies are, in a sense, born prematurely and need care for a long time before they can become independent, means that primates need a different sort of family background from animals which mature in a comparatively short time. I asked Janet Proctor if she was implying that because of this fact some sort of extended family was necessary for child-raising. 'It's not just babies who need it. I don't think that a mother/child dyad in any human group can exist independently. I also don't think two men can exist independently! Humans depend on a social group of some size beyond two or three people for basic survival, not for emotional reasons, but for practical reasons, from shelter onwards. We humans can't live in absence of artifacts: we have to have tools, whether you manufacture them yourself or get them in an economic situation like ours. Our food gathering is more elaborate than chimps and apes who just wander around eating and playing all the time, but even they need each other to defend themselves against predators, or the climate. You have to exist alongside others. Yes, you're right – for single mothers the state can become the surrogate husband or extended social group, so they're not really doing anything new because they're not actually living *independently* of others, even when they have money to pay their own way.'

Kate Millett saw the family in a different light, believing that in a patriarchal society the chief function of the family is to socialize the young so that they fit in with prevailing mores according to patriarchal needs, and that schools, other children and the media would complete the socialization. Patriarchy obviously insists upon legitimacy and since the family rely on the father for their social status and the financial background, his position is extremely powerful. Although from a biological point of view, she continues, there is no reason why 'the two central functions of the family [socialization and reproduction] need be inseparable from or even take place within it, revolutionary or utopian efforts to remove these functions from the family have been so frustrated, so beset by difficulties, that most experiments so far have involved a gradual return to tradition.' Experience to date shows quite clearly that without a full understanding of the political and social aspects of the existing society, change is very difficult if not impossible.[12]

There are other kinds of changes, though, besides planned political ones. Whether we are in the middle of a genuine change of mores as far as family is concerned or whether factors such as the economic recession, unemployment, fear of the loss of personal happiness in the face of the appalling divorce figures, will mean a reversion to traditional family units is impossible to tell at present. I suspect that thanks to the women's movement there has already been too fundamental an alteration in the way women perceive themselves and their role for them to let themselves willingly collect up their apron strings and tether themselves once more to their oh-so-easy-care kitchens. And yet, and yet. . . . Listen to what some of the married or cohabiting women have to say about how their husbands actually perform in this new and 'equal' world.

Sonia (lived with then later married Saul, an Israeli artist, who eventually took their children permanently to Israel in spite of her desperate attempts to gain custody): 'When I first got pregnant Saul flew into a total panic and started screaming about abortion and wouldn't let me sleep all night, shouting and stamping. I just stuck to my guns and said, if you want to go off, go off. I wanted a child, and I wasn't worried about being on my own, I knew I could support myself. I hadn't cheated him, he'd known I wasn't taking precautions. In fact, when our son was born, Saul almost loved him to death, squashed him tight against himself like a 2-year-old would a toy. But then the real difficulties began. He didn't help with the baby at all in the middle of the night – that was my business – and also I was having to get up at five or six. He was still very nervous and he'd shout and scream at me. We were living in one room so I used to sleep on the kitchen floor after I'd fed the baby rather than go back to bed and wake him. Anyway, I got through it somehow and got pregnant about ten months after the first one was born, and he did the same number again. No, neither of us thought about taking precautions, isn't that odd! Perhaps he just needed the panic? He started shouting abortion again, but not too seriously this time, and I just flatly refused. Then one day he suddenly said, we're going to get married now, and so we did, more or less immediately. I didn't mind whether we married or not, but he had this Jewish thing about families, and I had to get converted or the children wouldn't officially have been Jewish.

'When the second one was about 3 months old we moved into a two-room flat. The children had one room and we had another, a small room with a huge double bed: he worked in it, he had his work all over the place, he entertained till one or two every morning, and it was very hard. Everything happened in that room. The children played in there, we slept in there, we ate in there, my husband worked in there, everything went on in that one room. I couldn't sleep until the guests went – I was totally exhausted. He complained bitterly because I was tired. He helped somewhat with the kids, shopping, laundry, things like that, he did his best, and I started doing some work at home, because we were very poor on top of everything else. It gradually got worse and worse. At the same time his career was getting more and more interesting – he was invited to go to the States to do a show, and gradually he went away more and more, and the less he was there, the happier I was. When he wasn't there we had a wonderful, very close and free sort of existence, the children and I. Eventually I insisted on a trial separation and he was very upset. It took three years to finally break it off, but in the end I knew the marriage was finished.'

At the beginning of this chapter I wrote how after the divorce Sonia fought for her children but the patriarchal Israeli law awarded Saul custody, with deeply upsetting results for her son especially: 'I was given unlimited access, and they were supposed to come to me every summer, but they didn't for about three years, so I had to go to Israel instead. There was a lot of bitterness and anger between Saul and myself and it was terrible for the children. Everything was so different with my third child, whom I had later by a lover I didn't want to live with. There was just no comparison! It was wonderful, all the way through. I was able to do what I felt was right all the time, and even the way she was born was quite lovely. She was the first official Leboyer baby in this country. And afterwards – well, I think it's a lot easier for the child, to have one point of reference only – perhaps with an alternative viewpoint from an important person, but just the one point of reference as to what's done and what isn't done, right and wrong.'

I have already written about *Julia*'s 'husband' (Julia lived with her lover for three years after their daughter's birth) who, like Saul, liked going to bed late, would play music long after their baby had been put down to sleep in their single room (the standard picture of marriage so often assumes affluence, but for huge numbers of couples early married life with a baby means sharing with in-laws or living in one or at most two rooms, with no spare cash and conditions quite as stressful as any single mother knows), and refusing to compromise his lifestyle in any way. 'On reflection I think he found it very hard – coming home and having a baby crying a lot of the night. No, he never got up to help. Sometimes he'd wake up for a few minutes, then go back to sleep. He says he always felt I wouldn't want him to do it, but he never offered, and I never pushed him. The thing is I didn't like to because right at the beginning I *did* ask, I used to ask him to do things, and he was *so* bad-tempered that I just stopped asking. I think that was sad, really. Now I'm on my own I feel I'm a lot better off. Financially as well, oddly enough, because although I'm on social security at least I feel the money is mine and I can make decisions about it. I always felt so guilty about what I could spend money on, not allocating any for clothes for myself, or treating myself in any way, even though he was never tight on money – he'd always give it if I asked him, but there was such a grudgingness in general. I like to be independent about money, I don't like to lean on people. Another thing, I'm moving again, and that sort of decision is easier too, because it's only me who has to decide.'

Ann Oakley, in the Preface to her book *Becoming a Mother*, writes how although she was delighted with her two children when they were born, what followed was a depressed time of 'nappy-washing and pill-taking', when she felt nothing but tiredness, isolation and resentment at her husband's freedom. Eventually she had the strength to drag herself out of the depression and to begin work on her PhD, an understanding of feminist principles helping her to realize that it was society itself and societal expectations that were at fault rather than her husband or herself.

This understanding lies behind much of her work. Specifically, for example, she reports in *Becoming a Mother* that when she asked her sample of married or cohabiting mothers how much help they got from their husbands once they had returned home with their babies, the answer was very little. She found that the mothers' satisfaction with this situation depended on their expectations, and since they expected so little in the first place they would say things like their husbands were 'very good' or 'marvellous', when the truth was they were hardly doing anything to help at all. It was the *attitude* of the men that seemed most important to many of the women – as long as husbands expressed willingness to help they didn't seem to mind that in actual fact they didn't. Perhaps one of the reasons the men did not do more was that their wives didn't ask them to, but most women know too well how men manage to slip out of this kind of work, either by being so slow or deliberately hopeless at it that the women give in and take over, or by creating such an uncomfortable, even resentful atmosphere that for the sake of peace the women learn not to ask. A breakdown of the mothers' responses to this questioning was that over half, 54 per cent, were satisfied with the fathers' help. Yet asked how much help the fathers gave with looking after their new babies, only 11 per cent of the mothers replied 'a lot', 24 per cent answered 'some', and a huge 65 per cent replied 'little or none'.

Men rarely changed nappies or bathed the babies, wouldn't push prams, mostly left night feeds entirely to the woman and didn't do much other feeding, but they did enjoy playing with their children. They mostly refused to change soiled nappies at all. Only one man was prepared to do this, and he would even do it at night and hand his wife in bed the changed, clean baby to feed: is there some message in the fact that unlike most of the parents in this sample this particular couple were not legally married? To answer the cynic's obvious comment, they had lived together for seven years, so it was not exactly a case of love's young dream![13]

The researchers also found that men did less and less housework after the birth of their child. All of the women did jobs until a short time before the birth, and none of them returned to work after they had had their child. This meant that men now expected their wives to take over chores they had often done for themselves before, especially laundry. Twenty-two per cent of the men helped their wives 'a lot' during pregnancy, but this figure fell to 14 per cent five weeks after the birth, and to only 6 per cent five months after the birth. Forty-eight per cent reported that their husbands gave little or no household help during their pregnancy; this figure remained the same five weeks after the birth, but by five months after the birth 61 per cent were getting little or no help. When the mothers were asked if looking after the baby was anything like they thought it would be, a huge majority, 91 per cent, answered 'no'.[14]

It seems that in men's eyes washing the floor is the same as washing the baby – anything domestic now becomes the woman's chore, and not just during the weekdays when the man is away working, but also at the weekends when he is home. I remember my own resentment at this – it seemed impossible to make my husband understand how worn down I was by the evening by the perpetual *caring* for others, and how much difference it would have made to my feelings to have a cup of coffee made especially for *me* and for it to be given to me with a cheerful smile, instead of the resentful grimace that usually accompanied an evening drink if I persisted. I was at home all day (writing, but that didn't count as work since it was mostly very badly paid) while he was out all day, and in his eyes that entitled him to twenty-four-hour-a-day personal service. This was how marriage was in the 1960s for many; because I was brought up in a very different atmosphere I thought in those days I had been unlucky in this aspect of my marriage, but listening to other women I'm now no longer sure that such behaviour was all that unusual after all.

Sadly, Oakley reports that while emotional relationships between spouses improved during pregnancy and immediately after the birth, they then soon deteriorated: 73 per cent of her sample wives reported a drop in marital happiness.[15] I mentioned earlier an important study by Professor George Brown and his colleagues at Bedford College which found that 25 per cent of working-class women in Camberwell in London would have been diagnosed as clinically depressed if a psychiatrist had examined them, compared with 5 per cent of middle-class women. But in fact less than half had even been to see their family doctor about their symptoms, let alone a psychiatrist. 'When the sample was reduced to mothers with children under 6 years of age the class differences became even more marked. Forty-two per cent of working-class mothers were psychiatrically disturbed while the proportion of middle-class mothers remained unchanged at 5 per cent.'[16] The reasons that Professor Brown and his colleagues found for this discrepancy are complex, and have been summarized in my book *Web of Violence*, but briefly it was found that what the researchers called 'life events' – loss of a job, unwanted pregnancy, eviction from house, etc. – affected working-class women more than middle-class women, who in any case usually suffered far fewer of these events while their children were young. Also, importantly, middle-class women had more to look forward to in the future and felt more in control of their lives. Interestingly, close intimacy with a husband or a lover was found 'to give almost complete protection against the onset of psychiatric disorder caused by a severe event . . . faced with such a happening only 4 per cent of the women with an intimate relationship became disturbed.'[17] There is not space to look more closely at this very interesting and important study here, but the point I want to make is that we can see from this study and the earlier quotations that marriage does not ensure happiness in a mother, and to assume that a child or children brought up in a single-by-choice family must necessarily be unhappier and more disturbed than children brought up in a 'normal' family is clearly erroneous.

A number of women referred to the lack of tension when for one reason or another there was no partner around to be consulted or allowed for. Even women with happy marriages commented on this when I was discussing the subject with them; they may miss their husbands' help, but there are also rewards. Psychologist Karin Meiselman: 'I remember when Herb had gone away for a business trip I worked terribly hard being a single parent, maintaining my job, chauffeuring the kids around to the places they had to go to and stuff like that, but there was a reduction in tension in that there was no question about whose job it was, it was all *my* job, and so although it was a great deal of hard work at the same time there was an absence of tension – you know, why doesn't *he* do this, or whose job is it to do that? Some of the confusion is reduced, and it's all very simple. Herb's always been very helpful, he's never rigidly defined housework or cooking or things like that as female duties, but from time to time there still have to be little renegotiations about whose job it is to do what, and so on.'

I remember very clearly the tension that would build up before my tidy-minded husband was due in from work when I would suddenly realize the kids' things were all over the place, and the resentment I felt that I had to bully them to tidy up when I really didn't care either way as long as it wasn't too awful and they were happy. And yet when he got home I longed for the children to go to bed so that I could talk like an adult after a day with only children for company, and I wished there were time to make myself look reasonable so that I would please him and he wouldn't leave me for one of his female colleagues, etc. etc. What until then had been easy and amicable would suddenly become a rush, and I'd nag the children and probably moan at my husband when he finally did arrive.

The relief of not having to please another or take another into consideration may or may not be balanced out by the fact that there is somebody else to *share* problems with you, another shoulder to lean on when it all gets too much. *Felicity*, medical researcher before she had her child, said, 'I think I'm better off without a man, quite honestly, seeing some of my friends and the problems they have with their husbands. I have only got myself to consider, only got to concentrate on the two of us. I know where I am, I'm the one that makes the choice and the decisions, and I haven't got somebody else giving an opinion that I have to listen to.' *Charlotte*, a part-time researcher: 'I know so many people who are in unhelpful marriages where they don't get ordinary help like holding the baby while you do the washing up – perhaps not so many, but enough to know it must be awful, and far, far worse than having to do everything yourself. Because you've got emotional aggro and fury and anger and wanting to kick the baby away from you because your husband isn't looking after it, whereas if you're on your own you've just got you and the baby, and you find ways of coping, it's as simple as that. I think it's probably still best to do it as a couple – I know some marriages where it does work and they have fun, but knowing a few where it doesn't work I'm terribly grateful I haven't got that problem.'

Women in happy unions must at this stage be longing to rush to the defence of marriage, but it is natural that women who have made the choice to be single mothers should be more conscious of their advantages than of their disadvantages. Yet virtually all of them would rather share with another person than remain alone, *if* – and what a huge 'if' this is! – they could only meet that right person. I don't think the reason they are alone is that they are asking too much, or that they have emotional problems to solve before they can live with someone, though that may be true in some cases; I think the truth is that we are all asking more and more, wanting more and more, out of our intimate relationships nowadays. The old kind of rubbing-along marriage just won't do for most of us any more. It may be the time will come when people will realize that the kind of full relationship we have been hoping for is just a pipe-dream for most of us, that men and women *are* two different species almost, and some of us will decide to compromise for the sake of companionship, and others will prefer to stay alone.

As I commented before, one of the very happiest couples I met were lesbian, and certainly the understanding they shared would have been envied by many a straight mother coping simultaneously with small children and a husband who wanted his own share of attention. We will look in a moment at what Stella and Jan had to say about how they cope as a lesbian family, but first let us glance briefly at some advantages and disadvantages of being married. Museum curator *Elizabeth* pointed out one obvious advantage: 'it was a real operation even for me to go to the cinema when David was younger – round here all my friends belong to baby-sitting circles, but if you're single you can't do that, you can't ever reciprocate, you can't leave your house to baby-sit for someone else because you've got no one at home to do *your* baby-sitting while you're out paying back your evening off. You can never make a snap decision to do anything when you're on your own.' This was a comment that many mothers made to me.

Another advantage is the one that Dr Elphis Christopher pointed out, that children learn about the relationship between two cohabiting sexes, which is great if the relationship is a good one – on the other hand I know individuals who have been put off all relationships for life because of the physically and/or emotionally abusive homes in which they were brought up. We will be looking at role models in the final chapter of Part 2, but thinking of fathers in a more personal way I recall the sheer delight my children had in bouncing around on our double bed wrestling with their father, the pleasure on their faces as they rode him piggy-back down country lanes, the pride of my daughter one birthday party when her classful of small friends decided to use him as a cushion and leapt, all sixteen of them, at him and on him, and good-humouredly he caught them and threw them around, amid shrieks of laughter. There can be a lot of pleasure in a father's presence, but we should not forget the reverse side, that of breaking marriages: at least single children in single-by-choice families don't have to cope with that.

The advantages of single mothers are surprisingly many: *Carolyn*, theatre director, pointed out that a lot of married women are much lonelier than single women because they expect when they become mothers to have companionship and support from their husbands and when they don't get it they really suffer. 'I knew from the start I had to find my own support, so I ended up creating a network around me of friends of different ages that's really intense, and I think there are a lot of married women who figure their husbands are going to do this and they don't, and they suddenly end up being really alone because they've dropped old friends and not thought it necessary to make a new support group.' Another advantage pointed out by Dr Afton Blake is that it is easier for single career women to let their older children break away from them than for 'a mother who's never worked and who goes into a deep depression about what is the meaning of her life when her children leave home'. Talking about symbiotic child-rearing, Afton also pointed out that not many men would be happy with a child sharing the family bed for two or three years, and with the child suckling night or day at any time it felt like it. *Jane*, a lawyer, also commented about women at home, 'Too many women have children because that's what they feel they're supposed to do. You know, the real definition of being a woman is being a mother, etc. Oftentimes what it means for them is that they get totally invested in their children, have no life outside of their children, and that's when you get frustrations and resentments. But anyone who's made a conscious decision to do it after having established themselves as an adult, not just in terms of a career but having a sense of yourself as a person – they're going to feel very different about it.'

Finally, *Stella* and *Jan*. For a variety of reasons they decided after Stella had been back at work for a month, when Gene was 4 months old, that it would be best if Stella stayed at home. Jan carried on with her demanding work in one of the caring professions. Stella: 'Now that Gene's in his own room I get up to see to him at night and don't wake Jan because I have the option of taking a nap during the day when Gene's sleeping.' Jan: 'But he does take a bottle, and when I come home from work I try to feed him dinner and I spend time with him while Stella relaxes. I usually cook dinner, and during the weekend I'm usually the primary caretaker. Stella gets free time to be by herself to go out and do something, or as a family we go out and do something together.' Stella: 'We belong to a support group from when I was pregnant, and one of the heterosexual women is real envious of us at the moment. Her son is a month older than Gene, and she just doesn't have that even though her husband really loves her son. Even in the night, if he cries, she's always the one who gets up, her husband never gets up though they both work.'

'*Aren't there any tensions between you two at all?*'

Jan: 'Well, there is a little stuff once in a while. Sometimes I'm real tired when I get home from work, and I think one of the things that occur to any couple whether they are heterosexual or gay or lesbian is there are always little things that come up, where one person's had a good day and the other hasn't. If I've had a really bad day at work, I'm reluctant to. . . . I always offer to take over Gene, but you know . . .' (she prefers not to spell it out). 'But for the most part I'm trying to be as supportive and take care of him as much as I can, knowing that Stella's home with him all day.' Stella: 'We've had different sorts of days. I've put all my energy into Gene doing things at home, and I need a break and some time to myself by the time Jan comes home.'

'She's been with adults all day – do you think she's had a better day than you?' (Here they both talk simultaneously and I cannot hear what either of them says. I repeat the question to Jan instead, saying that perhaps Stella's been able to get out into the sunshine and has had a lovely relaxed day, while she, Jan, has had to be in the office all day. Is she resentful of that? I ask.)

Jan: 'No, not at all, because I know from weekends when I take care of him just how much work he is. You know, I saw a bumper sticker the other day that says it all – EVERY MOTHER NEEDS A MOTHER. I don't put our work at different levels. I really believe being home, taking care of a child or doing stuff around the house is probably one of the hardest things to do and would drive me crazy if I did it all day. I enjoy my job, and it's just *tiring* kind of hard. The only thing I resent is that I may miss some stuff that Gene does during the day. But I don't resent Stella's position, I really respect what she does.'

To Stella: *'You don't ever feel resentful that it was you who had the child and who stays at home?'*

Stella: 'No, I never felt that. Jan has bad days too, and if she's had a bad day at work then I take care of Gene. We work it out somehow – it's never been a problem.'

Jan: 'Maybe it's because Gene's not difficult often!' (He has been beaming and giggling at us all through the interview, his chuckles a continuous accompaniment to almost the entire tape. I have no difficulty believing them.)

There are heterosexual marriages as good as this, and it is possible for a heterosexual couple to understand each other as well as to be as sympathetic to each other as Stella and Jan are, but society places such pressure on men to behave as men are traditionally supposed to behave, and such pressure on women to behave as they are supposed to behave, that however much today's couples want to depart from the norm and achieve the kind of sharing and loving that Stella and Jan so patently do, they face tremendous difficulties which few can fully overcome. No one looks askance at Jan if she behaves in a thoroughly womanly way with her baby: her male equivalent may have to face snide comments at work, or amused, rather patronizing smiles from passers-by, if he does the same. Men who want to share fully and who do so quite often report the opposition they face, not to mention basic snags like there never being anywhere to change a baby's dirty nappy in a men's lavatory or female strangers who rush forward to help if the baby seems to be in trouble because they don't believe a mere man can possibly know how to cope. But it can be done and it is being done. It requires extreme tact and love on both sides: it is not only men who have to change – women will have to cope with sometimes feeling unneeded, that their role is being usurped, and those feelings may be far more difficult to deal with than they first realize. But it is quite an intense pleasure, being with such a family for any length of time, and I can imagine no more hopeful outcome for the future than that at least some of tomorrow's children will be brought up in this way.

Can single parents make a family?

Most but not all mothers who have chosen to be single families by definition feel the answer to this question is yes. Usually they enlarge the family of two by ensuring a close network of friends and/or relatives. Some encourage the father to keep in contact with the child. *Frances*, who runs her own art gallery, is one of these – she was one of the rare mothers who felt a single family was incomplete: 'But I never wanted Heather to feel we weren't a family unto ourselves, even though *I* felt that way – there were just the two of us and were all alone and it didn't feel big enough, solid enough somehow, but I tried not to give her the feeling we weren't enough by ourselves. I think to have a male person who is father is real important to little girls *and* little boys. When she was small we saw her father maybe a couple of times a week – now we've moved she goes up to him for a couple of weeks in the summer and another three to five times a year for a week or ten days at a time. I think father figures are important for children; they want to know what their roots are, what their history is. "Tell me stories about when you were little", she says to her father.'

Clinical psychologist Afton Blake, herself a mother, has no doubts about herself and her son being a family, but she has ensured a family of more than just two in what at present is rather an unusual way but which in the future may become less so: 'My very closest friend has just had a baby half-sister to Doron – it's the same donor – and we already say to him, Doron, here's your little sister. As a psychologist I don't see any problems with it: it's not any different from half-brothers and sisters in reconstituted families. I myself have half-brothers and half-sisters from the same father and I'm very close to them. And artificial insemination babies won't have the feeling of being so different, with another similar child being brought up right close to them.'

Mary, children's nurse: 'What law says there has to be a *man* in a family? *We're* a family, me and my son. Who says there has to be a man around to make it a proper family?' Psychoanalyst and mother *Stephanie* answering my question can a mother and one child make a family, said, 'No. To me a family is those who love you and care about you and respect you and are there for you when you need them. But it doesn't necessarily have to be a blood family. So I do have a great family, with my *friends*.' Child psychiatrist Tony Baker answering the same question: 'It depends how you define a family. I suppose I see a family as being any group of people of more than one whose lives are bound together by reasons of economy, finances, accommodation, sharing of resources, sharing of space – you don't need a marriage to make a family, you don't need two parents to make a family – you need a common interest of space and money and resources to share. A commune can become a family.'

Sarah, languages teacher and unwilling single mother: 'I'm afraid I can't really reconcile myself to being a single family – I wish I were strong enough, liberated – if that's the right word – enough, to be able to say, OK we're a family, just you and me. But I can't feel that – it goes against the grain, it goes against my inner feelings. If I'm lucky I shall meet someone who can fill that gap. If some women feel they and their child make a family, then they *are* a family: I don't feel it's particularly good for the child, but then some children grow up very nicely and very happily, brought up in peace by one parent rather than in distress by two. But I wouldn't have chosen it that way for myself.'

Clinical psychologist Hendrika Vande Kemp feels that you cannot have a family without a marriage: 'You can't have a baby without a man's sperm and if you're going to take his sperm then I think you should also find a way to take him. I cannot settle for using a man as a stud, especially not as a Christian; I think it is dehumanizing. I cannot even settle for it as a professional.'

But it seems to be inevitable that the future will contain huge numbers of single-parent families; Professor Chambers predicts that by the year 1990 41 per cent of children under 18 in the USA will be living without one or both of their biological parents, and shortly after the year 2000 the figure will have risen to half of American children.[18] British estimates would be lower because of our lower divorce rate, but a similar trend is clearly there. Whatever stresses and strains children of single-parent families will have to face, that of being unusual, different from their peers, won't be one of them.

We have been looking at single-parent families with one child only, but of course single mothers by choice can have more, though most of them feel that coping with two children would be more than they could manage alone. *Felicity*, medical researcher; 'No, I shan't have another one. I felt broody a little while ago, but that's as far as it went. It's a twenty-four-hour job, and I just couldn't cope with a second baby.' Theatre director *Carolyn*, who has a 1-month old baby: 'I'd like another one, but it's occurred to me in the last couple of weeks this could be a thousand times harder if there were a 2-year-old running around – to have another one and to be alone in the house sounds more than I could handle.' *Charlotte*, part-time researcher, 'For a long time I thought I couldn't possibly have another baby when the relationship with this one was so close, but as the relationship gradually changed I realized I could because each child would be different. I don't know I could go through with it, though – partly because having accepted the first one so wonderfully my family mightn't be all that keen on another one – once is forgivable, but twice looks like carelessness! But yes, I do begin to hanker after having another baby, and I suppose I'm curious to know what all the other babies waiting inside me are like, though in practical ways I think it would be too difficult.'

However, several of the mothers have had or are planning to have more children. Afton Blake intends to have a second one when she considers Doron is old enough for a sibling, and she will use the same donor. *Nora and Adina* would like to adopt several children and make a large family, but they have each other and so are in a different position to single parents. Jessica Curtis has a son by her first marriage, and a daughter as a single parent, while museum curator *Elizabeth* would love to have another one but probably won't – 'in fact when I begin to bleed with my period I think, oh bugger, I'm not pregnant! It's ridiculous, I can't possibly afford another one, and anyway life's too complicated as it is. Anyway, if I started again I'd be jolly nearly 50 by the time another child was David's age, and I don't think I'd want that.'

The question of age is of course a perennial difficulty with single mothers and makes it unlikely that many will decide to have more than one child, but if the idea becomes more popular and single women start having children earlier then we may see larger single-parent-by-choice families in the future. Either way, the consensus to my opening question seems to be that, yes, a single parent with a single child can make a family, *provided* a really close, permanent support group is involved. But I suspect the general public at large may well have different views at the present time, and for the time being single parents may find themselves coping with a certain amount of hostility if they live outside the more 'progressive' urban areas.

The future of the family

People talk about the virtues of family life as though our present nuclear family has existed as a sacred entity since the creation. But family life as we know it is a new creation of the last two centuries, and contraception, modern medicine and social changes have reduced it to a pale shadow of what it had become by Victorian times. By 1982 the average number of dependent children per family was down to 1.83 as against 2.01 in 1971, according to the 1982 General Household Survey. Between 1971 and 1982 the proportion of households with six or more people in it fell from a mere 6 per cent even lower to 3 per cent. Twenty-three per cent of households consisted of people living alone, 16 per cent being people over 60 years old. Not only are married couples having smaller families, they are also delaying longer before having their first child, and the proportion of those having three or more children after five years of marriage has fallen from 12 per cent to 3 per cent during the decade. Nearly twice as many births were illegitimate in 1983 as compared with 1977. In 1977 one in ten children were born outside marriage: in 1983 the figure was almost one in six. Fifty-nine per cent of parents having illegitimate children put both mother's and father's names on the birth certificates in 1982 as against 53 per cent in 1977, which presumably means that even more couples are now living together without legalizing their union. (In Sweden in the late 1970s 40 per cent of babies were illegitimate.)

The average family, then, is no longer what it was by the end of the last century: 'maiden' aunts no longer exist – an unmarried women is unlikely to be the virginal spinster that phrase suggests, and in any case she will almost certainly be a working woman living in her own accommodation; grandparents usually live separately now; old family friends, bachelor uncles, orphaned nephews and nieces who might once have swelled the numbers of a family are today comparative rarities. In addition, from lower-middle-class families with their one over-worked servant to the large households of the rich, there would have been a certain number of hired people around, sometimes well-known and trusted, sometimes almost strangers, to enlarge the household. In poor families neighbours would have played a far larger part than they do today, and very likely there would have been close relatives living nearby.

Today's social mobility means people often live far away from their place of birth; the extended family hardly exists except at Christmas (which is surely why so much nostalgia is heaped upon this annual holiday, its religious symbolism being almost entirely forgotten in the sentimental emphasis on the 'holy family'), or other festivities such as Thanksgiving or Passover. If we also take into account the divorce figures and other statistics given at the beginning of this chapter we can see that in fact there is no way the minute proportion of mothers who have chosen to have children on their own can conceivably make much difference to the future of the already mutilated affair that people profess to treasure so. What, on the contrary, seems to be happening is that these single mothers are moving back towards the richness of old-time sharing, forming extended families that are no less 'family' because the ties for the most part are ties of friendship and utility rather than of blood. It may be argued that blood links are more stable, but families move away, split or die – individual members of a loosely knit community may come and go, but if the community is a viable one the unity of the group as a whole will remain.

We looked earlier at the reality of family life as it is today in comparison with that of single mothers. There were certain aspects of marriage hardly touched on: for example, the fact that it is now normal for women to be working outside the family while bringing up children, partly because the cost of living makes it difficult for families to live on one person's wage, and partly because increasing numbers of women prefer to be away from the house during the day.

Child psychiatrist Tony Baker, talking of children in the modern family, mentioned another alteration in family life: 'I see an insidious change in the quality of childhood, in that children now are much more conscious of material possessions. They are very product-centred, there's tremendous competition for ownership, and sadly this trend in children is being manipulated and organized on a grand scale by the industries who are using the power of children within the family to sell their product. It's altering enormously the quality of childhood. I mean, you're no one if you haven't got whatever's the latest craze – this week it's Star Wars and next week it's Action Men or Cindy Dolls or whatever. The *modus vivendi* of children now seems to be "what have I got and what can I have next?" I think this comes largely through the swamping effect of the media and the fact that parents are prepared to give up some of their parental role. Yes, you're right, this has been so for some time, but we're seeing the second generation now – it's become the norm and the parents don't think there's anything odd about it because that's how they were brought up themselves.'

'*But quite a few young people are becoming involved with alternative ways of living, or they're concerned with spiritual movements or meditation groups, etc.*'

'I guess they've realized the belief system they've grown up in is a jungle belief system rather than a family belief system, and that it's actually superficial and shallow and empty, and they're struggling for something a bit deeper and more real.'

Jessica Curtis makes a point that I think is important: 'I don't think marriage will go away, that's to say marriage as a unit involving a man, woman and children, but it's not a sufficient unit by itself, there's not enough people in it. You can't get all your needs met if there's only one other adult and children in it. You need a firmer and supportive larger intimate group – and when you have that, it's fine. When you don't have that it puts a tremendous amount of pressure on the marriage. You need an extended family – it doesn't have to be a family of origin, it can be friends, or a shared household, like the one I live in, for instance.'

Findings recently published by the British National Marriage Guidance Council suggest that marriage is adapting rather than changing radically. Marriage guidance counsellors found that nearly all young people say they want to get married, they see cohabitation only as a preliminary stage, most of them expect faithfulness in their partners, they want to have children, and they agree (at least in theory) that men and women should share housework, though the men were less happy about changing nappies and similar jobs.[19] A report on teenage pregnancy published in 1984 showed that although teenagers are more likely to have sex at an earlier age, they are no more promiscuous than their parents were twenty years ago, and it was similarly reported that the teenagers wanted and expected to get married.[20]

It is difficult to make sense of the huge increase in divorce figures when one reads the previous paragraph, unless it means that young people are going into marriage with little or no idea of what it actually involves, and since in many ways as adolescents their needs have been catered to more intensely than for any previous generation they are not prepared to stay in a marriage that gives them less than they expected. When you add the increasing trauma of joblessness and redundancy, which must be having a very depressing effect on the hopes for the future of the younger generation, you can begin to understand why it is that marriages are breaking up so fast and that it appears the family is falling apart.

There is a further point brought up by actress *Catherine* that applies to many people in her age group. 'It just so happens that people in my exact generation – I've just turned 35 – seem to have different ideas about family life. Somebody said to me the other day that this is the year of people living alone. It's true, really. I mean it's mostly people of my generation, but suddenly men are living alone, too. They've tried relationships, they've tried marriages, and they've come out the other end thinking, well, the most important thing is to feel you can cope with yourself, and then perhaps something will fall into place. But the thing is that once people learn to cope with themselves, they're very reluctant to give that up. I think in many ways we've been a generation of guinea-pigs – and that's why such a lot of relationships are going wrong. It's the generation of the sixties, when a freedom suddenly hit and you were allowed to live with a partner and not get married. It was less so in New Zealand – I think every single person I was at school with has since married and settled down, though they may be getting divorced again by now – but coming to England gave me such freedom, it was like wiping the slate clean. Although I suffered enormously when I got here – I had some very lonely years to begin with.'

But books and articles are beginning to appear which suggest Catherine's generation is being left stuck out on a rather lonely limb. *Time* magazine has published a major article called 'The revolution is over' which basically claimed that the sexual revolution was finished and that close relationships – 'meaningful', 'significant' relationships – are in. 'Caution and commitment are the watchwords' is its sub-heading.[21] *New York* magazine published a mainly unsympathetic article called 'Mommy only' about single mothers by choice, in which psychologist John Ross is quoted as saying, 'We've emerged from the sexual revolution with a renewed feeling of commitment to the family. Fathers are assuming more responsibility for child rearing, and that's the direction in which we should be heading.'[22]

This last comment is, I think, the vital one as far as the future of the family is concerned. If men can take this on board, then I think the continued existence of the family – whether legalized or not – is assured, at least for the foreseeable future. But without men's genuine commitment to a more sharing kind of marriage as opposed to the older, more conventional version, I foresee disillusionment followed by increasing divorce figures and perhaps eventually an almost total abandonment of the idea of two people settling together for life. Variations on this theme came up time and time again in my interviews, whether from married or unmarried people, psychiatrists, psychologists or other professionals.

Marilyn Fabe: 'Ideas about what "family" is are increasingly becoming more tolerant, and I think that different ways will co-exist. I think the heterosexual impulse to have a child with someone you love is very powerful, the trend now being towards the man taking equal responsibility. Inflation means changes too – I don't know who can afford to stay home, so I think the family is going to have to change with men sharing, but the family will become a stronger place because of this. The more that men become involved with children and women become involved in the world of work, so that it balances out, the more likely it is that the family will be saved, because these last years the family has been cracking apart.' Psychologist and mother

Afton Blake: 'I think many men are way behind many women in consciousness, but not all of them – there are some men with a highly evolved consciousness. Women are demanding more, they're putting up with less, but even now there are many married couples where both of them work and there are children to look after, and the wives say to me, "I come home and I'm still expected to do all the usual things, I still somehow end up doing the cooking and housework and the child care as well.'

Even psychologist Hendrike Vande Kemp, who is unsympathetic to the idea of single mothering, believes that men must change: 'This question of single mothers can't be looked at in isolation. The whole structure of the family is changing. But I don't think we should necessarily accept that, just go with the flow. I think we may need to fight, because many things are only going to get worse rather than better as a result of the changes. I would like to highlight the issue that as women are changing so men need to change too, and we haven't found a way to make that easy for them. It doesn't help men to change if we sit and bitch at them and tell them how awful they are. You know, when I get into those sorts of moods I want to make it a personal issue for them, but that's not very helpful – people should be supported through their personal struggles and we haven't found a way in society to do that. I feel that if enough women rally together and say we're not going to marry men on their terms, that they have to change, then I think it would have an impact. In that respect you're right in what you were saying earlier, that single parenting could have a good effect on the family in that way, though I still worry about the children.'

We have to remember that both mothers *and* fathers can 'mother' when we are considering the kinds of changes that might be possible. But mothering in this sense implies reliably consistent warm caring and loving, and there is no question that, especially where very small children are concerned, whoever is doing the mothering must regard her or himself as coming second to the needs of the child. That does not mean that the needs of the self are unimportant or that they should be ignored, but if a small child is hurt, ill or upset, its urgent needs cannot be set aside while the parent goes for a quick jog or a meditation session. Children's demands are often immediate, and mothers soon learn to handle half a dozen things at once while thinking of a couple of other things at the same time. Men usually find this continuous splitting of attention very hard to cope with, but they can and do learn if they have to. There are other problems men have to deal with as well, such as the undeniable fact that men who attempt genuine 50/50 sharing will almost inevitably find themselves held back in their jobs to a certain extent. Employers, especially big companies, expect more than an eight-hour working day from their rising stars, while academics will find it difficult to produce the stream of learned papers and books that is expected of the brightest. A man who takes time off to take his children to the dentist, or to help nurse them through an illness, or who merely insists on leaving sharp at five or whatever the official leaving hour is, will probably find he is thought not to be taking his career very seriously. (Women, of course, have the same problem, sometimes in reverse in the sense that often childless women will *not* be offered the higher jobs because it is assumed that sooner or later they will have children and will therefore become unreliable in the eyes of their employers.)

Sometimes family patterns are changed unexpectedly. Bereavement can be one cause. Another is unemployment, which is happening to more and more people. Some fathers finding themselves at home against their will may take the opportunity to become more active in the family but, because so many men define themselves by their jobs, when this prop is taken away from them most find the total change of lifestyle extremely difficult to cope with.

Some benefits may occur as a by-product of something else – job-sharing, for example, not only gives two people employment instead of one, but where a couple shares a profession such as teaching it may be possible for them to split a teaching post between them and thus be able to genuinely share in the upbringing of their child. *Rosa*, a Dutch child psychology specialist, talked about other changes she saw as being necessary: 'I want society to be changed – educating, bringing up children, that must be something that comes from the whole society, so there must be more collective activity, like day playgrounds where you can leave your children in proper care; restaurants where you can go for cheap meals where you can bring your child and it will be made welcome. The way houses are built is very bad, you are too isolated from other people. Dirk is helping me a lot now, having Alex for two or three days a week, but he will have a problem when he gets a full-time job. Now he is studying and it is OK, but what will he do then? Most men choose full-time jobs and that must be changed too if they are to help. It has to be possible to have children and do a part-time job or to share. I find that most of the women who decide to have children on their own are intellectually trained – they work three days a week and have good money for that.'

David Chambers sees the family of the future much as psychiatrist Tony Baker sees it: whether or not it is linked by blood or by marriage will be unimportant; what will make a 'family' will be the fact that a group is living together in intimacy and has financial interlinking. With regard to the last, Professor Chambers, thinking of families where step-children – perhaps from more than one other family – are involved, writes that in the family of the future if a child is living with a step-parent then that step-parent would be responsible financially for the child, whereas a blood parent who has either never lived together with his child, or who left the family home long ago, would not be thought of as a member of the child's present family.[23] With so few absent fathers paying maintenance anyway, this is in fact the current situation in many reconstituted families.

This last section may have chilled some people who yearn for a return to old-time certainties, but the fact is these certainties never really existed. Women used to die in childbirth; babies and children died of practically everything in horrifying numbers: pneumonia, tuberculosis, a fall, appendicitis – so many physical ailments easily curable today would kill previously healthy adults and break up families; people married, were widowed, remarried, and had large numbers of replacement children. But nowadays a marriage can last uninterrupted for fifty years or more, and this in itself raises an important question – is it reasonable to expect people to know at 25 what they will need to make them happy at 75, or even at 30 or 45 for that matter?

The world has changed dramatically in so many ways in the last hundred years and will continue to do so – we must try not only to stay attuned to what is happening and to attempt to retain the best of the past in so far as it is possible, but also be prepared to try new ways of coexisting with each other in whatever form the family of the future will take. I don't think we have any choice, because children need secure backgrounds and for the sake of the future of the world itself we have somehow to improve the very insecure backgrounds in which so many of today's children – tomorrow's adults – are being raised.

Part 2
PRACTICE

6
Action

'Single parents have probably deliberated more over what it's going to be like than most married couples have. They've really thought about what it would do to their life and what changes will be made, and they know what they're getting into. In order to do it comfortably you need money, and it usually takes a decade of your twenties and even some of your thirties for most individuals to establish themselves.' (Afton Blake)

'The main thing I learned is that you can't do it alone. That's the irony of ironies. That's what I tell people in the Single Mothers by Choice group. We run three meetings for women who are thinking about getting pregnant, and the thing I most try to get across is that you really have to be prepared to get help, to get support, to learn what your limits are and find other people who can help you when you reach your limits.' (Jane Mattes, founder of SMC)

Getting pregnant: (I) the traditional way

Getting pregnant is the first hurdle. For most mothers this proved surprisingly more complicated than they had anticipated. Very few chose a man purely as stud: some looked for one but as we saw in Chapter 3 couldn't find anyone, while others like *Stella* – 'I'm not into casual sex like that, I just couldn't do it' – disliked the whole idea. Marilyn Fabe told me that when researching her book *Up Against the Clock* she never found anyone who straightforwardly went out with the intention of picking up a suitable father and succeeded. One mother who prefers to be nameless about this particular episode tried advertising, but got such 'awful men' she soon gave up and – like many others (Afton Blake,

Lynn for example) who refused to have a baby from a casual relationship – turned instead to artificial insemination.

Joanna, graduate student of Third World studies, was one of the few mothers who organized finding a man with an almost military precision. 'I wanted the healthiest, most intelligent, most beautiful child I could have. In selecting the father time was a crucial factor. I was studying cultural history in the Third World, and my plan was to get pregnant after having become detoxified by living for some time without chemicals in my food and with clean air in an unpolluted environment, then, shortly after I was pregnant, my intention was to go to Europe for about three months so that I could finish my research and to make sure I was having proper medical care, which I couldn't expect in the economically poor area I was then in. Then I wanted to come back to the States to have the baby and stay home with him for six months so that I could start him on solid foods before getting back to teaching and putting him into day care. I was 40 then, but I'd built up my health through diet and was convinced everything would be all right – as it was – the gynaecologist said it was ridiculous, he'd had 22-year-old women who weren't in as good shape as I was, and when the baby was born the paediatrician said he'd never seen a more alert newborn. Anyway, I met the man I'd been looking out for – he was a colleague in the university department I was attached to – he was racially different from me, but that was unimportant. I even made sure that our facial measurements matched, I didn't want any gross imbalance. I did not go at it in a thoughtless fashion. I wanted somebody with characteristics that if the child inherited them I would be able to live with him comfortably, so that every time I looked at this child I wouldn't hate him because he reminded me of something unpleasant in the past. Not only physically – I wanted that my child's personality characteristics would be ones I would like. I found I really liked the man as a person, and at first we became very close loving friends but without a sexual relationship. When the time came, I told him I wanted to have a baby nine months later. He agreed, and when my temperature was right we made love and I became pregnant instantly.' A success story for a rather extraordinary woman – but even Joanna found that although she and the father were not in love they realized she was becoming dependent on him and within a month the man had 'pulled out' of the relationship.

At the other extreme of this highly organized planning were the few who had got pregnant 'by accident'. I put that phrase in inverted commas because in most cases the mothers who fell into this category admitted that if they had been really determined not to get pregnant they would have taken better precautions. Only for one, *Catherine*, the actress, was it a totally genuine accident, because, as she said, 'If you've been reasonably promiscuous since you were 15 or so and you've reached 29 then you'd expect you would have already fallen pregnant if you were ever going to. I was on and off the pill, I knew I'd made slip-ups – you know how young girls are – you try to be careful, but I mean. . . . Then in addition to that there was a period when I was actually trying to get pregnant with a fellow I'd been living with for a couple of years – we tried incredibly hard for nine months at my peak periods, but it just didn't work. So I assumed I couldn't get pregnant even if I wanted to. Then some time after that I was having an affair with a married man – it was wonderful, no responsibility, just fun – when clang! I got pregnant! It was the furthest thing from my mind: I remember going to the doctor saying my breasts were really swollen and tender and that I thought I must have been sleeping on them in the wrong way, and she said, "Well, my dear, there's only one reason your breasts are like that, and that's pregnancy." I laughed at her and said it wasn't possible.'

Sonia, who was married to the Israeli artist, was also amazed to find herself pregnant after her children had been carried off to Israel by their father. She was so delighted she said she felt as though she 'had had a gift from God'. It happened after she had been to Israel in a vain attempt to win them back. On her return to London, desperately unhappy, she fell ill. 'I had peritonitis and it ended with one of my tubes being removed and the other badly scarred. The doctor said I was very unlikely to get pregnant again, and didn't need to bother about contraception. It was quite a time before I was fit enough to go back home, but when I did I fell pregnant within a month.' The interesting thing is that the relationship with her lover was coming to an end and in fact they separated almost straight away. As I wrote earlier in the book it sometimes seems that getting pregnant has more to do with the mind than with the body – in Sonia's case she wasn't planning to become pregnant but she was distraught at the loss of her children, and although medically speaking conception was almost out of the question she became pregnant almost immediately on sleeping for virtually the last time with her departing lover. 'I thought, well, there is a God somewhere, after all,' she said.

Jenny, the young mother of 20 who feels that having a child at her age was almost disastrous, nevertheless admitted a certain ambiguity about her feelings beforehand. 'It's true that when I went to live with Robert, Ben's father, I was almost quite keen to have a baby because I was so much in love with him that I wanted another piece of him, as it were, in case anything happened to the real Robert. It wasn't that I wanted a *baby*, I wanted a replacement Robert. But we took precautions – the rhythm method – only it didn't work and I got pregnant within six weeks.'

As I carried out more and more interviews I became used to mothers telling me similar stories, and marvelled at how powerfully the mind can affect the body. After all, apart from *Jenny*, these were not young women and normally one would have expected it to take them some time to get pregnant. *Felicity*, medical researcher; 'I'd been taken off the pill because I was over 35 and smoked, but I had a few packets of pills left and when I went over to Paris to meet this man I'd fallen in love with I relied on them, though I shouldn't have because you are supposed to use other methods as well for the first month, and I didn't. I told him about it, and I suppose I thought that would put the ball in into his court, but he said afterwards when he was trying to make me have an abortion that he'd misunderstood me. Yes, I suppose I was taking a chance, but it was the safe time for me – I'd had a period just before I went to meet him, and I was only with him for five days, so I really thought it would be all right. But it's true, if I'd been absolutely determined not to get pregnant I would have used another method as well as the pill.'

Several mothers like *Sonia* became pregnant by somebody they were on the point of parting with, as though subconsciously they felt it was now or possibly never. *Sarah* was one; *Julia* (who lived with her lover for three years after the birth) said, 'The affair with Bill was really on the rebound, and when I got pregnant the relationship was at the point of ending. I wasn't using a cap or anything and we had this arrangement that he'd use a sheath and if he wasn't using one he'd withdraw instead. But that time he didn't withdraw, so in a way I felt it was his subconscious decision rather than mine. But it's true I knew he wasn't wearing one, so I could have stopped him, I suppose. It was like that was the high point of the relationship, in a way.'

Most of these mothers were in relationships that were never intended to be long-term, although some at one point or another in the relationship had considered the possibility of settling with the man. The position when these women got pregnant was usually that they either felt they were not quite ready yet to have children though they had been exploring how to do it for some time already, or they feared the relationship was unsatisfactory and were unsure about what to do. Again, conscious mind and body often seem to be at odds. *Carolyn*, the theatre director, said, 'I was pretty sure I didn't want to just randomly sleep around with men and not tell them what was going on, and then not know who the father was. It was real important to me to be able to tell my child when he said, "where's my father?" I wanted to find someone who was willing to be involved in that with me at whatever level, even if all he wanted was to get me pregnant and then disappear. But then I met a man I found myself beginning a good relationship with, and I felt I couldn't do both things at once – working out a relationship *and* getting pregnant. So I thought, OK, I'm still young enough to say I don't need to get pregnant right now. I was real upfront with him – he knew I wanted to get pregnant but at that point I was using birth control, and wasn't attempting to get pregnant by him.

'It was a difficult choice – it was a new relationship, not

anything enormous at that point, but it was interesting enough to me to postpone what was this very big desire in my life. But although when I met him he was separated from his wife and he said he was getting a divorce, when it came to it he couldn't make up his mind and sort of bounced backwards and forwards between us, you know? Around Christmas last year we broke up, then it started up again a little later – I knew very well I needed to stop seeing him but it was hard to clinch it. Then I was in a car accident and hurt my back quite a bit. He was wonderful during that period, he spent a lot of time taking care of me – emotionally it was not the time in my life to tell him to go away. But I did not mean to get pregnant. I was using a diaphragm and it had always worked before but this time it didn't. I blame it on the fact that I had dropped a whole lot of weight right after the accident without realizing it. When I'd been fitted for the diaphragm the doctor had told me to come back and have it checked if I were to lose or gain ten pounds, but I was still spaced out by the accident and wasn't really myself so I just didn't think about that. That's my only explanation because I'd been very conscientious about using the diaphragm every time. I always *intended* to plan my pregnancy. I wanted to have a child, but I always intended to be in control over it when it happened. But the minute I found I was pregnant there was no question I was going ahead with it, I never considered doing anything else. I know I didn't do it on purpose, yet I was mentally so prepared – I'd thought through the economic realities, I had worked out every detail about having a child, except how to get pregnant.'

Serena, acupressurist, also wanted to have a child, but did not actually intend to get pregnant at the point when she conceived. 'My baby wasn't an accident – it wasn't intended in the sense of now I'm going to get pregnant, but the time was right, I was with somebody I really cared about and was thinking about the possibility of this man as someone I could settle happily with. We were having a very intense relationship – the energy just pulled us together very fast, and I can't help but think now, looking back on it, that somehow we were intended to come together for the reason of my having this child. I was taking precautions because I intended to be sure before I got pregnant, but I always watch my cycles very carefully and don't put the cap in when it's a safe time. So it might have been one of those times, because I had gone to Europe to be with him, and travelling changes the cycles, and everything was thrown out. Perhaps too I wasn't watching them as carefully as I usually do. So I feel now we were really meant to come together. But in fact when he came here to the States to see me – we were both very pleased I was pregnant – I saw he just wasn't the person I was to share with: his view of the world was too different from mine – very traditional European, male dominance – and I knew it wouldn't do.'

Half the mothers I interviewed had their babies by a man they had had some kind of fairly involved relationship with: quite a few at one point or another had even considered marriage with the man. This was not at all what I expected to find when I first started researching this book, which only goes to show how cautious one ought to be when thinking about any 'new' phenomenon – modern archaeology may suggest that mankind has progressed in 'jumps' rather than with Darwinian slowness, but human nature doesn't alter much over the centuries. What has changed, however, is the expectation that a woman who gets pregnant will pressurize the man to marry her, and that the man will succumb to the pressure. Of the relationships where marriage was ever on the cards, in half the cases it was the women who either broke off the relationship or who refused to actually marry the father, and in a further third it was a mutual decision. (The other 50 per cent of the mothers who were not involved in relationships became pregnant by other means, including artificial insemination.) There was only one mother, *Sarah*, who was embittered by the refusal of the man to make a permanent relationship, and even she had never demanded marriage.

Some of the relationships broke up soon after the birth – *Rosa*'s deliberate affair with her Greek ex-sailor who scarcely spoke English, let alone Dutch, was doomed from the start as a living-in relationship, since she never intended to accept the restrictions of Greek peasant life and he was quite unable to earn a living in Holland. *Jenny*'s boyfriend wanted her to live a solitary life in the country, and at 20 she found nuclear family existence intolerable. *Anna*, the Dutch child psychologist, fell in and out of love with the father of her two children – he was younger than her, only 23 when the first child was born, and far too immature to cope with fatherhood, although he knew about and agreed to help her with her desire to get pregnant: 'I have found out over the years that when I really need him he doesn't love me, and when I don't need him he loves me a lot. I find that when I feel sick and small he is not proud of a woman like that, but when I'm looking good and I'm there with the baby on my arm and talking on radio and television about BOM [the Dutch single mothers group described later in this chapter] he is really proud of me and is loving me. So at the birth it was really terrible – he didn't know me as somebody who was dependent and he got angry with me for little things like when I asked him to pass the sugar because I was so sore, I'd had a big cut and it really hurt me to move – and I nearly kicked him out. After three or four days I said OK I prefer to be alone and doing things for myself than you being there and not understanding my situation as a mother who just gave birth. We tried to resolve it, but it was such a change in the feelings we had had for each other before, it just wasn't good any more.' It took her decision to have a second child before their relations became as they were before, but by then he had another girlfriend in Paris, and after the birth of the second child they both accepted that though they would stay friends they could not live together.

Angela's relationship was of a different kind. Both graduate students, they lived together for about two years in all, including nine months after the child was born. Unlike most of the mothers she had not worked out the whole business of having a child in advance: in fact, it was the man who suggested the idea. 'I'd been proposed to before, for marriage, but no one had ever asked me to have a child by them. Ben loves children, and all his partners since we split up have been women with children. I hadn't been meaning to get pregnant – I was only an undergraduate student then – but I knew motherhood would be just as difficult as a graduate student. We took a trip across country and when we came back I decided I did need some sort of stability in my life, and I just kept thinking about having a child. I thought it would be an enrichment, and so I made a very quick decision. I had my IUD taken out and got pregnant. No, I'd never wanted to have a child or get married before. It wasn't anything to do with being in love or anything like that. As a matter of fact, after I was pregnant I considered once or twice having an abortion. I saw how difficult it was going to be. I'm studying East African history, and I will have to travel a lot, and that was one of the reasons I hadn't thought about having children. I always knew I was going to be a very mobile person – it's always been my dream to travel around and to live in different places. I didn't come from an academic background at all, and I was meeting a lot of people who were academics, professional people – I realized I wanted to be that kind of person, and I saw that I could have the life I wanted as well as having a child. But when I was growing up it was assumed automatically that having children meant staying home, doing the nappies and so on.

'When I got pregnant Ben wanted us to get married. It was more his family than himself – they're very religious, evangelical, and there was quite a pressure. But I wasn't sure I wanted to stay with Ben for very much longer anyway, though for a while I convinced myself I could work it out. But I couldn't, and about nine months after the baby was born I decided to leave him. There were terrible scenes! Ben threatened to take me to court and not let me have my son – it was because he was so emotionally upset he did that, but yes, I do worry a little he may take me to court some day if he thinks I'm living too much of a gypsy life, which he knows I will be because of my work. He still tries to make me conform to certain standards that he considers right for a parent – there's a big class difference between us and already although he's a student he's made a lot of money, while he knows I'm never going to be materially wealthy.

'At the moment we share the care of our son without any legal arrangements, and it works very well. He's 4 now and he's very happy – everyone says he's a wonderful child.

What will happen when I have to go to Africa for at least two years to do my research I'm not sure – we'll have to have a real legal agreement for that. We may have problems then.'

Julia's boyfriend, on the other hand, had not wanted a child, though it was he whom I mentioned a few pages back who had agreed to withdraw when they were making love if he wasn't wearing a sheath, but in fact had not done so. As I wrote, they were on the point of breaking up their relationship when Julia became pregnant, although they were still and have since remained good friends. They had not been living together previously, and all during the pregnancy 'Bill didn't know whether or not he wanted to be part of it. I felt very frightened about that, although I never had any doubt at all I wanted to keep the baby. I had the birth at home. I managed to find a midwife and a doctor who were willing to do that with me, and in the end Bill was there too. He hadn't planned to be in advance. I think he felt there was something in him that could manage either by taking full responsibility, or not to cope with it at all – he couldn't manage a sort of middle thing – so it was either like we had to live together or he had to leave town. He couldn't imagine seeing me in the road with the baby and not living with me, things like that. At the birth I was supposed to have a girlfriend there too, but that fell through and he was worried I wouldn't be able to cope if it happened in the middle of the night. He was worried and felt responsible. So the night I went into labour he was with me and he supported me through it, making phone calls and things. In the morning he was actually going to go to work even though I was in labour, but in the end he didn't and he stayed with me. He said he was really pleased he hadn't missed the birth – it was very moving. I'm glad he was there, it was very good to have him there. The doctor came round too late – it was a very fast birth – and afterwards when the doctor and midwife had gone I sat up and persevered and in the end my baby took the breast. Bill stayed that night, and then he just stayed on.

'Of course both our parents wanted us to marry, but we wouldn't. He stayed on for a month, then we decided to give living together a try, so he gave up his flat and moved in. I was glad, I wanted him to be part of it, and I wanted to share it. But I knew he hadn't come to terms with being a father, and so I wanted him to be able to make a real decision about it. But it came out more and more in our relationship that he just wouldn't make decisions, about finding a home and things like that. I was ready to move, the house we were in was dirty, we had to share a loo, a bath, there was broken furniture, it was just awful, actually. He found it very hard, too, but he never offered to share looking after the baby and I never pushed him.'

I wrote about this aspect of their relationship and Bill's reluctance to share care of the baby earlier in another chapter. In the end, after three years of indecision about many things, including moving (Bill had quite a good job, so money was not too much of a problem), several times finding then rejecting various houses, Julia decided to move out, which she found was a great relief once she had brought herself to do it.

The question of marriage – traditionally of great concern to women – did not seem to be overwhelmingly important to the mothers I interviewed, although nearly all of them said they would happily form a permanent relationship if ever the right man came along. Only one, *Janice*, a research assistant, is still living with the father of her 2-year-old child. They have shared a seven-year long relationship which has been described elsewhere, and the only real difference between their union and a marriage is that Janice has always insisted on having total rights over the child, although the father shares completely in the care and upbringing.

One mother, *Sonia*, had given in to the pressure to marry (to the Israeli artist) and look where that got her – her two children legally abducted and taken away to Israel. *Sarah*, the languages teacher, didn't get married, ended up alone, and look where that got *her* – hurt, angry, even embittered. Several women had affairs with married men whom they never expected to marry, like *Elizabeth*, the museum curator, who was eventually on such good terms with her lover's wife she still goes with her son and spends

weekends with her 'step'-family. *Laura* had picked out the
father of her future child when she was 16. She knew him
and his wife well and although she became very close friends
with him she never wanted him to be much more than that –
she had no intention of breaking up the marriage. *Catherine*,
the actress, was enjoying a 'lovely irresponsible' time having an affair with a married man whose wife was frequently away and certainly did not want to marry him
when she unexpectedly became pregnant.

Of the remaining 50 per cent of the mothers who were
not in a relationship of one kind or another, some chose old
friends to become pregnant by, some searched for an
amenable male, some gave up and chose artificial insemination. A few chose the last quite deliberately for a variety of
reasons.

Some of the women chose gay friends to father their
child on the grounds that they were unlikely to marry and
fight – probably successfully – for custody of their children,
the courts being more likely to grant custody to a male
parent in a married situation than to a single mother. (This is
a particularly important consideration for lesbian women
who are very vulnerable to prejudiced courts.) *Charlotte*,
part-time researcher, didn't make a positive decision to sleep
with someone on a particular night and get pregnant – few
of the women did – but like so many she gave herself every
chance to get pregnant, that is to say she slept with a friend
without any contraception at her fertile time of the month,
and afterwards knew that she had, in effect, been saying to
herself, 'right, it's time I had a baby, I'm jolly well going to
make sure I get pregnant.' The father was a gay friend of
long standing: 'It's strange being with a man who is a friend
and terribly close without feeling any sort of sexual
attraction together, you sometimes wonder about it and
think if only I could fancy him, it would be so *nice*. That
night we'd had a good evening together and we were both
feeling jolly, and you know . . . so we tried the experiment.
When I think back to it, I think I wasn't ready at that stage
to be involved in a relationship with a man, so I got
pregnant by a homosexual. That all sounds terribly premedi-
tated – it wasn't, but sometimes you can analyse what

you've done and it seems to make sense.'

Sharon, assistant professor of women's studies, got married at 20 having been brought up in the expectation of doing just that, and divorced after a couple of years having decided she wasn't 'cut out to be a wife'. Now she is 37, has been thinking she would like to have a child ever since she was 30, but has not met anyone she would be prepared to have a long-term relationship with. 'I'm trying to get used to the idea, and I may have to get pregnant some other way. My first choice would be a man I was very seriously in love with for four years when I was in graduate school, who is now one of my closest friends. He lives elsewhere, and is now gay, and is involved in a long-term relationship with another man whom I'm very fond of. But he's not prepared to do it – he thinks it's a little too weird. I'd want someone who'd be prepared to co-parent anyway, and he wouldn't be able to, so it's not on in any case. His attitude is that there would be this child in the world, and what would his relationship to it be? It doesn't feel right to him. I said to him, well, it would be just like we got divorced very early in the child's life. . . . I'd like it to be some man I feel very close to who I know is going to be in my life, child or no child, and whom I trust. It feels strange to me, the idea of just having sex with a man who would have no connection to the child at all.'

Catherine, the actress, also said that if she decided she wanted to have a second child and she wasn't in a relationship she would ask one of her gay friends – of whom there is no shortage in the acting world – and pointed out the advantage of having someone as a father who would love to have a child in his life and who would come and visit it regularly without trying to take away any of the woman's independence.

Pat, midwife, is a lesbian, and like several of the other lesbians I interviewed she told me she had had 'a long coming-out process, and I wasn't really out until Josh was born. I'd got engaged to an Englishman when I was studying in England to be a midwife, and I only broke it off right at the last moment after buying the dress and sending out the invitations and everything. My first major lesbian experience some time after that was really pathetic! It was a real crisis; I felt like it had to work because it was a big change for me, like straight women do with their first boyfriend after a divorce. Anyway, it was all a terrible mess and I ended up after I'd finished graduating having a breakdown. But I had some therapy, got myself together, and I think that's where the decision to have a child came in. It was some time before I felt like dating anyone, but my first choice was a man, which shocked me. We broke up after six months of living together. After that, I lived alone for a year then started dating women again – but there was always this thing about wanting a child. What happened then was I met the man I'd lived with – he lived nearby and we went out together maybe a couple of times a year. This time we ended up spending the night together. I hadn't been using any birth control for a long time because I'd only been with women, but I'd been taking my temperature, and had kept a chart for three months. I said to this guy, 'Oh, I've been keeping this chart and I think it's an OK day.' In fact six weeks later when I took my positive pregnancy test I looked back at the chart and it was clear it was absolutely the wrong day not to take precautions! It wasn't an outright lie, it was a close call, only a couple of days from the dip, and I always wonder when I look back, why I did that? I think maybe I believed what I told him myself. I don't know. I would probably have slept with him anyway, because I still hadn't made the choice to become fully lesbian, not until the day I took that pregnancy test. The day that test was positive I knew that that was my choice, and I had freedom at last to be a lesbian.'

Having a child by an old lover was an idea that came naturally to other women as well. *Jane*, the lawyer, had also intended to do just that and would have tried that route if an investigation into the possibility of adoption hadn't surprisingly borne fruit almost immediately as she had approached a new adoption agency which as yet did not have a waiting list. Since she had some fertility problems which she knew would make conception difficult, though not necessarily impossible, she decided to go ahead with adoption.

I have already written in the chapter 'Man as stud'

about how Jessica Curtis had asked various friends to father a child for her. Later in the interview she elaborated on what had happened: 'I knew I didn't want to get married – I wanted to have a kid and that was my main focus. I just wanted a guy to get pregnant by, and I used to tell them that – it's not that I'm against getting married, but at that time the clock was running out, and you have to put first things first. That's one of the main themes in Single Mothers by Choice groups, it's not that you don't want to get married, but to find a guy and to establish a relationship, to solidify the marriage, by that time you're 40 or 45 and it's getting late. I'd find the man would say yes, but I didn't get pregnant, and they wouldn't come back the next month, they'd had second thoughts about it. One guy got impotent – he was a very irresponsible kind of guy and I think the idea scared him; another guy decided he'd rather get married and have his own kid, which he proceeded to do; a couple of friends were vasectomized, and there was another guy who was willing but I just didn't think he'd be a good father biologically speaking. What would happen was I'd get them to agree before they'd had second thoughts – I'd tell them the same night what I wanted to do, and it would be OK – but when they'd had time to think about it then they'd change their minds and decide they weren't interested. I respected them for that, for being clear about their motives. So in the end I went to a fertility specialist and got myself pregnant through artificial insemination.'

Getting pregnant: (2) by artificial insemination
The idea of single women deliberately getting themselves pregnant through artificial insemination arouses more hostility than any other aspect of single mothering. Part of this hostility – felt by women as well as men – is an objection to the mechanical, institutional feel of AI, expressed by acupressurist *Serena*: 'For me, the philosophy behind the idea of a child being conceived in love is very important. I'm very romantic by nature, and this takes over my relationships on every level. It's such a wonderful beginning for a child to be conceived in love.' Few would disagree, but alas

there isn't that much love around in the world, and some women must make do with less than the ideal. Even Serena said that AID (artificial insemination by donor) might have been a possibility in the end for her had she not managed to meet a man she fell for.

It is interesting how people manage to fall in love when they *need* to be in love; I noticed this happening occasionally among some of the mothers, who became disillusioned with their partners quite quickly once they had conceived or borne their children. This may sound cynical, but it is not meant to be – falling in love is such a special emotion, compounded of so many factors, one very important one being a strong desire to actually *be* in love, to live for a while in that incredible, energy-giving, totally absorbing near-blindness that is like no other experience in the world. As a romantic myself, I think the emotion is worth all the pain it frequently brings, but as a basis for choosing a long-term mate it has its risks. As a basis for choosing the father of your child it is less controversial – one is hardly likely to fall in love with someone really incompatible, there has to be some common ground – always providing that a suitable temporary mate is all you are asking for. A few mothers did it that way, others preferred to remain totally clear-headed about their choice, or just didn't meet a man they felt sufficiently attracted to to allow the emotion of falling in love to take them over.

Another reason for the hostility against AI is felt mainly by men, but also by some women who perhaps feel threatened by its implications. Traditionally women are supposed to be passive creatures dependent on men for their happiness as well as their physical well-being, while men are supposed to be independent and aggressive. It seems from available evidence that women who are independent and successful in their careers are less likely than their less energetic, less successful sisters to build around themselves a homely nest of their own, while exactly the opposite is true of males, unsuccessful men being the ones who are more likely to come home at night to a lonely bed.[1] To openly flout such conventions, to have your cake and eat it, is something that must strike at the root of men's self-confidence (what, they ask plaintively, are we good for, when we're not even needed for *that*?), while women who have made child-bearing their reason for not 'succeeding' in the world's eyes, also find their self-confidence undermined. Letters used to appear in the press from career women defending their choice to work and not stay home having babies – now it's the housebound mums who write such letters of self-defence.

Single women choosing artificial insemination (mainly American women at the moment, although the innovation is spreading in Britain too) are making the clearest possible statement – I'm doing this completely alone, it's not an accident, I'm not a woman abandoned by some man, I am an independent, capable woman making a choice that is entirely my own responsibility and no one else's, thank you very much. If less confident mortals quail before them, they should not be surprised.

What makes a woman take this route to pregnancy? Afton Blake: 'I would not have a child from just a casual relationship. I did think seriously of inviting one of several men I respected and cared about as a friend to co-parent, to be in every way the father without us having a relationship, but when I began to think about values and education and child-rearing, plus arranging holidays and so on, it began to seem like it could be as messy as a couple getting a divorce, trying to solve those issues, and I decided I didn't really want to get involved with all that. Plus I wanted to leave the road open for a new man to come into my life who would want to adopt my child and not find himself in a triangle situation.'

Dr Blake is well known as the second mother who had her baby through what is commonly known as the Nobel Prize winner sperm bank, actually called the Repository of Germinal Choice, founded by Dr Robert Graham, millionaire inventor of the plastic lens, who felt that because of contraception intelligent people were having fewer children than the less bright, and that the gene pool needed strengthening. Unfortunately for Dr Graham, Nobel Prize winners either rejected the whole idea as genetically unsound or politically frightening, or were too old to have sufficiently viable sperm. Now Dr Graham contents himself with potential Nobel winners instead, but insists that they are also healthy, tall, good-looking athletic men preferably with some musical skill and with a sound family inheritance of long and healthy life.

Because it is easier to select donors of verifiable intelligence from among successful men of science than from artists or authors Graham at present chooses his donors from among scientists. However, this is beginning to change: Afton Blake said, 'The fact that all the donors at the sperm bank are physicists, mathematicians and computer scientists bothered me, because I'm much more into the fine arts. But now they're trying to branch out from scientists and are interviewing various men – I've arranged some interviews for them with philosophers and men I like who would be suitable. People always make it sound as though I went there because of the genetic side, but though I'm quite happy about that the reason I really went was because unlike all the other sperm banks available at that time this one was very personal. It's not a profit-making organization, they're not a commercial venture. I was able to find out such a lot about the father, which was very important to me. Now the other sperm banks are beginning to follow suit, but at the time I was pursuing it they would not tell you anything about the donor. In fact I have just become psychology consultant for a new sperm bank which especially caters for single and gay women, and enough information is given about the donors for women to be able to make a genuine choice.'

Dr Blake has sent me details of this new service, which supplies frozen semen from carefully selected donors in – if needed – 'a "dry shipper" cooled with liquid nitrogen which can be sent through the Post Office anywhere in the USA', and which can be used for home insemination. Recipients 'other than a licensed physician . . . must sign and return the "Consent Agreement for Artificial Insemination" ', which places certain responsibilities on the mother. Details of the necessary technique are included. It is too early for me to make any comments of how successful the service is, but I do think it has certain implications that need to be carefully examined – not all people wanting to set up a sperm bank may be as highly reputable as the originators of this scheme, and not all hopeful mothers as responsible and thoughtful as the mothers I have been writing about. For details write to 'Heredity Choice', P.O. Box 42245, Los Angeles, CA 90042.

I asked Dr Blake about her own choice of donor when she had Doron. She told me: 'I was able to choose from about ten donors – what I wanted was somebody who was intelligent, medically and emotionally from a secure background, and this one was also a classical musician and somebody who enjoys sports a lot. He has the same Nordic good looks as my family – in fact the family joke is Doron is cloned, with my eyes, nose, mouth and forehead and same blond hair and blue eyes. He looks exactly like my dad in early photographs of him, which is fascinating. As important was the way I was treated. They brought the sperm to my house, taught me how to do it myself so I could be very romantic and really loving and I didn't have to go to a cold, sterile doctor's office and wait for an appointment and do it in their time.'

'How do you mean, loving?'

'Well, I would burn incense and light candles and play my favourite music and you know? meditate on inviting this soul to come into this world – to me it is very romantic, creating a child. I'm very much of a loner person, and many of my peak experiences have been when I've been alone with music, with nature, and I brought Doron into consciousness in that way. For me it was as loving as any man I've ever been with, the way I brought him in.'

'Can you tell me how you actually did it?'

'You simply insert a little syringe with the sperm in it, and some months I did it ten or eleven times every twelve hours, and some months only two or three times. It took me ten months to get pregnant – it's very hard, waiting. I currently have women in my practice who are working on inseminating, and waiting, and I know what it's like, how you can get very depressed at times.'

'It must have been difficult to arrive at a meditative state while carrying out what perhaps was a rather messy, very medical sort of procedure?'

'After the first month when I learned how to do it it was like putting the diaphragm in – after you get used to it you do it automatically. One of the criticisms I've heard of AI is that it is not done with love, but – granted that many still have to do it much more technically – all the women I've heard of wanted the children with such passion, such love, it couldn't possibly be any greater with a couple relationship, and in many cases I think it's much greater. Because of the publicity I've been on several shows, and on one of them I was told that at Berkeley sperm bank they've actually created a room with pillows and candles and music and champagne, and the staff there celebrate the insemination, which if it's true I thought was marvellous. That goes along with my spiritual belief that the soul should be invited in with love – it doesn't have to be the physical love between a man and a woman, it needs to be the love of the body and the soul.

'Yes, waiting was painful, but this must be the same for a married couple waiting for a baby. After the first couple of months I knew it was going to happen sooner or later, because I'd been pregnant before. What really worried me was that I'd miscarried three times before and I was frightened it might happen again. Some months were a little depressing and others I just felt great joy – I lost the need for it to be immediate and I knew in the long term it would happen. When I finally discovered I was pregnant it was the chief experience of my life.'

I told her I had been fascinated by how frequently the mind seemed to rule over the body among the mothers I had interviewed, and asked her if she had any theories why she had miscarried the earlier pregnancies and not this one. 'I think I wasn't ready before. I was over 30 but I was in a bad relationship, and at one level I must have known this wasn't somebody I should have a baby with. I was in an apartment, I had no money, it would have been a nightmare to have children then – in retrospect I can see that now. I wanted them, though, they were planned, but now I can look back and say that that was not a good situation to have them in. Then I got so depressed with the third miscarriage I separated from the man I was with and just immersed myself professionally and the energy went into my profession.'

I have written a lot about Afton Blake's experiences because I think they refute the charge that AID is necessarily a very unspiritual experience, and because meeting Afton's son, Doron, I cannot help but be impressed favourably by him. I realize that some people on reading the above must have thought her account weird in the extreme, but what came over to me as I talked to her was that she is a very sympathetic, balanced, aware person. Later in this chapter I want to write about her views on 'symbiotic' child-rearing, but I think it would be useful now for mothers who are contemplating artificial insemination to see for themselves the processes as they were explained to me from a professional point of view by three gynaecologists, two American and one British.

The first important point is that it seems single women are likely to find it difficult to discover a doctor who is willing to help them. Some gynaecologists are totally against the idea and won't even consider it, others are prepared to help with fertility problems but will not do more than that, although in some cases they might suggest a doctor who would help with the insemination. Dr Ted Nagle, gynaecologist, of the Department of Obstetrics and Gynecology at the University of Minnesota, only treats couples who have been attempting for some years to have children and who finally after trying every other avenue are referred to his department which deals specifically with infertility problems: 'I feel I would rather provide a service for these people than for some woman who is single and decides she wants to have a child. I think it's hard enough to raise a child in a stable situation, or not necessarily stable but one that is the societal norm. Also I think raising a child is not a part-time activity, and when a couple elects to have children one of those two people ought to feel the children are their primary responsibility rather than their career or their job. I don't care whether it's the husband or the wife who stays home – yes, I think the caretaker can work part-time, but I don't think it's a good idea for a child to grow up in a day-care situation. I'm willing to treat these women to enhance their fertility if they're having problems, but in terms of actually impregnating them, I would rather not. I will certainly help investigate why she's not fertile – I've had single women with pelvic infections, etc.; hormonal problems so they're not ovulating; blocked tubes and they want something done surgically to repair the tubes – most of them have come because they've been having pain and they would like to be painfree. Now of course some of them may also want to become pregnant and don't tell me that.'

I argued that I couldn't really see much of a moral difference between him getting them ready for insemination and inseminating them, and eventually Dr Nagle arrived at the conclusion that for him the vital difference was that one was a medical problem, which was his proper concern, and one was not. 'If the woman is just looking for sperm she doesn't need to come to me. I'm not happy with getting couples who are psycho-social disasters pregnant, either, or couples who want a child to cement their shaky marriage together. In such cases I try hard to persuade them against it, usually successfully, but it's difficult for me to refuse them because in the current legal climate they could take us to court on the grounds our decision is too arbitrary, unless we have strong medical reasons to refuse them. But if ever there's a situation where the norm for society is a mother and children and peripatetic fathers, well – that's the norm, that would be different. But I think it's very difficult for kids to be born into non-normative situations.'

Dr Ed Cohen, obstetrician and gynaecologist, a private doctor in California who also teaches, feels much the same as his Minnesota colleague. 'I personally have reservations about it – not from the medical viewpoint but from my own personal morality. I don't think that a single parent is an optimal situation for a child, and since that is my belief I don't think I would contribute to the situation. But other partners in my office will do it and have done it, so I would pass someone who wanted it on to them. There might be certain circumstances where I would do it – if it's somebody who's been a patient of mine for ten years, for instance, and I know her very well, then I might consider it if I felt sure she could provide an emotionally, financially and in every other way sound upbringing for the child. You might raise the question, is this playing God – but I think you might raise the more general question, is artificial insemination playing God? I think physicians have a responsibility to make sure their work does not negatively impact on society in any way, and from what I understand at the present, though things may change in the future, in general children coming from homes where there's only one parent don't do as well in society.'

I asked, as I frequently did during my interviews, whether it was fair to compare single mothers with married women as though the latter were invariably part of a perfect marriage, refusing to treat the one and accepting the other. What, I said, would he do if he were presented with a couple he felt would almost certainly make bad parents. 'I have on occasion told a woman that I find certain personality differences between us – I put it on my own shoulders – that I have a problem dealing with her and that for her best interests she should probably see another physician. Most people don't like the idea of being rejected, which is why I present it as my problem, that it's not their problem they're a paranoid schizophrenic or they're neurotic as hell! I have done that, not frequently, but more than once, maybe three or four times in the last ten years.'

I tried to find a gynaecologist who *was* prepared to inseminate a single woman, but none of the men I talked to were prepared to do it, and although I tracked down a woman doctor who had previously been prepared to help single women she had now changed her position, partly due to th fear of litigation which controls much of the behaviour of American doctors. In Britain, also, doctors are not at all keen on the idea. I interviewed Dr Bridget Mason, whose infertility clinic in London has helped more than 3,000 babies to be born, and she told me that she only knows of one London clinic which will treat single women not in long-term relationships, and that is the British Pregnancy Advisory Service, which places no bars on who they see or help (for information about their eight clinics throughout Britain, including London, write to the Information Office, BPAS, Austy Manor, Wootten Wawen, Solihull, West Midlands). She knows of no clinic at all that will help a single woman under the National Health Service and only of two which will give treatment under the NHS to married women – King's College Hospital and the Middlesex Hospital, where they have long waiting lists. Various other centres outside London will also treat married women, but whether or not they will provide this service under the NHS should be checked with local GPs.

Dr Mason took the same attitude about who she would treat as her American colleagues: 'I'll see women of the kind you describe if they're having difficulty in conceiving – I'll investigate their fertility. But if they haven't got an infertility problem as far as getting pregnant goes, and it's simply they don't want to sleep with someone, then that's another question. I'll treat their infertility problems but I will not inseminate them because I'm not at all happy about helping single women to have babies. I've got three children of my own, and a grandchild, and I think it's quite hard enough bringing children up in a stable marriage even with a partner who's extremely helpful.'

I have dealt with these objections at length because they seem to be fairly universal and it is important that single women considering insemination be aware of this very basic difficulty before they make up their minds to get pregnant this way and then find their problems are by no means solved. However, these were top-flight gynaecologists accustomed to using their expertise on fertility problems I was talking to: where sperm is easily available from sperm banks no doubt it will not be too difficult to find a private doctor willing to carry out what seems to be a relatively simply procedure. In Britain the situation at present is that there are no commercial sperm banks of the kind that exist in the US, but as one GP said to me, 'You can get anything done privately if you're prepared to pay for it,' and certainly some private clinics or doctors are prepared to help unmarried women for a fee. Also, some women have inseminated themselves without any medical help at all.

Before discussing this last method, let us look at how the procedure is carried out by doctors. I have already written in Chapter 4 under the sub-heading 'The biological clock, or the age factor' about Dr Mason's clinic which uses fresh sperm and an ultra-sound scanner to make sure that insemination is only carried out on the days when a patient is ovulating, and in the same section I gave details of how long it generally takes for various age groups to get pregnant. But using fresh sperm presents certain problems that can be avoided by obtaining frozen sperm from sperm banks. Dr Cohen describes the process his practice uses: 'We generally refer the patient to a sperm bank that is reputable by our standards, and we assume they continue the standards they had when they were originally set up. The bank we use is run by a urologist and a pathologist. The urologist treats diseases of the urinary tract predominantly in men, and the practice is also the male fertility counterpart to our own practice which specializes in female fertility, the sperm bank being a sideline of this. It's run as a business partially, yes, but then everything we get paid for doing is a business in a sense. When we need semen for a patient we call over and tell them that so and so is coming back to pick up a semen specimen, and when the patient brings the specimen to us (it comes in a little plastic package, enough for one treatment) we go ahead and inseminate her.

'We usually use two inseminations forty-eight hours apart, unless the woman is one of those rare people who has her menstrual cycle every four weeks on a Thursday afternoon at 12 noon – there are a few who have it so regularly you can pin-point ovulation – but most women have a variation of a day or two at least with each cycle, and in order to maximize the chance of getting pregnant we have to use two inseminations approximately forty-eight hours apart in order to bracket the most likely time of ovulation. If there is no other problem her success rate should be in the 85 to 90 per cent range, within the year. The average infertility in the population is between 10 and 15 per cent, and those people may have a cause for their infertility that is amenable to treatment, but not necessarily. Among that percentage there will be a certain number who will never get pregnant and will never know why.'

Mary, who works in a children's nursery with newborn babies, described from the patient's point of view what happened when she realized that time was passing and she hadn't yet found a man she wanted to have a serious relationship with: 'At 29 I decided to make my plans. I thought of going to UCLA – I think there's a sperm bank there – but it's such a huge place it didn't really appeal to me, having to walk up to the front desk and say, excuse me, where's your sperm bank?! Then I read an article about a sperm bank in Century City (Los Angeles) and I thought, gee, this is just what I'm looking for, so I called the bank and they told me I needed to have my own personal physician call them to assure them I had a physician who was going to take care of it and to give them permission to go ahead. I work with newborn babies, so I was able to choose an obstetrician I was familiar with and whom I like a lot. He'd never done it before but he agreed and he called the bank. Then I had to go down there and fill up various forms – among other things you have to sign a paper signing away all rights to the donor so that you can't go back and insist on knowing who the father was. After that you can either pick up the specimen – it's frozen, of course – or they'll deliver it to the doctor's office: I chose the last. He did it for me right there in his office. I took four or five months before I actually got pregnant. My cycle is regular enough that when I ovulate I get a little cramping pain, so that I know almost exactly, but when I wasn't getting pregnant after the first few tries then he had me start taking my temperature and making a chart. The bank recommend using two separate specimens on two consecutive days, so I figured I'd just use one, but it didn't work. My obstetrician did a sperm count after he'd done the insemination and he said, well, ordinarily this would be a low count. So we did what they'd recommended – I guess they can't concentrate enough sperm for one go only, because the freezing process does destroy some of the sperm – and it worked immediately.

'When you fill up the forms, if you're a couple you write down a close description of the husband. If you're single, then you put down a description of what you want, like build, and hair and eye colouring and things like that. No, they didn't ask a whole lot of things like IQ and interests – this was a pretty small bank, though some of the bigger banks go into all that. In one they have a whole book and you can see what the fathers actually look like and what they do, their IQ, what they're interested in, their business and things like that. I just picked out the characteristics that I would have liked in a partner – I chose fairly tall, because most of our family is pretty tall, and dark hair and blue eyes – I knew there was a pretty good chance the baby would have blue eyes because my father has them, and it turns out he does have blue eyes, but he's very blond, though my sisters have blonde hair, so. . . .

'There are a couple of ways of doing the insemination – the one my doctor chose is to use a special cup – it looks almost like a diaphragm only smaller – and it has a plastic tube that comes down. He puts it in so that it fits right over the cervix, and he injects the specimen right up the tube so that the sperm just sits around the cervix, and you have to keep it in for a couple of hours. Afterwards I got teased a bit at work, the girls say why do it that way and miss out on all the fun, but I told them, just because I'm getting pregnant this way it doesn't mean I'm celibate: it's just that at this point it's the only way I'm going to get a baby!'

Most donors are medical students. Bridget Mason described how her clinic chooses theirs: 'We interview our own donors – all medical students – we have our own panel. Most of the samples are fresh and the donors produce the samples here – we do have a sperm bank but this is only a back-up service in case a donor can't get here in time. We screen the donors very carefully, and only accept about one in four. (We allow only a limited number of pregnancies from any one donor – about twenty – because of the faint possibility of half-brothers or half-sisters marrying unwittingly. It happens to a large extent anyway in this country – there were two large-scale trials done on blood groups some years ago in Britain and the research had almost to be abandoned because among the families being looked at so many of the children couldn't possibly have been fathered by the men who were supposed to be their fathers. Geneticists don't consider it a hazard to the population unless it happens generation after generation, but because of the anxiety of the lay press we feel we should cut down on the possibility.) The donors are paid a little just to cover their fares – we do that because it's difficult to run an entirely voluntary service and insist that people come at a particular time! They have to fill in a very detailed form before I even see them about their family medical history – one of the reasons we like medical students is they can give you a good family history. We then ask them to produce a semen sample to make sure they're fertile enough. Then they go on to have blood tests to make sure they're not carrying hepatitis, that they haven't got any venereal disease. When they've got through this initial screening process they're interviewed and examined and everything's double checked. We do take personality into account, yes, but the chances of somebody really unsuitable getting into medical school are quite low – there's a big screening programme to get into medical schools in the first place. We also feel they do it because they can understand the problems – they go to the infertility clinics and see couples who are childless and the problems it causes. I mean, adoption is nearly a myth in this country – the total number of babies adopted is falling every year, and I talked to one adoption society recently who told me they'd had 2,000 couples on their list approved for adoption and they hadn't had a white normal baby for two years. So the students feel it's a way they can help people.

'We keep all the details of the fathers until the last baby has been born from them and we've done a rigorous follow-up to find out about their children, then about a year after they've left we shred their records so that there's no way a child will ever be able to find out who their father was. As far as I know there aren't any proposals to change this in Britain – in some of the States in the US the names have to be filed, but there are no penalties for not filing them and most of the doctors I've asked don't file them. They're told they should do it, but there is no penalty if they don't. I think if there were legal requirements to keep records in this country you'd have great difficulty trying to run a donor programme because it would be a difficult thing to agree to, to risk having a child arrive in twenty years time and claim you for their father.'

Dr Nagle in the US asks for 'permits signed by husband

and wife accepting legal responsibility for any offspring produced as a result of artificial insemination because if a couple parts we don't want the father saying, "that's not my child, that's some donor's child and the doctor who did the insemination and the donor ought to be responsible for the support of that child." Nor do we want a donor who finds himself in an infertile marriage turning up and wanting visiting rights to a child he had from the days he was a medical student, so we don't like to maintain records as to who donated to whom, as they'd be able to trace who their semen went to.'

Jessica Curtis deliberately chose to go to a private doctor instead of a clinic as she felt a private doctor would keep records and she feels her child ought to be able to find out who her father is when she is older should she want to do so, but whether or not when the time comes the details will in fact still be available (regardless of what the legal position is) is problematical, according to what the specialists have told me. One way of overcoming this anonymity is to choose the donor yourself and to either find a doctor who will then help you, or to resort to what I learned was called 'turkey-basting'.

When I first heard this term I thought it was just a joke phrase, but far from it – turkey-basters (for British readers this is simply a large syringe for squirting the drippings from a cooking turkey over the bird) are literally used; as one of my interviewees explained (she doesn't want to be named in case somebody decides to try to bring in a law against it): 'It's very simple. All you need is a donor and a jar and a syringe! People think it must be very complicated because doctors do it, but it isn't at all. I had thought about doing it through a doctor but it was much too expensive – something like $40 an insemination and you usually have to inseminate two or three times during the ovulation period, and there are no guarantees how long it would take to conceive – it can take months so you could be looking at hundreds and hundreds of dollars. This way was free!'

I asked Dr Cohen what he thought about this idea, and at first he, like me, had difficulty in believing the term 'turkey-basting' was no more than a phrase, but I assured him I had spoken to several lesbians who had themselves used the method successfully. 'Given how delicate the process of conception is, it's surprising it works so frequently with any method you use. But turkey-basters are so huge you'd think a little semen specimen would get lost inside there!' I asked him if the method could cause any medical problems. 'I don't think so, not as long as there wasn't any detergent inside the instrument, because detergents and certain types of cleansers that might be used to make the instrument sterile could also kill the sperm, unless they were well washed off. As far as I know that would only kill the sperm, it wouldn't deform it in any way, no.' I had in fact asked the mothers who told me about it how they had ensured absolute cleanliness, thinking of my days of sterilizing baby bottles for topping-up feeds, and we all dissolved into laughter as one of them said with a straight face, 'Well, you don't exactly get a man to boil up his penis before he uses it, do you?'

One of the lesbian couples said that when they told their parents they were having a child through artificial insemination, the mother said, 'Whooh! What's *this*? Science fiction!' But in an age that now is faced with extraordinary legal decisions about frozen test-tube embryos – such as the embryo's legal rights if both parents should die (as has happened in Australia); the question of when embryos may be used for medical experimentation, if at all; and what rights 'spare' embryos remaining from an in-vitro fertilization have, etc., etc. – a little turkey-basting sounds almost cosy in contrast.

Getting ready
Dr Afton Blake: 'Single parents have probably deliberated more over what it's going to be like than most married couples have. They've really thought about what it would do to their life and what changes will be made, and they know what they're getting into. In order to do it comfortably you need money, and it usually takes a decade of your twenties and even some of your thirties for most individuals to establish themselves.' *Carolyn*, theatre director: 'I've never

been married, usually unattached, for the great majority of my life. I've been operating as a single person and I was comfortable with that and I didn't imagine it was going to change. But slowly evolving in my mind was that I was going to stay single, and that I did want to have a child, so I had to work out how to do that. I began to talk to a lot of people, and think about it a lot, found out that I had plenty of support from friends, men as well as women. About two years ago I realized this was going to be the next step in my life, and I began to consider the various options.'

We saw earlier how meticulously *Joanna*, graduate student of Third World studies, had planned her pregnancy, down to making sure the facial measurements of the prospective father matched hers. She was 40 when she had her child, but her planning began ten years previously. She realized the job she was doing then would not give her the time she needed, 'so I went back to school to start all over again because I wanted to get into a field where I would have to spend very little time away at work and would be able to do much of my work at home so that I could have time for a child. It all took longer than I thought but I ended up where I wanted, right down to having my baby exactly as I planned.' Several other women also chose their careers quite deliberately in order to have time for children, or went into branches of their chosen fields that would allow them comparative freedom.

Nearly all the mothers had given a lot of energy to sorting out how and where they were going to live before taking the plunge. *Lynn*, the nurse with two daughters: 'I was thinking about adoption, and I talked to a physician I knew. He said it was practically hopeless for an unmarried woman to adopt and he suggested I had a baby on my own. I said I couldn't just have a baby by a casual affair, so he suggested artificial insemination. I was amazed – I didn't think they'd do it for a single woman! He said he'd help me, and I told him I wasn't ready yet, that I was not going to bring up a child in an apartment, that I wanted a home with a back yard with green grass and a sand pit. So I waited about two years after I talked to him and then bought the house. Then I waited another year to make sure I was going to be able to handle the house payments. It was only then that I went back to him to say I was ready. Now I have two children, and sometimes feel I have the best of two worlds.'

Like Lynn, for most mothers getting together a safe nest is a priority. *Laura*, who had 'earmarked' an old friend as a prospective father when she was only 16: 'I wouldn't have gone ahead with it if I hadn't known there was a little bit of financial security there. I've got a roof over my head, which is mine, and that's something that my mother instilled in me since I was small – do what the hell you want, but make sure you've got a roof before you start producing children so that if he boots you out you've got somewhere. The house I'm getting is big enough to let rooms out, and I've got enough money to support baby, house and me for about a year without having to feel a pressure to go out to work.'

Jane Mattes, founder of Single Mothers by Choice, said, 'Many of the mothers coming to the groups have put aside a lot of money and are taking off six months or a year to be able to be full-time mothers for a while. They've either been successful enough to be given time off or they've planned to do it and chose the kind of job they could always go back to when they were ready.' I found that the American mothers I spoke with tended to be more highly qualified professionally than my English interviewees and therefore were better off financially, but I think this is mainly because American women in general have been in a more advantageous position than British women as far as independence and choice of career goes. But I believe this situation is changing, and also feminist pressure against child-bearing which has had quite a strong influence on many educated English women has lessened.

Money, housing, pre-planning – few of the mothers had not sorted out these important things in advance. They had also talked, questioned and read, although as acupressurist *Serena* said, 'I read books on single parenting, but nothing told me what it would be like in reality.' This was a general comment, but in America women are fortunate in having a group that will help them find out what reality really is like.

Associations and self-help groups

The only group I know of at present that was founded by the kind of mothers I am writing about and which is growing daily is the American one called, unsurprisingly, 'Single Mothers by Choice', or SMC as they usually refer to it themselves. I will write about it in detail as I feel other countries could follow suit with profit. In Holland, also, several mothers got together and began to form groups in a not dissimilar way to SMC, but BOM (Bewust Ongehuwd Moeder – literally, consciously unmarried mother) never became a cohesive continuing group as SMC has.

Jane Mattes, a psychoanalyst and psychotherapist as well as founder of SMC, described how it all came about: 'It started as a coffee clutch in my apartment. I was pregnant and everyone I met seemed to say, oh, I know someone who's had a baby and isn't married, or I have a friend who has a friend. . . . So I finally sent out the word to all those people, and said, come round or tell your interested friends to come to my apartment on such and such a day, and we'll have coffee. So about ten people showed up, pregnant, with babies, or thinking about the possibility, and we really got excited that we all had this in common. We decided to keep meeting, but to organize it more formally.' An article in issue no. 1 of SMC's newsletter brought out in July 1983 continues the story of the first meeting in October 1981: 'we were not SMC at that time, just a group of about twenty women half of whom were expecting or mothers, responding to an interview which had appeared in the *NY Daily News* featuring two therapists in their late thirties. One had deliberately gotten pregnant without any expectation that the father would marry her; the other was trying to conceive but had run into fertility problems. We met at the former's apartment. It was her idea to form a group for the dual purpose of sharing information and experiences with those who were thinking about single parenting and meeting other women who had chosen the same path to discuss issues while exposing her son to other children with a similar background.' The meeting went extremely well and 'after three intense hours we decided to meet again [the next month]. A bond had been formed; we knew we were not alone.'

As the meetings progressed it became apparent that there were two strands present – those who had already made their decision and were either pregnant or had already had their children, and those who hadn't yet made up their minds and were thinking hard about it. So it was decided to 'split into two segments . . . and to choose pertinent topics to discuss and a leader to run the meetings. One of our members found a church whose pastor offered to let us use the facilities . . . flyers were passed out and members encouraged to spread the word amongst interested friends. A Board of Directors was formed . . . we discovered there were five of us who were willing and able to devote our free time to organize SMC. Starting off as a steering committee we began to list topics of interest, volunteer our views for public exposure through the media and contact other mothers and thinkers to urge them to attend meetings and contribute their unique viewpoint. Eventually we coalesced into a Board and began the tedious task of putting together a national program. We arranged for a telephone line and at this time of writing [1983] are awaiting formal notification of our incorporation.

'We realized almost immediately that we have a great responsibility towards those women who came to us seeking information in order to make the decision whether or not to have a child. It was not and never will be our objective to act as an advocacy group. Obviously, we had decided in favor of motherhood and could very easily encourage the thinkers by expounding the joys and downplaying the hardships. We felt that by being totally open about the economic strains, loss of independence and lifelong emotional commitment along with providing information about our doctors or clinics we would be meeting our obligation. *Over one hundred thinkers have attended meetings, and only a handful have decided in favor of single parenting.*' (my italics – author)

Jessica Curtis, the president of SMC, explained to me what happens in the thinkers' groups. 'There are three Monday nights of about two hours each, and there are between ten and fifteen people each session. We go through everything: why do you want to have a child; what having a child means to you; how to get pregnant; fertility problems you might have; the rights of the father if you use a father; the kind of experience people have had with fathers like where people have had a strong relationship with the father, and when they haven't, and whether they could marry the guy; going through pregnancy by yourself; how to give birth; how to arrange your birth experience so it's optimal; how to arrange support systems while you're pregnant; having somebody be a labour coach for you; what kind of care you should get; planning finances; what it's like to work and have kids; how to get disability and maternity benefits, day care; how to get started *now* thinking about day care for when the time comes. At the first meeting we have mothers come along who had their children in different ways – artificial insemination, normal, adoption – to talk about their experiences for a few minutes. At the second meeting we have people in different financial situations – somebody really well off, like a psychiatrist, say, and somebody like myself who makes a living wage but isn't rich, and somebody who's on welfare. Then the leader goes through the information that's been presented and you can ask questions. Then at the third meeting Jane Mattes tries to bring out people's feelings – it's a kind of introspective meeting – so that they have a clear idea of what their own motivations are. I've not been to one of them because if I went it would contaminate the process – some people who were training to run the other two sessions went to one of hers and it really messed things up.'

For those who already had children or were pregnant a different sort of structure was necessary. At the beginning they found that with toddlers playing around everyone's feet it was difficult to have a coherent discussion, and anyway people soon knew each other's stories by heart. 'Several mothers became bored and dropped out. So we choose a facilitator to think about a topic, suggest an agenda and moderate the discussion. The meetings immediately settled down, with each person assured she could be heard', and discussion was able to develop satisfactorily with a hired baby-sitter looking after the children.

'People who join the group say they are taking charge of their own life – other people say they're being assertive. Whatever it is, just having made a decision to have a child by yourself seems to select out an amazing group of women. I don't feel we're superior copers, so that doesn't mean child abuse will never happen, but I think we're much better able to get the resources we need than the average mother.'

I could easily write a whole chapter on SMC – how they have grown into an organization with many chapters across the country, the breadth and interest of their regular newsletter, the picnics and parties they arrange which members obviously enjoy enormously – but lack of space prevents me, though I hope I have given enough information to encourage mothers in other countries to consider setting up organizations of their own. For people who want to get in touch with SMC the address is: SMC, P.O. Box 207, Van Brunt Station, Brooklyn, New York, NY 11215.

For some people this organization must sound ideal – for others it is antipathetic. Jane Mattes: 'Our group is in some degree self-selective, yes. People who come to a meeting hear the way we talk – we're not bemoaning our fate, we're just talking about the difficulties, which is different. But some of the women who come along once or twice say, "let's not talk about the difficulties, there's nothing to talk about, you just do it and that's it," while others who may have gone into it accidentally or without thinking are tearing their hair and saying, "I wish I'd never done it." But *we're* saying, "we wanted to do it, and let's talk about how we can do it better." It's not that we say to women we don't want them, it's just that they stop coming to the meetings. The men-haters don't come either, because we're not men-haters here. And no, there aren't any lesbians who've stayed with us yet, either.' Clearly, SMC suits people who like to be in an efficiently organized set-up and feel pretty happy about themselves, but who have made an important discovery. As Jane Mattes said to me, 'the main thing I learned is that you can't do it alone. That's the irony of ironies . . . you have to learn what your limits are and find other people who can help you when you reach your limits.'

BOM, the Dutch 'organization' has never achieved the
coherence of SMC and has never seriously attempted to. It
seems to have had a much more consciously feminist
background, though its beginnings were similar. In 1977
Cecile Jansen, a single woman who was pregnant, put an
advertisement in her local newspaper in Amsterdam, and
twelve women came to meet her. They formed a group, it
began to be written about in newspapers and the word
spread. The group then organized a general meeting to be
held in Utrecht, and about one hundred people from all over
Holland came in response to their advertisements. *Rosa*, a
specialist in child psychology and child education, who at
the time was thinking about getting pregnant, was one of
these women. She went to Utrecht with two girlfriends:
'Addresses were collected at the meeting if you wanted to
make a group. The two girls who went with me didn't join a
group – they just wanted to hear about it, and decided not to
do it. Most of the people at the meeting were not pregnant.
It was held in a small place – I think perhaps it was an
alternative theatre – and we heard women talking about their
experiences. Many of the ideas I heard were my ideas, and I
was very enthusiastic about it – so some of us started
another group, the third one here in Amsterdam.' Rosa
found, though, that at her group, which met every two
weeks, there were only one or two mothers with similar
ideas to her, and so gradually she dropped out.

I must admit I found it very difficult to sort out exactly
what had happened and what is still happening to BOM. I
am not even certain that the above facts are absolutely
correct as everyone's story was very slightly different. It
seems that the originators had quite a lot of publicity,
appeared on television, radio shows and so on, but the idea
of a national organization never took off because the
mothers couldn't agree on terms of definition, exactly who
BOM mothers were, and whether the group (if it was a
group) should be called BOM anyway. *Anna*, child
psychologist, who was involved very early on, felt that
names and definitions were not important: 'no, we never had
an office; in Amsterdam there was just my phone number
and we organized a few meetings. We had a lot of publicity

because we were the first, but other groups formed in Amsterdam too, because we felt that ten was enough people in one group and then another group had to be started.' In true feminist style there would be no leader or organizer in a group: 'Everybody in the group was running it. But we found out that when a group had existed for half a year it was splitting up again, because although we were all unmarried mothers by choice, *how* we did it was so different. The thing is that every group was splitting on this – we don't agree how we have to be a mother when we have the child – some of the women are very traditional, others want one thing, others another thing. As long as we were pregnant or the child was just born there were no problems at all, and we really needed each other, but as soon as we have to start to educate the child a little bit we didn't agree. I think the only thing BOM mothers have in common is that we are not married and we don't give the name of the father to the child.'

Rosa felt differently to *Anna* – she wanted a more firm structure: 'I am involved in politics, I believe in structure, I don't believe in . . . softly . . . waving . . . things. I tried to get a decision whether we were an organization or not, what democratic level, what contacts, if we should start an office. But I couldn't get this done, so then I say, OK, it's not a movement. I am always ready to help with things but as long as it's not a good structure I cannot work with it because if Cecile says something on the radio everybody thinks that is BOM and if I say something or Anna says something then they say that *that's* BOM. I know that people are still contacting each other – but people have to make up their own groups, organize each other.' Anna, explaining this, said, 'My experience at the moment is that a lot of women still are phoning me, but just talking once is OK for them. If they want then I give them the address of other women if they want to talk to them, but they don't need it so much – everyone knows all about single mothers now.'

At the time of writing I have not heard of the existence of any groups in Britain – Gingerbread and the National Council for One Parent Families do very good work, but they are aimed primarily at people who had not originally intended to become single parents. The latter organization was founded in 1918 as the National Council for the Unmarried Mother and Her Child; in 1973 it took on its new name and extended its role to help all parents bringing up children alone. They give free advice on legal, housing, pregnancy, social security, taxation, maintenance and many other problems; they also press central and local government to provide single parents with the services they need. In one of their pamphlets they point out, 'Society is centred around the two-parent family. Economically, legally and socially it tends to be seen as the most acceptable way of bringing up children. But one in eight families in Britain is a one-parent family. There are now around a million divorced, separated, single or widowed parents caring for over one and a half million children.' They will provide information on any aspect single parents might need it on, from housing to child benefits, and all single mothers whether by choice or not can benefit from their help. They are, however, concerned with the problems rather than the joys of single parenthood and are a very different organization from SMC. Their main address is One Parent Families, 255 Kentish Town Road, London NW5 2LX (01-267-1361).

Gingerbread is closer to SMC in style, but the majority of members are divorced or separated parents of both sexes, and although some mothers are single women, it is thought that few had their babies by choice (this sort of statistic is not kept by Gingerbread). Gingerbread was begun in 1970 by a 'lone mother living in London, who faced difficulties bringing up her children alone, and who wanted to bring together people who were experiencing similar problems.' From such small beginnings Gingerbread has grown into a nationwide organization reaching out right through Britain, this area being divided up into fourteen regions each of which contains a number of groups who send representatives to the local regional meetings. The national organization is a charity managed by democratically elected National Council of Gingerbread members drawn from all over the country.

The National Office in London has a small staff which co-ordinates the groups, and acts both as an information centre and 'as a catalyst to foster self-help initiatives'. Julie

Kaufmann, General Secretary, explained to me: 'All the groups are very different, some small, some large, some merely providing a meeting place, companionship and family activities, others providing a comprehensive range of sophisticated services for one-parent families. How a group operates and what services it provides is entirely up to its members. National Gingerbread provides support in a number of ways – by training, seminars, information, advice and a quarterly magazine which goes out to all the groups.' All groups are based on the same principles, but how they function varies enormously, some being more effective than others. Groups aim to provide 'a meeting place for parents and children, and a new social life to replace the one lost with the lost partnership' (as I wrote earlier the assumption is that members had never intended to be alone), 'friendship, information and advice, moral and emotional support, practical help', and many groups also arrange 'baby-sitting pools, clothes and toy pools, skills exchanges, transport, a library of relevant books, a "listening" ear service, savings clubs for holidays and outings, support and discussion groups'.

It is a very interesting and for the most part a highly effective organization. Any one group is precisely as good as its members make it, each group being run entirely by lone parents for the benefit of one-parent families in the locality, although they do in fact have a system whereby groups that 'operate to a very low standard' can find themselves disaffiliated, but this only happens after attempts have been made by National Gingerbread to help the group become more effective. Some of the larger groups even run day nurseries, because 'Gingerbread has always regarded day care for children as a crucial service which enables lone parents to earn their own living rather than being dependent upon Supplementary Benefit.' Gingerbread's National Office is at 35 Wellington Street, London WC2 7BN (01-240-0953), and they will send information to anyone who writes to them.

While it is true that single mothers by choice have a different focus from most Gingerbread members, I do feel that for many women who do not have as extensive a circle of supportive friends as they would like or who are finding certain problems difficult to cope with, it would be helpful for them to contact their local Gingerbread group. Even more useful for them might be to write to Gingerbread for a copy of *The Gingerbread Handbook*, an extremely informative and well-planned basic guide to running a group, and to then consider whether it might be feasible to set up a single mothers by choice group in their own area, possibly connected with Gingerbread, and perhaps with national ambitions at the back of their minds. Or perhaps there might be set up some kind of affiliated group alongside Gingerbread which could, like SMC, on the one hand help 'thinkers' to decide whether or not to have a child, and on the other provide a place for those already pregnant or with a child to meet and bring their children?

Extended families

The importance of extended families has been referred to frequently throughout the book, and will figure importantly in Part 3. The message unquestionably has come through to me that to attempt to have a baby alone without the support either of family or of really close friends is to ask for trouble. People involved in the women's movement have sometimes reported their disappointment that the movement itself did not supply the extended family as at first it had seemed to promise, and this applied particularly to women who were having babies. Mothers either felt they were letting the movement down by having babies at all, or they sometimes found that while they were expected to help out in collectives where other children already existed, if they themselves got pregnant they were not supported. In theory communities are a marvellous idea – unfortunately the practice is often not so agreeable.

But informal communities – such as where housing is shared or where several friends live close by – can often provide invaluable support while lowering the risk of the ill-feeling and domestic disputes that can build up when people live on top of each other. *Jessica Curtis*, who bought a house and shares it, charging lower rents in exchange for some baby-sitting: 'The worry was, suppose I fell in the bath tub and banged my head and the baby's 6 months old, asleep in bed – who's going to notice if it screams for three days and nobody comes? But living like this has made things so dramatically much better I'd probably never live any other way. All these people living in expensive little apartments, paying high rents – I can't understand it. Living here with other people in the house I can go out jogging in the morning, I get free baby-sitting, and there are men living here so she has male role models.'

Tam, clinical social worker and therapist, considered sharing the upbringing of a baby with a girlfriend (they are not lesbian) but when the other girl's lover came back into her life she married him and soon became pregnant. The husband then suggested Tam had a baby and moved in with them to share the household, but Tam felt she would not be comfortable living alongside a happy pair without a viable sexual relationship of her own, though she did consider it might work out if she lived alone nearby. Variations on this theme are being worked out by other women wanting to get pregnant, sometimes with the idea that the husband will impregnate the single woman out of a desire to help, but human nature being what it is problems almost invariably seem to arise, usually before anything positive is achieved.

Stella and *Jan* had two support groups – one, already mentioned, the group of five mothers who first came together in pregnancy and who still meet, the other a group of lesbian mothers who discuss things like how their children cope with school and other matters of specific interest to lesbians as well as all the usual things mothers like to talk about. Mothers, straight as well as lesbian, who have had artificial insemination find it helpful to get together. Dr Afton Blake: 'There are things to work out with sperm bank children, like what to tell them about their fathers. I have accumulated about fifteen different women in this area who have sperm bank children, so they'll grow up knowing each other, and I think other sperm bank mothers should do this too.' The reader might also remember that Afton's close friend chose to be inseminated with sperm from the same donor as Afton, so that their children are half-brother and sister. Margaret Wood, who in 1935 was adopted by her unmarried mother who ran a nursing home, told me how helpful it was that her mother's greatest friend who lived nearby also adopted a baby, and that the two children were brought up together like cousins, sharing Christmases, birthdays and so on.

Some mothers found blood-related family a great help. *Mary*, children's nurse, lives close to various members of her family, and when her married sister, who had a son from the marriage, divorced she moved in with her. Now that Mary has a child of her own she finds the arrangement of sharing works beautifully. For *Charlotte*, part-time researcher, it is her mother and sisters who provide her main support – she has many friends, 'but my family is very important to me – I can ring up any time of day or night and tell my mother things, ask her things, moan or exult, and I know that she wants to know.'

Of course, not everything always goes according to plan – inevitably some mothers have found that even long-standing friendships can falter or change. *Anna* had a girlfriend who once a fortnight looked after her first child for a whole day and a night. 'It meant I was free to go to the centre of Amsterdam and just sit and read my newspaper and have a coffee, or just to walk and buy my clothes, and in the evening I could go out and make appointments with people. But just before the birth of my second child this girlfriend made a new relationship, and she didn't say directly to me I don't want to do it any more, but she was always too busy. My free day and night had meant so much to me, I think she didn't realize how much.' *Rosa* had two girlfriends who had helped her with her pre-natal exercises and stayed with her during the birth, even changing their holiday plans when it turned out the baby was going to be late. But 'afterwards I hardly saw them. The problem is you have had a different life before the baby comes and you have to change. Your life becomes different from theirs, and you lose a lot of your old friends.'

So single women especially have to be ready to make new friends. You have to be prepared to talk readily with neighbours, other mothers met at nursery school or at toddlers' groups, search out friends of friends who like you are single mothers. Often married women too will be glad to look after your child sometimes for the weekend in exchange for your having theirs, or they will be pleased to share daytime baby-sitting with you – several of the mothers I spoke to had arrangements of this kind which had evolved into deep friendships. People at work, too, can be supportive – *Julia*, who lived with her lover for three years after the birth, but not before, felt that the office she was working in was not very sympathetic: 'it didn't feel like the right environment to be an unmarried mother, somehow, so I found myself a place in a health food shop. I didn't want to be where I felt I'd be disapproved of, I just didn't want to have to cope with all of that. The health food shop was a much more open, understanding sort of place, and it worked out very well.'

The message, then, was always the same: as mothers-to-be these women knew that if they were to be successful and happy having a child alone, they had, in fact, *not* to be alone. How successful they were in making close friends, developing extended families, depended to a certain extent on their personalities, but I was interested to find that not one of these mothers by choice was cut off from society, and that all of them had good support, though some of it was not as consistent as they had hoped. Above all, they were all prepared to make positive efforts to achieve close friendships, and they succeeded. I think this says quite a lot about the kind of women they are, and might act as a warning for those more isolated, non-communicative types who are hoping to secure the warmth they lack and need by giving birth to a child. First, it seems, they must learn how to go outwards towards others before they should risk going inwards towards what they hope will be the most intimate relationship of their lives.

The birth

So many books have been written about pregnancy and birth that there is very little I can add except to say that of the mothers I interviewed some had experienced good pregnancies and some difficult pregnancies, some easy births and some difficult births. Age did not seem to make much difference: *Jenny* who had her son when she was 20 had a thoroughly unpleasant pregnancy, while *Joanna*, who had planned it all down to the last meticulous detail, had a very easy pregnancy and birth at 40. The mothers used various methods of preparation: Lamaze exercises worked out together with a friend or relation as a coach seemed to be automatic for most of the American mothers, while English mothers mentioned the methods they used less frequently, though two had followed the Leboyer approach.

For those unfamiliar with these terms, the Lamaze method is based on the work of the French doctor, Ferdinand Lamaze, who taught the psychoprophylactic method of childbirth, which involves the mother in concentrating so hard on her breathing drill that she is able to control how she interprets sensations of pain. In Britain the National Childbirth Trust also teaches psychoprophylaxis. Leboyer, another Frenchman, concentrates more on the baby's perceptions of birth and likes deliveries to take place in near darkness, in quiet, with the baby being held and massaged by the mother immediately after birth and then immersed in warm water to help it feel it has been returned to a familiar environment. Battles over whether a mother should lie on her back or be permitted to choose whatever position she likes, be it squatting, standing, kneeling or whatever, are as heated in certain circles as the arguments over whether or not mothers should be given epidurals to take away pain.

An epidural is the injection of an anaesthetic into the back near the spinal canal which causes numbness from the waist down, but leaves the mother in full consciousness. Epidurals are not without risk, and have caused paralysis and even death, although doctors play down such danger saying it is so minimal it is not worth considering.[2] For hospital staff it has the advantage of producing a docile mother, and pressure is put on women to accept pain-killers at a time when they are most vulnerable, whatever they had planned to do in advance. Ann Oakley writes that of her sample only 29 per cent had decided before the actual birth to have an epidural, but 79 per cent ended up having one, while 59 per cent had their membranes artificially ruptured to induce the birth and 52 per cent had forceps or ventouse (a form of suction) deliveries. These figures strike me as showing an amazing amount of interference on the part of medical staff, the greater part of which – unless women's physiology has made tremendous changes in the past three decades – has to be totally unnecessary. Details of what all this involves, the way a woman ends up with a variety of tubes sticking out of her for the epidural, the glucose drip (which speeds the labour up), etc., are horrifyingly described at first hand by some of Ann Oakley's sample of mothers in her book *Becoming a Mother*, and I strongly recommend that women planning to have their babies in hospitals learn as much as they can in advance about what might be inflicted on them in the name of comfort and ease.[3] Except in cases of genuine emergency it is a great pity if what should be the fulfilling culmination of possibly years of planning and hopeful anticipation should turn into a kind of dimmed nightmare.

Sooner or later, though, for all the mothers who had planned their pregnancy, birth brought a time of bliss. In the next chapter we will enjoy some of their happy comments; this section deals only with a few practical matters that mothers might find useful. For example, *Mary*, children's nurse, comments, 'I worked up to three weeks before the date my baby was due, but if I were to do it again I'd work up to at least a week before. What happened was that I had three weeks of doing nothing – I'd got practically everything done before I left work, so there was nothing left for me to do, and as he was five days late I had too much time on my hands.' Several found it was difficult to believe it was actually happening at last. *Julia*: 'When the baby was born I was very shocked – the reality of a real baby, it was a shock! It had become like a fantasy, especially when she was about two weeks late. Part of me was saying, well OK, go back to work, it's not going to happen. Then there was actually a real baby born. I was quite surprised. The reality of it – gosh!'

For some mothers there were birth complications. The

nurse, *Mary*, when at last her baby came, found she had to have a caesarean section, so she wasn't able to be with him at first as she had planned. 'But I feel that you should be bonding with the baby from the time you conceive, so that if something comes up, like if the baby has a respiratory problem, or you have to have a C-section, it shouldn't make that much difference because you've been bonding for the last nine months.' Psycho-analyst *Stephanie* also had to have a caesarean, and was extremely ill afterwards. Unable to feed her baby and doped with medication, she lost the first few days of the bonding she had expected to achieve – in fact she says it took her two months before she was able to feel fully bonded to him.

Breast-feeding brought a great deal of pleasure to mothers. *Charlotte*, part-time researcher: 'It was lovely, and I went on with it until she was 15 months old. I didn't mind that all my clothes were covered in milk, in fact I positively liked it because it showed how much milk I'd got!' For women who worked away from home, though, breast-feeding presented problems. Museum curator *Elizabeth*: 'I went on feeding him at home morning and evening until he was 4 months old, but I had to stop because around midday I'd start leaking in the middle of a committee meeting – I'd have to hold my papers up to cover my dress up, you know? I had to go back to work when he was 6 weeks old – I'd rather not have but I'd taken all the statutory maternity leave public servants were allowed at that time – I know some people take their children to work to feed, but I could never have done that, I'd have found it too distracting.'

Breast-feeding on demand, literally – night as well as day – is something that some mothers have attempted, and one or two have achieved, but for women with a full working schedule it is usually too demanding. The specialist in child psychology, *Rosa*, had to rush backwards and forward between college (where she was taking her finals) and crêche: 'It was crazy, I was very tired all the time and no, I wouldn't do it again like that.' Nor would medical researcher *Felicity*. Robert, her 2-year-old son, still sleeps in her bed and wakes up every two or three hours. He was breast-fed on demand until he was 21 months, night and day, but now he has cups of juice from trainer cups when he wakes. 'I wake up instantly he does, and sleepily hand him his cup, then usually he curls up on my face or shoulder or something. I feel it's a comfort thing as much as anything. I think perhaps if I had another child, which I won't, I would try and force a routine, because I basically think they need one, whereas he's never had a routine. I wouldn't stop the breast-feeding early, and I'd stick to demand feeding because I wouldn't like to have a child crying for an hour because it was hungry. But I wouldn't share my bed again – he only came into mine when we moved here because he'd slept in a cot in my room before, and he didn't like being in a new bedroom all on his own. Now I don't know how I'm going to get him out of sleeping here with me, but sooner or later he'll have to do it.'

Dr Afton Blake, on the other hand, is a convinced believer in what she calls symbiotic mothering. Her argument is that 'nocturnal mothering', or keeping the child with you all through the night, 'dramatically alters the emotional experience of the child, having a profound positive effect on his emotional development and his capacity for adult intimacy.' She pointed out to me, 'A single mother is much more able to give that kind of care to him; many husbands begin to complain about breast-feeding after a while, you know, how long are you going to do that? how long is this child going to stay in bed with us? – and they begin to feel left out. I have a bed for Doron all ready in his own room and he can go there any time he wants, and I imagine he'll gradually use it more and more. I won't push him out, he will go when he has the wish to – his bed is there for him in his own room, his own space. The first couple of years of life are developmentally the symbiotic period, so the natural state for a human being is to be symbiotically merged with his mother, and symbiotic merging has to do with body contact. Then as the child reaches what they call *rapprochement* he needs mother there but not clinging. She needs to be there with arms open so he can initiate his independence when he wants but is able to immediately fall back to mother if he needs it, so that if the mother doesn't cling or push him away then he can move further and further away of his own choice in his own time. Eventually his own push towards autonomy will make him want his own space, and it will happen very gradually from maybe 2½ to 4 or 5 years, regressing when he's feeling sick or specially stressed, just as grown-ups regress when we feel under a lot of stress and would love to be held by mother again.'

I asked her if she had known any children who had been brought up like that and she told me she's known half a dozen such children closely. 'What we do know about them is that they are more independent in the latency stage, more secure, they are able to tolerate much more separation from their mothers. These were children both of single and of married mothers, where they were allowed the family bed and breast-feeding on demand.' It all sounded splendid, but when I asked her how well she slept with Doron at her side all night, she said, with a smile, 'I haven't had a decent night's sleep since he was born! I can't sleep really comfortably with him needing to nurse – like last night he nursed all night, and I always feed him literally whenever he wants. But to me it's well worth it. He's a very sociable, autonomous child, he makes friends easily with other children and with adults. I could leave him with you right now and he'd not show any of the usual 20-month separation anxieties, and I think that's because he's had so much access to me.'

Afton Blake is able to make her own hours of work, and has a devoted housekeeper. For mothers less financially well off, or with a less strong constitution, I feel that 'symbiotic' rearing, however advantageous it might be for the child, must be both exhausting and debilitating if carried out to the extent that Afton has. I know that for myself, needing regular sleep as I do, I would not have lasted out more than a few days before cracking up. Even if I had managed to become partially accustomed to the disturbed nights, without sufficient unbroken sleep I would have been in a perpetual state of semi-depression and sick thick-headedness. I therefore think it is very important to stress that any mother who wants to try this method of child-rearing without any adaptation to her own physical needs should realize just how much strain it puts on women, and not let herself feel the slightest guilt if she can't make it. As I said earlier, a happy mother makes a happy child, and however tempting a theory may sound it must be dropped if it doesn't work in practice for whatever reason.

7
Problems and joys

'I had a master's in child development, so at the point when I thought of having a child of my own I imagined I knew everything there was to know about young children, thought I'm perfect, you know? – I have money to take care of my child, I have a master's in child development, this is going to be just fine. I was an absolute set-up for major post-partum depression. Which I had! I was guilt-ridden constantly because I knew everything about how fascinating little babies should be, and I wasn't totally fascinated every minute.' (Frances)

'I'm still in heaven about this. I don't know whether it ever stops – but it's clearly the most wonderful thing I've ever done in my life and puts everything else into a back seat for a while, because she's just a wonder to me.' (Carolyn)

'I wonder what effect the relationships I've had with men will have on her, though. I've never cycled them through very rapidly – the shortest has been about three months, but the longest have been two to four years. . . . Recently she's been able to figure out what's going on, who's sleeping with mummy and what that means. I don't think it's been a problem for her – what it has forced me to do is to talk to her honestly about what I think relationships are about, and to talk a little bit about sexuality. I mean I can't take the line that you fall in love and get married and that's the only person you ever sleep with dear, right?' (Frances)

Fitting your career around having a child
When to have your child, what to do about your career,

working out priorities between baby and job, being aware
that the decisions you make now will affect not only your
entire life but also the life of your child – these are problems
that are inescapable for any single mother deliberately
choosing to have a child alone. To answer them demands a
certain maturity, and a great deal of thought.

Not all women, of course, go about it in this way – they
jump in at the deep end, get themselves pregnant and hope
for the best. But these are not the women I have been
writing about: either they tend to be very young, often with
unhappy backgrounds and wanting the comfort of somebody to love them (this can be a certain recipe for disaster,
as child abuse studies show[1]), or they are married women
who take if for granted that children are an automatic part of
the marriage packet.

I talked to Naomi Scheman about women and careers,
and although in this extract she is mainly thinking about
married women what she has to say about careers is equally
relevant to single mothers. 'I see with my students of all ages
there is still a tremendous pressure on women to have
children. A lot of young women are being led into a very
dangerous situation – they think that feminism and feminist
battles are things of the past and that they can have it all, and
they're wrong, they're headed for disaster. They cannot be
taken seriously in their jobs if they're only in their early to
middle twenties and they have a child. Marriage is still
enormously dangerous, it's economically, socially and
psychologically dangerous, particularly for young women.
They think they have a kind of power and they don't have
it. They've got a heady sense the millenium has come,
equality has come, and that false confidence is putting them
into a very dangerous situation. There's a lot of attitudinal
stuff on the part of one's hierarchical superiors; one's not
regarded as serious in one's career intentions. A lot of the
penalties are not a result of a decrease in one's activity but
rather a result of being seen differently by the people in
charge of making decisions. A lot of this would change a
great deal if high-quality child care were readily available to
any woman who needed it. Children pose unpredictable
disruptions in one's life, and the idea that one ought to be

able to have a child without this happening is a male fantasy, it's what men have essentially been able to do; only the gravest of disasters have interrupted the course of their careers or even of any individual work day.' But at the back of their minds men know perfectly well what having children entails, which is why they are so suspicious of married or pregnant women, however dedicated to their jobs working mothers protest they are.

Certainly in many careers having a baby to care for brings almost insurmountable problems unless full-time living-in help is contemplated. Wyn Knowles talked about her BBC radio programme: 'It's very difficult to have a child in my job *and* a career – I didn't have to get to work all that early, not until around ten, but I'd often have to stay on late at night, and that would have been very difficult if I had had a baby at home. Sometimes people you wanted to see would only be free in the evenings, or you had to edit something for the next day – there's always that kind of pressure when you work on a daily programme. When I was a younger producer it was even worse, because then you always seemed to be over-working – the pattern was you were very involved in making programmes to a deadline. I noticed that a lot of our married women producers would go off to have a baby, firmly convinced they'd want to come back, but they rarely would come back on the staff. They might freelance a bit, but I think your attitudes change a lot when you have a baby.'

So single mothers either accept that their careers will be held up, or they take care to put themselves into an invulnerable position first. Jessica Curtis enjoys her job as a public health nurse, and accepts that at least for the present her career is not progressing. 'You can't stay late and do extras and all the stuff that you need to progress your career. If I wanted to get on in nursing, I'd have to quit working and go to graduate school and that's impossible right now. But perhaps later. . . .' *Jane*, a lawyer, took the other path and firmly established herself in her career before she adopted her baby. 'In my current job I work three and a half days a week, and I had known when I took this job a year and a half ago that I was going to have a baby one way or another, so I told them I did not want to work full-time in anticipation of that. When I adopted the baby I took three and a half months off from work, but although I'm not in private practice there's still an expectation that because you are committed to the issues the organization is involved with you work harder than you would at a regular nine to five job. There are deadlines to be met, speaking engagements and so on. But I've various people who come in and look after the baby while I'm working, and the two women who live here do some baby-sitting as well, so it works out. She's wonderful – I've no doubts at all I've done the right thing.'

Jane was able to relax for a while in her career and take on only a part-time job because 'I've been established for many years – I graduated from law school over eight years ago. I've written many articles and I'm very well known in my field – it's connected with women's issues – so doing only three and a half days isn't putting me back in any way. I've had to make some choices, it's true – for example next semester I usually teach Law School courses, but I won't this year because I want to spend the extra time with my daughter, but I'll be able to do it again in future years if I want to. It would be harder if I weren't so established – even though I wanted to have a baby many years ago it probably was better I waited because there really isn't any question now about my career.'

Certain jobs leave mothers more freedom to manipulate their hours of work than others – therapists seem particularly advantaged. *Tam*, clinical social worker and therapist, who is considering having a baby, saw no problems in arranging her life to suit maternity, saying that she could put her baby into a baby community centre near her office so that she could pop into the centre to breast-feed it and would adjust the hours her clients visited her to suit the baby's feeding times. *Stephanie* has similarly adapted her life: 'I have a very fortunate situation. I plan my work hours around my child, so that I work six days a week instead of five, but I work five hours each day instead of eight. I arranged it like that so that I could be with him every morning, be gone some time during the midday or afternoon, and come back and be there for supper and bedtime. So I seem to be both a full-time mother almost, and a full-time worker, and I feel I am having the best of both. When he was a baby I stayed away shorter times, like I'd be away for three hours, come home for two, went away for three, came home to stay. I understand about child development and knew he couldn't hold on to me in his mind for very long. That's until he was 2. Then he got a little older and it seemed more disruptive than helpful, because he was saying – when are you leaving? and, what are you doing? So I realized he was able to handle my going – once he did an imitation of me dashing in and out that cracked me up! I thought it was really cute, he was standing there laughing, opening and closing doors. . . . So I changed it to four to five hours away, and once I was home I was home. Now he goes to a nursery school three hours a day every day, and two days I pick him up, one day Michael (his godfather and legal guardian) picks him up, two days the baby-sitter picks him up.

'Having to juggle all this is very exhausting, but I'd made my choices. I resigned from being a clinic director when he was two and a half; I was working from a part-time administrative position. It wasn't the time that was the difficulty, it was the emotional energy involved, and I just wasn't interested any more in hassling with the problems of being an administrator. I also gave up a teaching position I had in an analytic institute, because I'm teaching my child all the time, and my priority is him. I had accomplished in my career the things I really wanted to accomplish. So I gave up two positions that I had aspired to for years and was thrilled to have, but they'd really run their course in terms of my getting something out of them. I had proven to myself that I could do them, and the challenge and the satisfaction now was more in having the child. I feel my main interest at present is in running my home and teaching him, not in running a clinic and teaching psychotherapists how to do psychotherapy any more. Yes, I can take these things up again later if I want to.

'Financially I'm doing better than I ever did – my work seems to have improved tremendously since I've been a mother. When I think about some of the things I didn't know before! As a therapist I'm much better; my under-standing is much deeper of what it's really like to have a child, to be a child, to be a mother. Another thing I do, too, as a result of having a baby, is I'm very involved with SMC, and there's a lot of work to be done there, so all round I'm kept very busy.'

I think the profound difference between the way most women and most men regard their work is illustrated very well here by Stephanie. It is not that she does not take her work very seriously – she does. But work is *part* of her life, not all of it, and having achieved a successful career she is happy to relax for a while in order to achieve other aims: men, on the contrary, so often seem to be totally disorientated without the support of their daily job. What is also particularly interesting with regard to Stephanie is her comments on how motherhood has improved her work as a therapist – and I think this must also apply to many other jobs where human relationships are important. But it is also obvious that if women are going to get the best of both worlds, as Stephanie put it, they must first work out a way of earning their living that is compatible at some stage in their lives with bringing up a child.

Many jobs unfortunately do not lend themselves to sharing or to part-time work, their hours being relentless nine to five with occasional late nights that cannot be avoided. However long a mother with such a job may be able to take away from work after having her baby, sooner or later she is going to be faced with putting her child into the hands of somebody else during the day. Several, but not all, of the psychiatrists I talked to agreed that it is better for the child to either face this separation very early on or much later – to separate suddenly from the child when it is 6 or 7 months old is not desirable. *Stephanie*: 'If you have to do a nine to five job then the child is going to have to live with that, and I think the earlier it starts the better. You have to find a really good baby-sitter and start with that person as early as possible, at a few weeks, say, rather than have the child experience you as a full-time person then lose you. The first six weeks to two months are very important for bonding for both mother and child – that's the usual kind of leave people get anyway – then if you've got to go fairly soon it's better to go at that point.' (I should probably point out here that in America the term 'baby-sitter' simply means someone who is looking after the baby in her home or yours – in Britain it usually is applied to someone who comes to your home unless the opposite is made clear.)

Clinical psychologist Karin Meiselman agrees with Stephanie's attitude: 'I went straight back to work after three or four weeks, but I shifted my work load around so that I was working three days a week. When the children were very small I took them to a baby-sitter all day for three days a week, and they never had what's termed separation anxiety – they always knew that when I went I was coming back.'

I told her about my discussion with psychologist Hendrike Vande Kemp. Dr Kemp had said to me, 'The theory I most agree with says that it is harmful for a child to be separated from the mother, even if they are with a good person while the mother is at work, because the child doesn't have the capacity to image the mother, to hold her in mind during the time that she is gone, and so at best the child is going to internalize two part-time mothers, rather than one whole image of a mother. The first two to two and a half years are the most critical – after that once the child can hold the mother fully in mind I think full-time work would do. You're right, over half of married mothers are working too, and I can only say that raises a lot of serious questions about the welfare of the children who will be adults in twenty years from now.'

To this Meiselman replied, 'Well, all I can say is it didn't happen with me, the children responded to me very positively and never showed any kind of anxiety about my coming back or my leaving them, even. If I had left it until they were a year old, though, it's possible there would have been problems. I have a friend who was with her little boy constantly, then she tried to wean him away to a sitter's house when he was about a year old, and there was no way she could do that. He absolutely panicked, wouldn't let her go, and he was that way until he was 2½. I don't think it follows at all that the children will be split; it's always been quite clear to my children who their mother is, and they don't seem unduly attached to their sitter. They like her all right, but they always seem to prefer to be with me. I do think it's important for the parent to be around for the preponderance of the time, though, to really establish this is home, and this is mummy, and this is where you usually are – weekends, waking up in the night and so on – but that sometimes you're out at Mrs So-and-so's.'

Finding the right person to look after your child while you are working is one of the most difficult tasks of all. Few day nurseries will take small babies, and mothers anyway feel dubious about leaving babies in institutional care, however well run the nursery is. For very small children the most popular method, both in the States and in Britain, was to find a warm-hearted woman – perhaps with children of her own or one or two others she was also looking after – who would take the baby into her own home, thus avoiding problems of having to rush back to the nursery school or group before it closed. Midwife *Pat*: 'I found a local woman who had a licensed day care home – I talked to her and really liked her. She had her own 3-year-old and a couple of after-school kids, that's all, so that was great. It's difficult with nursing, because you have such different shifts. The worst was three in the afternoon to eleven at night, because then I had to pick my baby up after midnight, but that was all right for her because her husband worked nights and she was waiting up for him anyway.'

Lynn, the nurse with two daughters: 'To some degree I can adapt my hours, but most of the staff works from seven to five and I need to be available when they are there. At first I tried to find someone to live in with me – all I wanted was someone to be around to look after Heather and give her something light for lunch, and they'd have been free all weekend and in the evenings, and have room and board, but they wanted my take-home pay plus! It was impossible, I couldn't afford it. I looked for a long time, trying to find someone I really felt was qualified and capable and was going to give good love and care. Then I found someone who'd recently lost her husband, and had looked after her own children in the past. I really like her, and Heather was with her from 9 weeks until she was 18 months old. But I gradually began to have some reservations about her; I felt she was getting over-protective – Heather wasn't allowed to climb on furniture or do anything adventurous – and I felt she needed some socialization with other children.'

Day begins very early for working mothers with children. Americans in any case usually start their day earlier than the British do in general, and seem not to regard rising at 6.30 as very horrendous, but even so Lynn's description of her morning took me aback. 'My day's very packed. I get up about 4.30, because I have to take a shower in the morning, and I cannot prepare food the night before. I get up, shower, do my hair, get dressed, prepare packed lunches for myself and Heather, do odd things around the house, dusting and so on, maybe make a meal for the evening, though most of my cooking's done ahead on weekends and I'll stick it in the freezer. Then I get the kids up about quarter to six and we're out of the house about quarter to seven. We play a bit while I'm getting breakfast ready, but it's mainly things like Heather's very involved with the baby at this point, or she's helping me get breakfast ready, setting the table and that sort of thing – she's really a help. I drop the baby off first at the sitter's – she'll take children as early as 6.30. Heather's school doesn't open until 7.00 – lots don't open as early as that even. Then at night I pick up the baby at about 5.30 and Heather about quarter to six, then I bring them back and feed them and bathe them and put them to bed. The baby goes to bed at 7.30 and Heather and I have at least half an hour or so. There's not a lot of free time, but Heather and I generally read stories or we'll do something together, or sometimes she just likes being with me – she may be just sitting by me reading a book, and she's very content doing that. Then I'm home three days, and it's just straight family life – I do the cooking, the cleaning and the washing, the ironing, and going to the park and that sort of thing.'

I have already described this type of day at the end of Chapter 1 as seen from the point of view of Pat Verity who runs a British state-run day nursery, and the similarities are striking. I suspect at this point some prospective mothers may be wondering just what they are considering letting themselves in for! There are lots of joys, of rewards – but don't let anyone be misled: single parenting is hard labour, not just for a few weeks or a few months, but for years at a time. I think that to take on such a task and succeed, you need to be somebody rather special.

Actress *Catherine*, who adores her son and is happy with her choice, describes how much she had to put into their relationship when he was small: 'Tiredness was the first real problem I faced. I was doing a play in the West End and Tommy was too young even to go to a nursery school, he was only about 2½, so he was home all day – I'd always give him a really full day because I could only put him to bed myself one night a week, on Sundays, and bedtime seems the most important time of the day, so to compensate for this I'd give him as good a day as I could. By the time it was six o'clock and the lady came to pick him up and take him to her house (which he hated, but I couldn't get anyone to come here) and I had to get in the car and drive to the theatre, I would be feeling very depressed because I wasn't being a good mother or a good actress, I was falling right between two stools. I had a good part, and I needed to give it a lot, but after a whole day of taking Tommy to the park, to the shops, playing with him, all that. . . ! because at that age they need constant attention. I was giving him more attention than normally one would because I felt bad: I'd look at the clock and think, oh, in two hours I've got to leave, so I'd try to compensate for that. Then when I came back from the theatre I'd pick him up and take him home. Fortunately he'd usually stay asleep, but as he got older he'd wake up because he wanted to see me, and then I'd just put him in my own bed: he was so tired, he'd just happily fall asleep. That went on for six months, and I was exhausted. It was an awful patch: I wanted to have a nervous breakdown. It got to the point where I thought, well, how *do* people have nervous breakdowns, because you have to decide; and I thought, who'll have to fix up the mess – I will!

'I'd done one short job when he was six months – it was very brief and good money – my mother had come over from New Zealand and I was doing a bit of filming. We were in the country so my mother was sitting in a field somewhere and they'd put me in a van and drive me to the field and I'd get out my breast and feed him, and they'd pick me up again and I'd go back and do a bit more filming. That was great fun, but I turned down seven or eight other jobs, some of them very good: there was no decision, I just didn't want to do them, I was so happy to play mummy and be with him.'

Some things are easier to fit in with motherhood than others – creativity in the arts is something not many women manage to combine with small babies. *Serena*, the acupressurist, said, 'For a certain kind of creativity nothing takes the place of going inside and being quiet and allowing yourself to feel. I thought, OK, well, I'll put him to bed at night and I'll do something thereafter. I'll sit at my table and see what comes out. I'd start at around nine or ten o'clock, and then I'd forget that I'm tired and I get lost in the process – painting or writing – and already it's three o'clock – and I have to wake up early with him and then work next day, and I'm not clear-headed in the work that I do. But I cannot let myself behave like that; I have to be clear for my daily work – that's equally important.'

The financial aspects of single parenthood
It is obvious by now, I think, how much organization has to go into working out one's new lifestyle once the decision has been made to have a baby. Sufficient money is clearly a necessity. That doesn't have to be as depressing as it sounds – different people have different needs. Some people are perfectly happy clothing their children in hand-me-downs and cast-offs from stalls, understand about diet and know how to make nourishing food from the cheaper basic foods, compensate for cramped living space by taking the child to parks, friends' gardens, etc. – the only problem with this lifestyle is that it is time-consuming and difficult to fit in with regular daily work, and also for success it demands a competent, reasonably serene personality. Another type of woman wants 'the best' for her children – trendy clothing, the 'right' schooling, expensive toys and spacious accommodation. Such mothers have to make sure their income is

going to match their desires, or they will find themselves worn out, depressed and disillusioned. Social welfare, on which some mothers rely, varies tremendously in different countries – we will look more closely at this in a minute – while national attitudes also have a profound effect on people's expectations: what's OK in liberal Amsterdam, for instance, may be very much not OK in Manhattan.

How, then, do single mothers manage? First let us look at the worst off, remembering to bear in mind that the great majority of these did not choose to be single parents. Professor Chambers writes that in 1978 it was found that more than half the total number of children in the USA living in families headed by women with no husband around were living below the official poverty line, and this was *after* benefits from social welfare were counted.[2] In Britain in 1981 there were nearly one million one-parent families, involving 1,600,000 children; one-parent families make up 58 per cent of families with children on supplementary benefit.[3] In an Australian 1975 survey on poverty, Henderson found that one in every three lone-parent families were below the poverty line, and that 'lone mother families were found to have the lowest incomes. By 1979 Henderson found lone parents on benefits were much further below the poverty line [getting only three-quarters of a "survival level" income] than unemployed couples and age pensioners.'[4]

Recent figures on the actual cost of bringing up children, however, seem to bear no relationship to the above facts – they highlight quite horrifying social differences that must exist between children of different backgrounds. American research on divorce points out that few judges have an accurate perception of how much it costs to bring up a child, and that as a result they make insufficient awards to the parent who will have care of the child, usually the mother. This is also partly because they assume that if they award more than 30 per cent of the father's net income it will not be paid, and partly because they are trying to protect the father's future life with, perhaps, another wife and future children, however much his first wife and children suffer as a result. This misunderstanding of how much it costs to raise a child, the researcher points out, is common to many – parents in the middle-income bracket with two children estimated the cost to be 14.7 per cent of their annual income: in fact it was found they were spending approximately 40.7 per cent.[5] In the UK a survey by the Legal and General Insurance group on the cost of parent-hood, published in 1983, showed that 'it costs working parents nearly £70,000 to raise a first child to the age of 16, almost three times the price of the average house in Britain', the loss of the wife's earnings accounting for a large part of this sum. The survey also found that 'only one in seven couples takes financial considerations into account when planning a family'.[6] Single mothers by choice cannot afford to be so thoughtless.

Lynn, with two daughters, points out some of the day-to-day difficulties working single mothers have to face. It might be remembered that one advantage of the school her older daughter Heather attends is that it opens at seven o'clock. 'I love this school, and they go up to eighth grade, and as long as she maintains her grade she can stay there until she's 14. No, I don't know if I'll be able to afford it, but if she goes to public school [American style] what can I do with her when she can't go to school until eight o'clock and I have to be at work at seven? And what do I do with her when she's in kindergarten and she gets out at 11.30 and only goes half a day, and what do I do when she's older and gets out at 3.30 and I'm not back until around six? If she goes to public school I've got to find somebody who will take her early in the morning, who will then take her to school and pick her up and keep her until the end of the day. Or the YWCA has something called the Sunshine group, and you take the child to them in the morning, then they take them to the schools and later pick them up. But I like knowing for sure that Heather is at school and that she's going to be in one place. The quality of this school is excellent and yes, it'll cost me, but so far I've been able to afford it, and the fees will decrease a little bit as she goes into the main school, and when her sister is old enough they'll reduce hers a small amount too as there will be two kids there.'

The great majority of the mothers I interviewed do not

receive money from the fathers of their children, and prefer it that way. They wanted total charge of their children, and accepted that along with this independence went total responsibility. *Janice*, research assistant, who shares and has shared for seven years with her lover, is in a different position, but she has never demanded anything as of right, and their relationship is based on the accepted fact that if they split, Janice has full rights over their child and, with it, responsibility for her upkeep. *Sonia*, who had her third child after abandoning the attempt to defeat her Israeli husband's determination to keep her first two children with him in Israel, eventually after an initially very difficult period became good friends with the father of the new child: 'He lives very close and comes in every other day to see her. It's very nice for her and for me too. He's never given me any money, except a few pounds a week for a brief period. I never saw any point in expecting any, as I knew it wouldn't be reliable. Part of the time I was able to earn money, part of the time I was on social security. They tried to find out who he was, of course, to get maintenance from him, but I didn't tell them, so he was free of that. They pretend to have a legal right to know, but they don't, in fact.'

Catherine, the actress, who hadn't planned to have a child: 'He gives me about £500 a year, which works out to very little, but it helps that he gives it to me in a lump sum.' I asked her if she felt she was losing her independence doing this. 'Hardly – it's quite handy, but it's under £10 a week and that really isn't very much.' I asked her if it made a tie between him and his son. 'Not really. He's so clever at fudging any kind of ties. For all I know he might not ring me again now for ages: once he didn't contact me for a whole year, and the number of times I went to write a note, or pick up the phone not caring if his wife was there, to say what the hell do you think you are doing, because if you say one thing you must honour it. He knew I wasn't the sort of woman who'd fall to pieces and come and camp outside his home and disrupt his life: he knew that when I'd said I would bring up the child on my own that I would be able to cope.'

Charlotte, part-time researcher: 'I do a certain amount

of freelance work, so I have to pay a child-minder when I'm working, but my father gives me a bit of help, so that I feel my rates and so on are secure. I'd like to ask my child's father to give me money, but I never have asked him for any and I undertook to have the baby on the understanding he wouldn't be asked to do anything. He's never said anything, but I knew he'd feel put upon if I asked him – *he* hadn't asked to have the baby, after all, and I wanted very much that he should stay in our life and have a good relationship with the baby, and I knew that the only way to do that would be to be independent of him.'

This attitude was similar to that of other mothers who still saw the fathers – money was not invariably turned down, but independence was what really mattered and anything interfering with that was out of the question. As *Sonia* pointed out, they cannot force it but government agencies, both in the UK and in the USA, will try to persuade a mother to name the father so that he can be pursued for maintenance, not for moral purposes but in order to lighten the loan on the public purse. In the States the federal Child Support Enforcement Program was created in 1975 to pursue this very aim,[7] but there has to be an acknowledged father to be claimed against, and even when there is one it is common knowledge that success in making fathers pay maintenance is very limited. Single mothers by choice, of course, are particularly unlikely to name a father since the whole idea of being dependent on someone is usually repugnant to them.

In some areas the social services provide very good support for single-parent families. Holland, which is also generous with its social security allowances, is one such example. I had been commenting to *Anna* that it had struck me that the Dutch single mothers by choice were mostly younger than their American counterparts, who tended to get their careers thoroughly organized first before getting pregnant. Anna: 'The thing in Holland, I think, is that our social security is so good we can afford to do it even if we don't have a good job, or even if we do have one we can say, OK, we are stopping it for four years or what we want.' A Gingerbread member living in London praised her local social services when I asked her why the Camden Gingerbread group was not as large as some similar groups in other areas: 'It's partly that Camden's got excellent social services. I wasn't married, and from the time I was pregnant I had social services back-up. The first thing they said was you'd better go and see a social worker. I didn't think I needed one but I went to see her anyway, and she found me somewhere to live, booked up a nursery school place from when my baby was four weeks, though I didn't want one that quickly! Most of the nursery schools are also care centres, so if you've got any problems they would help you out. Most single parents in London automatically get an all-day nursery place if they've got a job or they're looking for a job. How much you pay depends on what you earn.'

Pat Verity who runs such a day nursery, however, pointed out that, while in theory social services would like to help all single working mothers, because of the shortage of places there sometimes has to be an additional reason before children can be accepted. Many nurseries also refuse to take babies under a year old: 'But what's happening here is that they offer what's called a day-fostering scheme, and there's also child-minding which people of the kind you're talking about would probably use. The minders are inspected and approved by Camden who limit the number they can look after so they do the job properly. If the mother can't afford a child-minder – it can be about £30 a week – and she's single she can sometimes get financial help.'

For some women the decision whether or not to work can be a difficult one, because in many cases part-time work is the only possibility and it may be that considering the very low rates of pay that most part-time jobs fetch they would be better off staying home and drawing social security, especially bearing in mind that if they earn more than a minimal amount they will lose their social security payments and special allowances. Some mothers don't mind staying at home, others dislike it intensely and, however much they enjoy their children, feel they want to have some life outside the home. But by the time a woman has spent money on clothes suitable for her job, fares, lunches, baby-minders, and forfeited her social security, etc., if she is going to be in pocket she needs a better salary than she is likely to be offered for part-time work.

Let us look at a few statistics. According to the US Bureau of Labor Statistics, 60.5 per cent of all women in the US with children under 18 are working, as against 42.1 per cent in 1970 and 21.6 per cent in 1950. It is now a majority of women with children under 6 who work outside their homes – 52.1 per cent. In 1980 the figure was close to 45 per cent, and only 19 per cent in 1960, and even fewer – 13.6 per cent – in 1950. A report published in 1984 in Britain showed that in 1980 40 per cent of the work force were women, 56 per cent of whom were full-time workers and 44 per cent part-timers, the latter mostly being mothers with young children. In 1950-54 it used to take women on average seven and a half years to return to work after giving birth; by 1975-9 they were going back after three and a half years. Only 20 per cent of full-time working wives had the same or more pay than their husbands, and few had top jobs.[8] The Economic Activity Tables of the British 1981 Census showed that the figures for women part-time workers had fallen to 39 per cent by 1981 while there were only 2 per cent of men part-time workers.[9] They also showed what at first sight seemed to be a triumph for women – the proportion of women in top jobs had nearly doubled in the decade from 1971 to 1981 – but just look at the actual figures: the gigantic leap is from 0.6 per cent to 1.1 per cent. The equivalent figures for men were 4.6 per cent in 1971 and 6.0 per cent in 1981.

It may be remembered that earlier I said that conditions for career women were better in the US than in Britain. This is borne out by the latest American Census Bureau figures which showed that the proportion of women in the executive, managerial and administrative jobs that are traditionally occupied by men rose between 1970 and 1980 from 18.5 to 30.5 per cent. These figures are not directly comparable with the previous British figures because the latter were classified as being in Social Class 1, while the American figures refer to the type of jobs and only a proportion of these women would as yet fall under the classification Social Class 1, but nevertheless the potential is there, which it certainly is not in the case of the vast majority of British working women. Nevertheless, even in the States, Labor Department figures show that the pay of full-time women workers continues to be around 60 per cent of men's pay.[10]

What all these figures boil down to is that women are at present almost inevitably going to earn less money than men of similar intelligence and drive, but if a woman wants to earn a high salary she probably will be able to do so provided she is prepared to make that her aim and to work hard to prepare herself educationally and emotionally, and to resign herself to putting off having children until she is well-established. If she wants, however, to be president of a corporation or chairman of a large company, until a proportion of men are prepared to turn themselves into devoted 'little wives' (one or more of which nearly every male success has) then she had better give over the idea of having a family altogether, unless she is a very unusual woman indeed.

Fortunately, though, women are prepared to put first things first, and are also sufficiently flexible to know that different things come first in your life at different periods of your life. When the time comes most mothers scrape together enough money to stay at home for whatever time they want to have with their child, then back to work they go. If they need extra money, they earn it. *Angela*, graduate student, who had her baby young, has borrowed a large sum of money from the government to see her through her PhD studies: 'Right now I'm working very hard in a bookshop to pay off my debts – I had to borrow a lot extra to do research in France last year. I work in the shop Tuesday through Saturday. I've got a lot of reading to do at present too for my exams, and I'm really tired. I feel a lot of fatigue. I've not been getting as much work done for my PhD as I should, but my supervisor understands my problems. It's money that's the biggest problem – I already have a lot of government loans out, and I've got to get funded to go overseas. But I'll get it. It's worth it. I enjoy the early evening with my son – he doesn't go to bed until around eight, so until then I play with him, we read together, listen to music. After he goes to sleep I get on with my studying. Yes, I do miss out a lot on university life – if I were on campus I'd have more of an opportunity to interact with other students, but as it is. . . . But I'm not the only one – I think in America a lot more of us students have children than in Europe. I know that in Paris I was surprised when I met a student who had a child, it was very much rarer.'

I have not attempted to go into the argument about whether or not women with young children should work at all, because for the mothers I am writing about this question is rarely relevant – they have to work, and that is all there is to it. Some people will answer, yes, maybe single women have to work, but they don't *have* to have children. But since, as my earlier figures have shown, over half of all married mothers with young children are working too, it seems to me this typical comment is beginning to smell of discrimination. It declares that women with a ring on their finger may work *and* have children, women without one may not. The simple fact is the majority of all mothers are having to work nowadays, whether they want to or not. Perhaps children are suffering as a result, perhaps they are not: psychiatrists vary tremendously in what they feel about this question, much has been written on both sides about the effects on children, and all kinds of statistics are being brought forward to prove whatever case the protagonist happens to be arguing. But there are so many things in modern life that one would prefer not to be a background to children's growing up: divorce; violence – local and worldwide; pollution; inflation; unemployment; the ever-present threat of the nuclear bomb . . . *if* mothers have to work, and most do, then isn't it up to psychiatrists and others to work out how best to adapt family life to cope with this, rather than to cry woe! woe! Or perhaps they could spend their energies working out how to tackle the horrors I have just mentioned, beside which a concerned though working mother appears to me to be positively benevolent.

Problems and . . .
Yes, there are problems – no one ever pretended there

weren't. *Pat*, midwife: 'When he was only 3 months old I just looked at this girlfriend one day who'd been a single mother for six years and I knew I couldn't do what she had done. I guess I've always been easily depressed, and I was extremely stressed at that point. I was exhausted feeding him, and I was taking care of my friend's daughter too, though she was at school most of the time. Nothing really terrible happened, but I was just so depressed. I decided I'd had it with this nurturing thing, breast-feeding every two hours, watching Donahue on the television twice a day and game-shows – that's all you can do if you're feeding every two hours! I'd have to go to the post office – we lived out in the country then and a lot of stuff was being sent to me – and the trip took two hours, to get in there, to take him out of the car seat and into the snuggly-pack – then I'd pick up all my packages from the post office, carry them out to the car, get him back in again, and by then he'd be screaming with hunger, so I'd pull off to a park and try to breast-feed him. . . . I wouldn't do it again, I wouldn't breast-feed another one on demand, I wouldn't stick the tit in his mouth every time he screamed, 'cos Josh has shown signs it wasn't good for him – he's very demanding, and when I have another kid I'm going to be more disciplined. I suddenly couldn't take it any more, and so I got myself an interview with a children's hospital where I'd worked before, and I rang up a lesbian mothers' support group that was listed in the yellow pages. That really changed things for me and it all got much better after that.'

Dutch child psychologist *Anna*: 'When Michel was 2 he was the best child in the world – his personality was really kind and you could drop him anywhere, he was used to going with people; but when I gave birth to Sandrine he felt jealous, of course. I was really tired at this period and I didn't have the energy to react right with him. There were times when I didn't like him at all, I really wanted to throw him away, and I hoped an accident would happen to me because it would mean that for a while I would have a rest – I was so tired, so tired. I think it was also the age for him to react to me, to see how far he could go, and he was finding out all the rules of society – so all this came together. I think it is very important you write about this; generally it is taboo to say such things, but these feelings happen. When he was 2 I thought my education of him was so good, it was a dream! I thought I would do it better than all the other women, than my parents, and so on. My God, it was really terrible then. I really went through the worst period of my life. I have never felt so bad.'

Art gallery owner *Frances*: 'I had a master's in child development, so at the point when I thought of having a child of my own I imagined I knew everything there was to know about young children, thought I'm perfect, you know? I have money to take care of my child, I have a master's in child development, this is going to be just fine. I was an absolute set-up for major post-partum depression. Which I had! I was guilt-ridden constantly because I knew everything about how fascinating little babies should be, and I *wasn't* fascinated every minute.' (I asked her if this was because, owing to a Caesarean followed by severe puerperal fever and two months' sickness, she had not seen her daughter for eight days after the birth and wasn't allowed to touch her for a while after that.) 'No, I don't think it was the bonding thing only. It was also that it was all so far from my fantasies, what this perfect experience would be like. I was constantly in pain that I wasn't doing it right, I wasn't bonding, I wasn't nursing, I didn't have her father, I didn't . . . you know? It was a very presumptuous thing to do, the way I went into it. It's not that it wasn't well thought out, because I think my way through everything, but I didn't understand some basic things about the realities of a young child, the demands of a young baby, the fact that I'd been basically very independent for years, and there I was at 32 with this brand new little baby.'

There was also another factor. Frances had been very much in love with the father of her child, but they had mutually agreed it was not possible for them to live amicably together. At this point he had found a woman whom he was eventually to marry. 'When Heather was about 5 months I went into a real depression. I think it was primarily the fact that her father had found someone else, and I was finally coming face to face that I was irrevocably on my own with this child, that he loved Heather and he'd help with her, but that basically it was *my* life, I was alone and nobody else would do it for me. I think it was a combination of responsibility and a loss of all illusions, the reality of not having somebody there who was my mate. She wasn't a difficult child, she was wonderful, and that made me feel even more guilty. I had the perfect child, why was I unhappy?

'One of the hardest things I'm still trying to sort out even now is how much of your life does your kid get, how much right do you have to some of your own life, and what is the balance? At all times I'm aware of the responsibility of a child – that's the hardest thing about being a single parent, I would say. As they get older it doesn't go away. I mean I'm always feeling I should spend more time with her, do more than I do – whether that's true or not I don't know, it's just that it's difficult not to feel guilty if I'm somewhere else.'

The mothers, including Frances, who had made a considered choice to have their child alone, eventually came through any depressions they suffered. Those who had made a less clear choice, or for whom maternity was unintentional, found life more difficult. Jane Mattes of SMC told me she had recently seen a television programme about single mothers, 'and four out of the five women on it were angry, sorry, regretful – I guess they didn't really feel they were doing what they wanted to do. They had chosen more or less – at the time they made a choice, but looking back they felt maybe it wasn't an educated choice, or a wise choice, or they were bitter about the father who they had hoped might be more involved and had let them down. They were disillusioned, disappointed people. What was interesting was that the one woman who was thrilled and happy had had artificial insemination' (which you can hardly do by accident).

I found that the few mothers who gave up work and stayed at home became depressed – they felt tied, too out of touch with the world. *Felicity*, the medical researcher who had expected to marry the father, denied she felt lonely or depressed, but she said in a far from happy voice, 'I don't think I realized it would be such a tying thing, and I thought it was going to be an extension of my life rather than a total commitment to somebody else. . . . I did try to take him out with me several times but I just used to end up in tears and come home again. What I discovered too, much to my amazement, was that I lost a lot of confidence, all my social confidence went. I think it was because I was emotionally drained, and also I suppose just being with other mothers and children, and not ever being able to carry on a proper conversation with the children running around. It's just a completely and utterly different world.'

Most married mothers staying at home will also know this last feeling – I certainly felt it myself – how do you have a semi-serious conversation at a party about philosophy or the latest film when for several days your mind has been occupied with whether it was the right time to move on from one teaspoonful of mashed banana to two? *Jenny*, who at 20 had never meant to get pregnant and who disliked staying at home, eventually rebelled and started part-time work, taking Ben with her: 'I felt so much better – I was alive for the first time in months!' But *Felicity* refuses to leave her child – she is determined to stay at home to look after him 'until he is 7 or 8 and over all the usual childhood illnesses.'

But single mothers by choice rarely opt to stay at home longer than a year at most. Of course they get frustrated and lose their tempers at times like every other parent. *Charlotte*, part-time researcher, said, 'I might as well tell you this because otherwise it all sounds far too rosy. I have hit her occasionally, when I've lost my temper. I've dumped her in her cot and gone away and left her crying – when I say hit her I've slapped her hand, slapped her on the nappy when she won't go to sleep; I've never actually hurt her, but I've occasionally been so angry and annoyed that I've done something stupid, like everybody else, actually. I thought I would be able to take a deep breath and walk away, but my temper does snap – I haven't as much self-control as I thought I had. Last night, for instance, she woke up in the middle of the night, and went to sleep again, then she woke up again and wouldn't go back to sleep, so I put her in my bed rather roughly as if to say if you wake up again this is the treatment you'll get, but she still wouldn't stop crying and I shouted at her to shut up. Of course it didn't work and she cried worse, and in the end I had to change her nappy and so on, and then she went back to sleep in my bed. Sometimes when I'm half asleep and desperate I do shout at her, though it never works – it's just the relief to one's feelings.'

But as *Jane*, lawyer, said: 'I don't have any spare time, things don't get done in my home, I don't read books any more, I can't go shopping for a couple of hours, I don't go out in the evening any more because I'm too tired. All of this is true, but I made the decision to accept all that when I made the decision to be a mother, so it's not that I'm not tired, and it's not that I don't miss reading books and having freedom to go out – I notice it, yes, but I feel OK about it: it's the choice I made for this period of time. I think the most important thing is that at the age I'm at now I feel like an adult, a whole human being, and I don't resent the time I spend with my daughter because that's just what I'm doing *now*, it's just one part of my life – it'll never be my whole life. She's obviously much more demanding now than she'll be in ten or fifteen years, or the demands will be different then, and that'll be OK too.'

... and joys

Theatre director *Carolyn*: 'I'm still in heaven about this. I don't know whether it ever stops – but it's clearly the most wonderful thing I've ever done in my life and puts everything else into a back seat for a while, because she's just a wonder to me.' Afton Blake: 'I don't have the standards of living I had before he was born, and I have a lot of debts, but I can afford anything I need for him, and whatever school I want. I've had to give up some of my earlier lifestyle – you know, wining and dining four times a week, but he's the greatest thing that ever happened to me. I've the feeling I have everything I ever wanted. I'm finally where I want to be.'

Sometimes the joy is outright, as in the two mothers above, sometimes it is a little muted. *Joanna*, graduate student of Third World studies; 'He gives me a reason to finish my work. I don't see how people work for the sake of the work alone – I know some people do it, but I'm not the kind of person who can sit and work eight hours a day, so that for me to have him away in day care for four to five hours a day gives me plenty of time for my work. He is very good company, and very athletic, and that gives me great pleasure. He has a baseball net already and we play catch.' When I asked *Angela*, also a graduate student but twenty years younger than Joanna, if she felt joy in her son she hesitated, then said, 'It's more than that. I feel a lot of pride in my son. The joy was mostly right after I'd had him, the first few months. It's a hard thing for me to say – it's not overwhelming joy, but I do have a lot of pride in him. I feel I'm a good parent, but I wouldn't say I feel extreme joy.'

'*What are the rewards?*' I asked medical researcher *Felicity*. She replied: 'Oh, lots. Real companionship. I do treat him a lot of the time as an adult. We talk a lot, and have tremendous conversations. Luckily he is very eloquent. He could say a few words at 7 months, and I've always talked to him a lot. He's also got a tremendous sense of humour. He teases me tremendously. He's now becoming quite a mimic, which amuses me a lot. He mimics advertisements on television, things I do or things I say that I don't realize I'm saying. And just seeing things through a child's eyes – it's me rediscovering the world as much as anything. I notice a lot more now than I did before, just pointing it out to him. I can appreciate things more. I suppose companionship is one of the main things.'

I have already reported some of the pleasures museum curator *Elizabeth* finds in her son; she also added, 'Since he's been about 8 the pleasures have far outweighed any problems – I mean he's a really nice companion now to have around, to spend time with, to go and do things with.' *Stella* and *Jan* had no doubts either – I can just hear what they are saying through the chuckles and giggles their baby son is making: 'We've said over and over again to each other that having Gene has been the best decision we've ever made.'

And finally I can't resist quoting again some of what *Charlotte* said about the joys: 'It's wonderful, it's lovely – I've never regretted it for a moment. To begin with, after she was born, it was very like what I imagine a very very nice love affair must be like. . . . It was the interaction between us that was so nice – the fact that she was there and I was here and yet we were both absolutely together.'

Later, discussing the future, she said, 'So far I've coped with every stage happily – each time I've thought, well, I can cope with this stage but what on earth am I going to do when – when she learns to walk and talk? But now I think how on earth did I manage when she was a boring baby and did nothing but bawl? But at the time I thought it was absolutely wonderful. I *do* worry a bit about being able to cope with the next stage, with things like asking about God, but I will probably know what to say when the moment arrives. The problems now at 1½ are not at all what I envisaged they would be when I was worrying about it when she was 9 months old, and the exciting things are much more exciting than I thought they would be – talking and thinking and watching her pass through all that – it's absolutely wonderful, and I didn't envisage it at all. I didn't foresee it would be such fun. I thought it would be more ordinary, but instead it's terribly moving.'

Appointing guardians
An important thing to consider very early on is who will look after the child should anything happen to you. It is not a welcome thought but it is one that must be faced. It would probably be sensible to sort this out before the baby is born, but talking with mothers who have appointed guardians it seems that most of them waited until their lives had settled down and they knew more clearly who their friends were and what they wanted for their children. Some mothers appointed siblings, most chose friends. Research assistant *Janice*, still living with her child's father in a long-standing relationship, wisely made him the official guardian, because if she were ever to have an accident he would not necessarily be allowed to look after his own daughter as unmarried men

have no rights over their own children (see the section 'Men's rights over their children' in Chapter 3 for details). This is something that all mothers ought to be aware of – it does not follow that someone who is living with you, has cared for the child, may even be the natural father, and wants in the case of your death to continue to look after it, will be permitted to do that. When you have finally made your choice of who is going to be the guardian or guardians you should consult a lawyer or your local Law Centre or Citizen's Advice Bureau on how to set about legalizing guardianship.

Having a legal guardian can be helpful in giving the child extra security. There is no need when the child is young to explain this relationship, but the guardian is likely to take an extra interest in someone who just possibly one day may become his or her ward, though usually the person is made a guardian just because this extra interest is existent already. Psychoanalyst *Stephanie*: 'The possibility of having a father substitute is something I felt very strongly about. Danny's legal guardian is also his godfather, so when people are in the house visiting for the first time after he gets to know them he drags them over to Michael's picture in our living room, and says, "This is Michael, he's my godfather – that's a special kind of father." I've been building that in ever since he was old enough to know what the word daddy meant. It's important you have somebody like a daddy who does the kind of things daddies do, who loves you the way a daddy would, and who will always be there for you. Michael takes care of my son every Thursday when I work for about four hours, then he has dinner with us. Occasionally we all go away on weekends together – he and his wife are my oldest friends. He got to know Danny at the beginning – he was not sure about how much involvement he wanted, but they grew to really love each other, and his status is now legal guardian. They're real old friends, we all go and celebrate the holidays together – it's like an extended family.'

Research assistant *Janice*, in addition to making the actual father a legal guardian, has been building up what she refers to as an extended family where she lives 'with close friends, women and men – for instance, there's one couple who are just about to have their baby. Hopefully we will do a lot of sharing child care between all of us, and my daughter already goes and stays overnight there and is sometimes looked after by them for weekends. There's another friend too who has a little boy – I'll look after him one day a week or take him away for the weekend and vice versa. I suppose we all see ourselves as the potential guardians or refuges for those children if anything should happen to their parents.'

Theatre director *Carolyn*'s chosen guardians take their connection very seriously: 'I had five friends with me at the hospital – it was fantastic, and two of them I made her guardians later. It's not an idle commitment for them – they say the chances of something happening to me and their having to take the kid into their house is so tiny that that's not the present reality of the commitment they've made. They see the fact they've committed themselves to be her guardians as having a meaning now while I'm alive, and they want to be an important part of this kid's life.' '*How do they do it?*' 'By being a family, that's the best way to describe it. I'm an only child so she doesn't have any uncles or cousins, and they see her every week or couple of weeks. Since they don't have any children of their own yet, they see it not as something they're doing for the baby, but as something they're doing for themselves. They're getting a great deal of pleasure out of being committed to this child.'

Rosa, the Dutch specialist in child psychology, made Dirk, the friend who looks after her son regularly, the legal guardian in her will (though she is not quite certain what would happen should she die because the child's Greek father who has registered his birth in Greece may conceivably be able to counter Dirk's claim). Most of the mothers felt it important the guardian should get to know the child well, but since they are usually close friends or relatives this is inevitable, anyway. The real fathers, except in Janice's exceptional case, are not made guardians. Languages teacher *Sarah*'s attitude is very straightforward: 'A married couple, very close old friends of mine, are her official guardians, not her father. Peter's down as the father on her birth certificate, yes, but I wouldn't let him be a guardian unless he were prepared to be a really properly responsible guardian, and he isn't. I would happily give him his rights, but he has to deserve them, he has to really earn them, and he won't do that. He never will, I know that.'

What chance of a new lover?

For mothers with young babies or small children the answer to that question was generally a groan and protests of when! how on earth! I'm too exhausted! But as children get a little older the energy and the desire returns. Art gallery owner *Frances*'s daughter is 9 now: 'I wonder what effect the relationships I've had with men will have on her, though. I've never cycled them through very rapidly – the shortest has been about three months, but the longest have been two to four years. I'm quite stable, it's not like her saying, who's going to be in mummy's bed tonight? Recently she's been able to figure out what's going on, who's sleeping with mummy and what that means. I don't think it's been a problem for her – what it has forced me to do is to talk to her honestly about what I think relationships are about, and to talk a little bit about sexuality. I mean I can't take the line that you fall in love and get married and that's the only person you ever sleep with dear, right? I hope she'll be responsible in terms of having relationships. Mine have all been serious, and they've been men who've also formed relationships with her, and who have all stayed friends and become part of what is quite a large circle of friends.'

Languages teacher *Sarah*, on the other hand, whose daughter is 4 now, said, 'Impossible! Absolutely impossible! Because you don't have the time, you don't have someone to look after the child, you don't have the energy, and also because it take a very generous man to want to be bothered with somebody else's child. There was one very brief affair – it was very nice after two and a half years having a short-lived affair, but it didn't last. Sophie was already calling her father daddy, she knew quite clearly Peter was her daddy, but at that age, $2\frac{1}{2}$, it was no worry for her to find a friend in my bed, it was all very natural to her. But now she is older it would worry me, I would be much more discreet.'

Afton Blake: 'I have a relationship with a man who stays weekends, and he loves Doron a lot. But my real difficulty is that my energies are really with Doron, I don't have a whole lot of interest in courting or dating, or what you have to do in the beginning of a relationship – it's a lot of work! – and I don't really feel like putting a lot of work into that, but I'm sure that in about a year I will.'

Charlotte, part-time researcher, also feels not quite ready yet: 'I don't have a sexual relationship with anybody at the moment, and it's quite hard to set one up if you're a single parent – I haven't so far even really bothered to think about it. I'm just beginning now to think there's room in my life for it and that I would quite like to share my bed with somebody else other than her – it interested me that it took so long. When she was very small it was so fulfilling – I don't mean one had orgasms or anything, but it was so terribly nice and cuddly and warm and gorgeous that I didn't feel any sexual loss. I have a feeling that some people who don't have children might sleep with people to get that, even when they don't terribly want the sexual part of it.'

Meeting new men isn't easy, even if you're not as unsure of yourself as medical researcher *Felicity* is: 'I just don't feel up to making a relationship with anybody. For one thing I'm terrified I'd be hurt again – that's a big part of it, and the other thing is I don't have the confidence. I don't want to go through all those emotional meetings and the wooings again; no, I'm not prepared for it. I think I could just about now go into a roomful of strangers and go up and talk to somebody, but earlier, no, I couldn't have. I was Robert's mother, I wasn't *me*. I hid behind him to a certain extent. I don't think I'll ever be the old me, the same me again.' *Rosa*: 'But where do you meet men anyway? You only meet people with children. I meet fellow students, of course, but they lead a different life – I have to get up early and go to bed early, they do the opposite to that. I don't know how to fix it now to meet men – I don't go to the places or do the things I used to do to meet men.'

Lynn, the nurse with two daughters, had tried to answer this problem before she became pregnant and was still looking for a relationship in a way that is beginning to gain popularity, but she won't try it again, 'even if I had the time, which I don't – I'm so busy at work at the moment anyway, and I barely have the time to get through what I have to do at home, with looking after the house and the children. But when I reached 32 I had got to the point where nobody was out there who wasn't married already, and since I've never been one to go to clubs or bars or socials to meet men I tried going through the scene of computer dating and dating services and whatever, and I just met the pits! the absolute pits! and I decided that was the only kind of man I was going to meet that way. Many people did meet some nice people, but I have never met anybody I'd want to bring back home!'

Actually meeting men is not the only problem: forming new relationships when you have a child at home can be very complicated. Dr Elphis Christopher, talking mainly about mothers who had become pregnant unintentionally, made a point that can also be relevant for single mothers by choice: 'When they make new relationships it raises quite a conflict. They may eventually meet a man with whom they can work something out, but the mothers can get into a very defensive position about the child. Either that child can be rejected – it may go into care – or they become ultra-possessive, hanging on to it and not allowing the man to actually be a father in any sense of the word. I've worked in the field now for seventeen to eighteen years and I've seen these girls in their adolescence, early twenties, going into their thirties now. I was thinking especially of a woman I saw the other day who had got married to another man, and his complaint against her was, she won't let me be a father to the child. I've heard that said an awful lot of times. She admitted, "I'm very possessive with him, I don't want my husband to tell him off, he's *my* child." That's what I mean about the symbiotic mother/baby thing – it's a nice sort of closed circle but when you've actually got to open it up and share it some way, how do you do that?'

David told me both how it felt to be a child in a single-parent family, and a man pursuing a woman with a hostile child. His father had left home when David was 10, though he continued to keep in touch occasionally: 'but we didn't have a real role model, so if my mother had a boyfriend who'd teach us boxing we thought that terrific. Any man that came to the house we immediately attached to if he was at all a *man* and could teach us boxing or something like that. But a lot of the men who came we didn't like, and my brother and I would give him a really rough time, because for better or worse we were loyal to our father. I remember one chap who used to boast about being in the Royal Air Force in the war as a flyer and was given all sorts of medals, and we twigged immediately it was all bullshit, you see, and we'd ask him these nasty questions and destroy his whole thing, and then tell mother.

'Then I had the same thing played back to me when I was dating a woman in the States back in the sixties. She had this little boy of 3 who used to drive me up the wall – he was terribly precocious, like a little old man, and she'd never wanted to marry the father but she was obviously insecure as all these women were then (they were mostly divorcées), because they really needed a man, a home and so on. So the child had this double role, not only of being the child but also of being the father, the one who looked after mummy. Also he was very competitive, he was instantly hostile to you as a possible father, a competitor for the mother's attention, so one of the worst problems was to have a decent relationship with *both* of them. In fact it might have been wise to woo the child first!'

It was reported to me several times that little girls especially tended to hang around men visitors, and occasional embarrassing questions might be asked. *Sonia*: 'I had a friend whose daughter was in therapy for a while, because every man who came to the house was a potential daddy and it got to be rather embarrassing for everybody – you know, "Are you going to be my daddy" or "Why don't you stay?" – this little child was clinging to all the men. She's better now, but the mother is in a quandary because she's had a living-in relationship with a man for two years, and she doesn't know if she wants it to go on, but she feels very tied since she knows, or thinks she knows, what it will do to the child if she broke it off.'

But it is not only girls who occasionally cause a blush.

Actress *Catherine*: 'Tommy likes having men around – he went through a period when he was younger of asking men if they'd like to stay – somebody came to fix the stove once and he asked him, "Are you going to stay in mummy's bed tonight?"! It's the one thing that upsets his father when Tommy asks him if he's going to stay with mummy tonight – Tommy likes us to be together, but his father hasn't been able to stay for ages. Yes, occasionally there've been other men – I had an affair with a man for about six months, and Tommy loved it because he had this huge house and a beautiful big garden. Tommy liked him a lot – he was a strong sort of man and used to tell Tommy off sometimes and Tommy quite enjoyed that, he liked somebody taking responsibility for him like that. But if I meet a man casually I much prefer to go to his place. If a man comes here I want Tommy to get to know him, because this is his home and my home and I think it wouldn't be fair for him to come up to my bed one morning and find a total stranger there. When he knows a man he loves bounding up in the morning to see him – he doesn't get jealous at all. In one way I wish I had met someone, because he'd be delighted – he loves walking between two adults, for instance, even with a girlfriend he loves it.'

Museum curator *Elizabeth*, whose relationship with her son's father, John, has continued at a deep level through the years, found that the two males already in her life made further relationships very difficult, although both she and John, the father, still fervently believe in the 1960s 'open' lifestyle. 'There have been other men, yes, but I think it would have upset my son if he knew I'd slept with them, I mean if he came in in the morning and found someone else there. So I try to make sure that nothing much happens in the home, you know? Yes, it certainly does make it difficult to develop a relationship with another man. I think if John didn't come regularly then perhaps I would have blinded on regardless – but John feels very much that this is a place where John, David and Elizabeth operate, and the introduction of a wild cell, as it were, would not be very fruitful. This has made for a very difficult period between us – there was a very old friend I wanted to see again, and what we finally settled was that if I wanted to see him it had to be when David wasn't here. It's a working compromise, I suppose, but had it been left entirely to me I would have done it differently. I think kids accept a relationship – David's going to have to accept it one day – I mean, you can't conceive a child in a certain lifestyle that you then deny. If you actually believe in open relationships, which I do, and which John does, then you can't shut it all out. I don't really want to discuss all of this, but yes, it was a very difficult time for all of us. I had to accept what John wanted in the end.'

Finally, there is one very important point several of the mothers made – that having a child had changed them, had made them more sympathetic and understanding to other people. I want to emphasize that they did not have children *in order* to 'grow', but almost any woman – married or single – finds that she becomes more whole, less self-centred, after she has had children – motherhood is a process that rubs off a lot of the spikiness of youthful selfishness. The result is that they become less demanding of men, more able to take other people as they come. Marilyn Fabe: 'The interesting thing I found with many of my friends is that the experience of having a child finally enabled them to get married. They were maybe 35, 38, 40 – had had one affair after another with impossible men, and they finally decided to go ahead and have a child. There's one friend in particular who met someone two months after she was pregnant, at eight months pregnant she married him – she is still with him and they're fighting it out. There are problems but she made an accommodation with him, she was able to live with someone, and somehow the experience of having her child has opened her up in a sense to the understanding of the give and take you need with another person, and it facilitated her making a marriage. I think it's fascinating that the experience of having a baby might help you work through problems you may have psychologically in finding intimacy with other people – you might have been afraid of it, say, or you're afraid of being overwhelmed or overtaken, but once you've had that experience with a child and you find your ego is whole and your integrity as a person is still there, you can be more venturesome and able to risk more.'

Letting go

Dr Elphis Christopher: 'I'm worried about the mothers not letting go of their children. You say they know about this, they're prepared for it, but always when you have a child you say I'm never going to make the mistakes my mother did with me, or I'm never going to do this, that or the other, but lo and behold you damn well do. It's the unconscious, and you can't control it.'

Not quite true. You can't control the emergence of certain feelings, but you *can* sometimes succeed in controlling how you handle them. And mothers have a long training in letting go. I remember the shock – and yes, jealousy – that I felt the day my 3-year-old son came home from his new nursery school and with dramatic gestures acted out for me a nursery rhyme I didn't know – 'Incy Wincy Spider climbing up the spout'. The point is, he was teaching *me* something I had never heard before, and I realized that until that moment he had never made a single comment or gesture the origin of which I did not know. I had taught him all his rhymes, my husband or myself had told him every story he knew (we refused to have television in those days), I was with him when he played with friends – I knew *everything* about him. Now I was faced not just with Incy Wincy Spider but the sudden realization that, from now on, the outside world would turn my son into a new person, an autonomous person who would not only be influenced by others but who would also have his own original thoughts, deductions. Of course at an intellectual level I had known this would happen in the future, had even looked forward to it with interest, but at that moment the pride I felt in his little achievement was certainly mixed with a large dose of sadness, regret and, yes, momentary jealousy that others now had an important place in his life.

All mothers I spoke to felt that their own liking for independence plus, in most cases, their involvement in their careers would help them to let their children go free when the time came. Karin Meiselman: 'I'm somewhat prejudiced towards career women myself, being one, but I do think that a woman who has discovered herself as an individual and also as a member of the working community has that basic knowledge that even when she's lost the immediacy of the motherhood role there's plenty out there for her – it won't feel like the empty nest situation so much.' *Jane*, lawyer: 'I think because my whole life will never be invested in her, because there'll always be other things in my life, it'll be OK. I'm not silly enough to think I know exactly how I'm going to feel as the years go by, but when you do it as an adult who already has a sense of self, that is not going to get lost in a child – it's much easier to recognize she's going to grow up and be a separate adult human being. I kind of look forward to that, actually, to having an adult mother/child relationship.'

Afton Blake: 'It's one of the strong reasons for having a second child – at least the energy would be divided, I can't say I don't worry about that myself. Doron's become so important to me and he's so close to me – I think he's much closer to men than many children are to their mothers who are married. I shall have to be real careful with myself and with him. But at least as a psychologist I'm aware of the danger and will make sure it doesn't happen.'

'*Other mothers say their careers will help them let go.*'

'Careers help, of course, but I don't think a career is a significant other – it's a very different energy that you put into your career and what you put into your significant others. But yes, it's a great deal better than not having one at all.'

Psychoanalyst and therapist *Stephanie*: 'If I let him make or break my day, or his successes are my successes to an extreme, or his failures make me enraged with him, that's when I realize I have to watch myself carefully. Most of us in SMC are extremely introspective, conscientious about what we do, and we have that awareness. . . . I know letting go is going to be very hard. I also know that that's my job. It would be terrible if my child was not able to separate from me, if I hadn't done a good enough job for him to go off happily.'

Elizabeth, museum curator, with her 10-year-old son,

has already had experience of letting go, and feels confident about where she stands. 'I don't think I'll have any problems, partly because I've always encouraged him to go away – he's been on one of those Colony holidays and things like that. Having been brought up in a boys' school I've seen the effects on children of mothers not letting go; I'm aware of the problems there can be. The thing is I've got lots of life myself, and I get pleasure out of his independent life anyway, I mean I like him feeling independent, I like him doing things which I haven't done which he then tells me about.'

I certainly felt that the great majority of mothers I spoke to would cope successfully with this final act of letting go – one or two may have problems, but then there are also plenty of married mothers who when the time comes are unable to let their children grow away into independent adults without a bitter, even traumatic, struggle on both their parts.

How other people react

Most people take it all in their stride. Here and there mothers have come across outright objectors, but not very often. Medical researcher *Felicity*: 'There's only one person, a friend of my mother's, who's totally ignored me – she's a woman who's never had children – but everybody else has gone on speaking to me and treated me very well, including my mother's friends apart from that one.' *Catherine*, actress; 'I've not really met people anywhere who don't accept it, and I think that's because I myself didn't think there was anything wrong in having a baby without a relationship, and so they accepted it too. I think if you feel unsure of something, or you look for disapproval, you'll find it. Some people do seem to need to cover it up for their own sakes – for example, in the hospital they insisted on calling me Mrs X, and I said, it's Miss X, but they wouldn't change. I don't want to disturb people from whatever they think's important, so I correct them occasionally, but I don't make a fuss about it.'

Within the family it is usually fathers who are the most

difficult, but as I wrote elsewhere, once the grandchild is born family pride takes over and peace is usually restored. *Anna*, Dutch child psychologist: 'In our group some women didn't dare to tell their parents – they just found out when they began to grow big. For me, I wrote a long letter to my parents telling them about it, and I said, either you can accept it or you can't, and if you cannot accept me with the baby I'm not coming any more back home, because it really is a choice of my heart, and I am really glad about it. So I hope you will respect it, and you will have me and also your first grandchild.

'My mother reacted very well – she understood why I wanted to do it. But my father was really angry – he said it was something he could have expected from me because I was the only girl from my village to leave and go to study at the university. I was 27 when I was pregnant, and 28 when I had Michel. My father was really angry I could do that to him, that he had to tell all the people in his village that his daughter was going to be an *unmarried* mother, and it wasn't even an accident, she did it by choice! But my mother said, OK, she is our daughter and she is staying our daughter; but she didn't feel comfortable about it because of how people in the village would talk about it.' But in the end all was well: 'My mother now feels good about my situation because she really likes my children and she sees I am well, and my father is really proud of his grandchildren. But at first it was really terrible for them; older people might accept it but they don't understand it and they don't feel well with it.'

In graduate student *Angela*'s case the opposite happened – it was her father who accepted it: 'When I called him he said, well, it's about time. But my stepmother didn't like it a bit – she's French Canadian Catholic, but anyway they've split up now.' Her lover's father had religious objections too. 'Ben's father is very evangelical, and he comes to visit me once in a while to try to save my soul by getting me to marry Ben – they'd love that, but I won't. They're very good grandparents, though.' Theatre director *Carolyn*'s parents didn't so much object as worry about her, her father especially: they worried about how she'd manage, about her health. 'But now they are like every stereotyped grandparent, they're bursting with pride, showing the baby off to strangers on the street.'

There were one or two out-and-out objectors. *Nora*, who is awaiting the birth of the child she and her lover are adopting: 'My family is practically disowning us – my mother is a hundred per cent unsupportive on every level to the point of threatening not to have anything more to do with me again – it's the combination of our lesbianism, our adopting a child, and adopting a child of a different race at that! Ninety-five per cent of it is what her friends and neighbours will say, but my mother is doing everything she can to make it all absolutely miserable. I mean she sends terrible letters and makes horrible phone calls. I think my mother is going to be one of the most difficult emotional situations our child will have to face in terms of racism and rejection. On the other hand Adina's mother is a hundred per cent supportive, and the child will know that.' *Adina*: 'That's right. I don't know what my father will come out with – they're divorced – he's just not talking about it; but my mother and sisters are beside themselves: they just can't wait.'

In general it was, not unexpectedly, the older generation who had problems accepting the situation. *Mary*, children's nurse, vividly describes the reactions of various groups of people, which were similar to that found by many other mothers: 'The only person I had to take aside and sit down and have a big decision with was my grandmother. My parents had separated when we were really young, and my grandparents took us and more or less raised us. My grandmother was 70, and I knew she was going to be the most difficult person. Funnily enough she didn't really react when I first told her, and I thought, gee – 'cos I'd expected ranting and raving and carrying on – but she never really said anything. It turned out she was in shock, because next day she called me up, and said *get rid of it*! She said, you can't have this baby, do something about it.

'For her the pregnancy was the most difficult thing, all the way through. She didn't want me to come to the church on Sundays because she didn't want to have to explain it to

the people at church – she's a very conservative woman. I
think it was mostly that I was pregnant and not married that
worried her, but it was the way I'd chosen to do it too. I
explained to her that I could have gone out and gotten
pregnant, but if you don't know anybody the only
alternative is to go into some bar or something, and then,
you know. . . . But this way at the sperm bank they screen
the donors, they have counselling, they have a complete
physical check and the men's history, and I thought I can't
get much closer to perfect than that. Whereas if I went and
picked somebody up, who knows what I'm going to get
into? I used that explanation to her, but I don't know. . . .
But relatives said, just wait, just wait until the baby's born,
she'll make a total turn-around – and that's exactly true, she
absolutely dotes on him now, she just dotes on him.

'Just before I was getting close to the due day she
started telling people, and yes, she told them how I'd done
it. When my grandmother told her next-door neighbour –
she knew us really well, her children and us we'd all grown
up together – she went straight home and called me on the
phone and said, I think it's *terrific*! So my grandmother,
she's getting all these very positive responses that she never
expected. She expected people to be ashamed and to look
down on her, and be terribly upset, but people haven't
reacted like that at all. She told her friends at church, she
told the minister, and a couple of people came up to her and
said, oh my daughter's interested in doing something like
that, maybe she could talk to her – she couldn't believe it, all
these people taking it like that. I was surprised myself at the
reaction at the church – it's Presbyterian, and I thought
they'd have a hard time dealing with it, so I'd better stay
away. But the minister came to visit me in hospital after I'd
had the baby, and afterwards I went to the church and
everybody came up to me and said lovely things. I was really
surprised – I thought I'd be cold-shouldered, you know?

'So my grandmother was the only one who had to make
a big adjustment to it – everyone else has been really
supportive. She said something just before I had the baby –
she's a fairly religious woman – she said, "One thing I'm
going to be sorry for is that I'm not going to see you in

heaven." And I said to her, "How do you know I'm not going to see you in heaven? The Virgin Mary's parents weren't very thrilled when she came home and told them that she was pregnant, either." She just kind of looked at me. . . .'

8
The children, and more about men

'There are a lot of qualities about our men friends that are very good – they're sensitive, they're uninhibited, not into the macho thing where they have to prove they're tough, and I would like our son to know that he can cry and still be a male, he can be sensitive and still feel he's himself, still feel good about being a boy. We're not raising our son up in an isolated kind of lifestyle, saying that all people live like this or trying to give him an unrealistic view of family life that is different from what society says it should be. . . . I would like for him to know that people are different from each other, and live differently, and not to be judgmental about how people live.' (Jan)

'What you live is the strongest message you give: whatever a mother says has no weight in relation to what she is living. And I think it is a tragic message to give to your children, that marriage is too much of a hassle.' (Hendrike Vande Kemp)

'I do think it is a distinct disadvantage of this sort of family you're researching that there isn't a father around, I think it's really desirable to learn how to relate to an adult male when you're growing up. . . . On the other hand I think there are lots of things worse than the plain absence of a father. A number of my clients have been from situations where the father deserted the family, or were divorced with the father never taking any interest in the kid, never coming round. I've known women who tried to approach the father from time to time to try to win some love and attention from him, and maybe got a vocal response but no real interest, and that to me is a heck of a lot worse than not having a father in the first place. There's a feeling of rejection and abandonment in that kind *of situation, a knowledge that their father simply doesn't want them.'* (Karin Meiselman)

'He's very glad I'm not threatening his marriage or his family situation, but at the same time he's very upset about it – there is this aspect that he feels the child is part of him and yet he's not going to have any part in its life.' (Laura)

The effect on children

In a book of this nature it is inevitable that everything overlaps with everything else. Children have appeared in these pages many times and comments on their present or future well-being have already been made. But here I want to isolate out the effects on the children of living in single-mother-by-choice families, looking at the children rather than at their mothers.

First of all I must make it clear that at the moment it is impossible for anyone to predict how the children will grow up, because there has never been such a situation before among middle-class educated women. Even 10-year-old children are not fair examples because ten years ago when they were tiny it was still unusual to live in a single-parent or reconstituted family and it was still very unusual for single middle-class mothers to deliberately choose to have a child: they were exploring a new way of life, and like all pioneers they mostly had to suffer a more pronounced social disapproval than today's mothers.

When they go to primary school these children of single mothers presently aged 2 or 3 will find that perhaps half their peers are also from families other than the traditional nuclear family, that more than half the other mothers work just like their own mothers do, and that instead of being a very unusual kind of animal they are merely a part of the herd. Very importantly, they will not feel themselves grossly different from their peers, nor will their mothers be made to feel like Jezebels or way-out weirdos. The children's situation will probably never be thought of as totally 'normal' because I think most people will continue to search out relationships and live in couples, but neither will they find themselves oddities to be treated differently from others.

Therefore I think because the whole situation is so new no one can predict whether these children will be in toto better or worse off for their background, or whether the advantages and disadvantages will balance out, leaving other more personal factors to be the major influences in the development of their personality. I found when talking to some psychiatrists that they would automaticaly trot out statistics and findings from old studies, but when I pointed out that the background of the genuinely disadvantaged children from single and broken families who had not done well in these earlier various tests was very different from that of the children I was discussing, they mostly accepted this objection, though some still felt very dubious about the outcome.

Mothers reading this section, then, cannot expect any definitive answers to the question they will be asking themselves – what effect will doing this have on my child? I can only quote what various people have said to me during the course of my research, and hope that they will find the following helpful when making their own decisions.

First, the objections. Hendrika Vande Kemp had just commented that children should grow up in a meaningful relationship, and when I referred back to the American one in two divorce figures, she answered, 'The research is only just beginning to come in, and it is very sobering – it's showing that divorce is very destructive to the mental health of children. OK, your mothers don't have divorce problems, but there are others – if the single woman is a professional, who is going to take care of her child while she's at work? I think the prognosis for that child would be very gloomy.'

'But over half all the mothers of children under 6 are working now.'

'But why make that choice? The theroetical literature around now makes it clear to me – don't do it. Another thing, in order for a child to develop any decent sense of identity they need to have both of their parents around and not five different men living with mummy, and they need to have a constant presence during the early years of their life.

You're teaching a child there is not room for a full relationship with two adults and a child at the same time. You're modelling that there's only room for one parent and a child, there's not room for another adult relationship. What you live is the strongest message you give: whatever a mother says has no weight in relation to what she is living. And I think it is a tragic message to give to your children, that marriage is too much of a hassle.'

I asked her about a worry of my own: small children can be amazingly responsive to parents' needs, so that even if a mother does her best to keep her own uncertainties and lonelinesses to herself, might not some children find themselves nurturing their mothers rather than the other way round? 'Yes. This leads to all the different things you see as a therapist. I think one of the key issues in people who have personality disorders – as opposed to neuroses – is that they are unable to make real relationships that are good, reciprocal relationships. They are either scared to death of commitment, or they are so afraid of being alone that they smother other people, and I think children who are asked to be parents to the parents wind up with those kind of relationships. They don't know what a good healthy relationship is that gives and takes.'

Karin Meiselman, asked the same question, had similar fears: 'Yes, one of the main dangers is that the parent is going to turn the child into a little spouse. If you have a really needy parent they may start relying on the child to supply all their emotional goodies – I'm not meaning to say there would be any sexual component in this, but sometimes there is. Single mothers will on occasion sleep with their little boy, getting a lot of physical warmth out of him, and that tends to be very disturbing to kids. I'm talking about any single-parent family, whether it's a mother or a father bringing up the child, and divorced or never married.

'I do think it is a distinct disadvantage of the sort of family you're researching that there isn't a father around, I think it's really desirable to learn how to relate to an adult male when you're growing up. You can make up for some of it by relating to male role models – schoolteachers, cub scout leaders, friends and so forth, but I think kids will probably wish they had a daddy like other kids they know. There's no denying that's a disadvantage.

'On the other hand I think there are lots of things worse than the plain absence of a father. A number of my clients have been from situations where the father deserted the family, or were divorced with the father never taking any interest in the kid, never coming round. I've known women who tried to approach the father from time to time to try to win some love and attention from him, and maybe got a vocal response but no real interest, and that to me is a heck of a lot worse than not having a father in the first place. There's a feeling of rejection and abandonment in that kind of situation, a knowledge that their father simply doesn't want them.'

Psychotherapist Dr Alice Fennessey is quoted in *New York* magazine as saying, 'One of the negative aspects of single mothering is that the relationship . . . can become overly symbiotic . . . [the child] tries to second-guess her underlying emotional needs and becomes a surrogate husband. This tends to backfire in adolescence, when the teenager begins to resent the mother for placing such unfair demands.'[1] Jane Mattes, founder of SMC, herself puts forward another related problem in the November/-December 1983 issue of the SMC newsletter: 'A potential problem can be the lack of emotional separateness when the mother looks at a child to meet her own needs, especially those that a spouse might meet, or the child may be seen as an extension of the mother rather than as a separate person. Too much oneness is very frightening to a child (who may worry about being lost in or taken over by his mother) and can be as anxiety-provoking as the fears stirred up by separateness. . . . When there's no one (else) there the child is likely to have a greater struggle with the mother during the $1\frac{1}{2}$ to 3-year-old phase of establishing separateness – where mother ends and toddler begins (saying no, testing limits, autonomy of decision-making).'

Among the older children I met this did not seem to be a problem, in fact, if sturdy independence in public was anything to go by. Museum curator *Elizabeth*'s 10-year-old son Alex is a very friendly, pleasant boy and I was amused when after he had gone to bed and I was interviewing her she told me the following little anecdote. 'He's a very intelligent boy, very highly strung, and he flies off the handle easily, but most of his friends are far more tolerant of him than I am. When he started school his teacher found him difficult, but I found out it was because she wasn't prepared to "take lip" from a 4½-year-old. He was the only child in the playgroup to tell his leader to fuck off – he's not at all aggressive, but it never occurred to him not to answer back! But actually that little incident with the playgroup leader made him friends with all the rest of the village, the word got round, and all the old village people, like the blacksmith and so on, they thought this was just the ticket, they thought it was absolutely hilarious.'

Catherine, actress, said about her 5-year-old son, 'He's a very balanced boy, he gets on very well with other kids. Once they go to school you begin to have some measure of how they are, because you see them with other children. It's a little local school just up the road, and it's very mixed, which is really good. What's interesting is that he's worked his way through the children who're middle-class like himself, and he's ended up with only black friends because they're the most lively, you see. The others were nice little boys and I met their parents and so on, but they just didn't have enough spirit, they were a bit quiet and one of them had every fad in the world – Tommy just finds the black kids much more fun.'

I think it is very important for the mothers to get over a positive attitude to their children's teachers. The effect of expectation among teachers is well known, and there has been some interesting Australian research (1982) which showed that when the researchers' tests were carried out on schoolchildren in a number of schools and then compared with the rating their own teachers had given them, the so-called 'intact' children did better than the 'disadvantaged' (single-parent family) children to a more marked degree in the teachers' ratings than in the research tests. This surprised the researchers since the teachers' own tests were geared to the individual schools (each of which has a restricted range of abilities), while the researchers' tests 'are designed to be valid across schools and would normally be expected to be more responsive to home background influences' (i.e. they expected the opposite results). 'The tests have a higher level of statistical reliability than the teachers' ratings, which would make the tests more discriminating. It could then be that some teachers are inclined to under-rate the one-parent children's attainments because of an expectation effect.' The more the researchers looked into the differences between the results, the more evidence they found that it was partly due to the teachers' expectations – as they point out, there are real differences, 'but some teachers may be inclined to over-state them, and, perhaps, award marks on this basis.'[2] Single mothers should therefore bear this in mind when they meet their children's teachers, and make sure they overcome any prejudiced expectation these teachers might have.

We spent some time in the last chapter seeing how mothers coped with finding day care for their children while they worked, and have already looked fairly briefly at the effect this enforced absence from their mothers has on children. Since it is such an important subject it is worth while considering a few more quotations. It will be remembered that most mothers preferred to leave their small babies with minders, not putting them into group day care until they were older. Most had difficulty in finding the right minder, but once they had succeeded they all found the arrangements worked very well, both for themselves and for the baby. There are in fact very few nurseries in Britain and the US which are prepared to accept babies under a year, and perhaps this is just as well. Jane Mattes: 'I have my own reservations about putting a child into a group situation at an early age, but the children who have to do it seem fine. Personally I wouldn't have put my own baby into a group situation like that if I had to work full-time: I would have gotten a full-time housekeeper or baby-sitter. I really think that one-to-one early on is very important, but I think once they're a year or two they do start needing social contact.

'The SMC mothers who've had to use nurseries have picked very carefully, and the children seem to develop very strong attachments to the child care workers in these places, so they aren't ignoring the fact that the children really need this tie: it just may not be as intense a tie as a one-to-one relationship.'

Graduate stduent *Angela*'s 4-year-old son, who spends his weekdays in a nursery, certainly seems to thrive on it: 'Adrian goes to a child care centre on campus from seven in the morning until five in the evening. No, I don't see him during that time at all. He's a very happy child, everybody says he's a wonderful kid, and *I* think he's wonderful. He reads stories to himself, he's very independent, he can vocalize really well, and most people are really amazed at how good he is, how well-behaved, how intelligent, and he's very well adjusted to his situation.'

I wonder aloud with a smile if it doesn't sound as though he might be *too* good, and she laughs a denial. 'No! Not at all! He doesn't have emotional problems, that's what I mean, he doesn't get temper tantrums, or anything like that.'

Languages teacher *Sarah*'s daughter, at 4, now bounces around the world with great vivacity and confidence, though when she was younger she was quite timid. She is a credit to her mother who – although she never wanted to be a single mother and has had her share of trauma – has obviously managed to keep her griefs away from her daughter. Sarah also had to put her child into full-time day care from early babyhood on but, between the day nursery and her mother, a happy, bright little girl has emerged. The reader might also remember how Karin Meiselman said she thought that if a mother was going to have to use a day care centre then the earlier the child went there the better – she had found her own children suffered no separation anxieties at all (but they were not away from her for a full day five days a week).

Many mothers thought the children positively gained from being with other children, especially when they had left the babyhood stage. Even *Felicity*, who refuses to leave her child and return to work until he is 7 or 8, nevertheless is planning to put him in nursery school when he is 3 for one morning a week, 'building up to two, for his own sake. I think he needs somebody else to give him a bit of discipline and at nursery school he'll get that. He's very clinging at the moment, so it'll be good for him to be away for a little bit –

there's about fifteen children there, which is a good number.'

Naomi Scheman comments, 'My ideal isn't that women get to have the kind of distance from child care that men have traditionally always had, but I think there can be some kind of middle ground, particularly with the move towards one-children families. I think group child care is in the child's interests, growing up with other children rather than in isolation with one person, usually a woman, who is probably feeling very trapped.'

However, Marilyn Fabe does issue a warning: 'I've five or six friends who work, and their children are in day care a lot of the day, and they almost always have sleep problems – they wake up two or three times a night. I've noticed that people who've put their children into full-time day care pay for it in subtle little ways, and one of the things is that their kids call for them at night and want a lot of them. We were talking about quality versus quantity time just now, and if you don't give them that quality time – playing, imaginative play – if you're coming home exhausted every night, it doesn't matter how much you love that child, that quality giving is harder, and children really do demand a lot. I'm concerned personally about this, because it would make my life much easier if I could do it. I drop my child off at 8.30 and pick him up at one – I feel that's as much as I could be away from him five days a week, but I know people who get along much better than I do in terms of their careers, and they're able to have their children *and* get their tenure [Marilyn is referring to her own academic career], but they put their children into day care from about the time they were 3 or 4 months old at eight o'clock and get them at six, and they all say there are ways they pay for it. Some of them are married, some are single. I'm not sure, though, that the children themselves are harmed in any way by this. There are studies that show that in some ways they do quite well, but what I'm saying is that if you have to work *and* have a lot of night-waking, to cope with it takes away your energy for your work and also for when you're home with the child. It can create tension with a partner, too, so maybe it's just as well not to have one!'

A worry that many people have is the effect on a boy's sexuality if he is brought up in a household without men, especially where the mother is openly anti-male. In fact none of the mothers I met were of this latter kind – even the lesbians were happy to have male friends. However, Pat Verity, dealing mainly with the children of divorced or separated mothers, said, 'I feel in quite a lot of the cases there's an anti-man feeling coming from the mothers using this nursery, without them meaning to project it, but it's there, and it has an effect on the next generation, their feelings about men and family life. I think you see quite a lot of aggression in the children when there's been a split, and perhaps they've witnessed something in the past. Something in the mother comes out – it may be quite unconscious – but often there's a feeling of anger towards males. There's also a bit about the children actually wanting men as well – when men come in here to play with the children they're a prize object, but they're being tested out all the time, too, both with boys and girls – they'll test out anybody who's male.'

Some researchers consider that boys brought up without a man around have exaggerated ideas about what masculinity involves, picking up from other boys at school or from television, comics and films, the macho image of an idealized kind of Clint Eastwood tough guy who can take endless knocks, doesn't seem to need emotional relationships, is automatically aggressive and rarely tender.[3] The inclination of many mothers will be to counteract this, sometimes possibly too much so. Child psychiatrist Tony Baker talks about one such mother he knows: 'I think where a mother has a very negative attitude or experience of men it will appear in a child during adolescence rather than childhood. I think there would be some control put on him perhaps in terms of boyish so-called masculine traits such as aggressiveness or what have you. I do know personally one single mother who deliberately chose to have two children, a boy and a girl, and those children are . . . strange children. They have so much to conform with their mother's various expectations that they will be peace-loving by nature, that they won't be aggressive, they won't express anger or hostility or negative feelings, that they will work extremely hard – at the age of $3\frac{1}{2}$ they were expected to read and write and to perform at a very, very high level. She had an enormous investment in somehow proving to the outside world that she could be a perfectly competent single parent, that she didn't need men, that men with male traits were bad.'

'*Certainly many women are very happy not to reinforce male social stereotyping of the old kind – perhaps much of it was social only and not necessarily innate?*'

'Absolutely. In fact, perhaps because of who I am, I'm for any movement which finds a replacement for the abuse and humiliation and sense of male superiority which is somehow inherent in our social and education system. But a mother attempting to do this on her own. . . ? Though maybe that's where it has to start, in the home. A child is going to run into those stereotypes in school, and there is potential for a lot of confusion there and a lot of negative stereotyping in his social systems outside his peer group, in other words he will be labelled a sissy, a weakling, a wimp or what have you. So I think these children may learn to behave in different ways in different contexts – it's like a child who isn't allowed to drop his aitches at home but has to in the street, otherwise he's beaten up for being posh.

'I think some children will naturally display aggression because it is part of their temperament. I think that needs to be dealt with effectively rather than simply squashed or disapproved of. How? Well, for one thing, children can learn that talking is better than hitting. Actually the emphatic treatment that this particular mother has given her children – "no, you will *not* have guns!" – is very authoritarian and there's been very little reasoning done. She's also dealt with both of them in a very unisex sort of way, so that they will each wear nighties or pyjamas, for instance – she's been trying to eradicate sex differences within the children, she's been trying to give them a very equal experience and she's actually run in the face of their natural wants and wishes.'

'*How do you feel about the children?*'

'Well, the boy is currently soiling in the day – he's 7 – and she won't identify that as being a problem because that would be a sign she's failed. I think he's doing it because he's under a lot of pressure – to achieve academically as well, to be gifted when perhaps he's not. The girl at 8 or 9 is much better adjusted, which is why I say I think for boys it may be more of a problem. The point is I think this particular lady is trying to impose a model of non-aggression on her children in quite an aggressive way.'

'*Perhaps it's her intellect rather than her spiritual self that's driving her – you know, you bloody well be good and loving and gentle or else. . . !*'

'That's right. I think negative experiences with men may lead women down this path, and I think they need to be very careful how they do it.'

It might be thought that one way out of some of these problems is for women to live in communities – we have already looked at the idea of sharing houses and having nearby friends in a previous chapter, and this less structured method can be very successful. However, to institutionalize this idea as in the Israeli kibbutzim has not seemed to work out so well, and many experiments of this nature have now been abandoned. Spes Dolphin describes in *Why Children?* a community where living is collective, with child care being shared as fully as the work on the farm which the community runs.[4] She writes that many of the mothers wanted to change their traditional relationship with their children, becoming a friend rather than a 'mom'. In this collective the mother looks after her own child only when she actually *wants* to, so that in theory the relationship between them should be a very positive one. There are always a number of other women around to look after the children, who eventually, it seems, learn that any one of a whole lot of women can give him or her the caring and the loving that all children need. However, apparently it can take many nights of the child 'screaming for his or her mom' before this happens, and I cannot see this as being good for a child's development – it may make for very rational, temperate human beings able to cope with many situations, but I fear that the development of an important part of a child's psyche would be being neglected under such circumstances.

Learning to share with others is very important, though, and it is something that is obviously difficult to teach in a two-person family. Mothers try to cope with this in various ways, and usually make sure that their children mix with others as soon as possible. Tony Baker feels this is not entirely sufficient: 'To share within a family system is different to organized controlled sharing in the way you've been describing. Those mothers are recognizing the need for there to be lots of external contacts, but that's different to a couple sharing the child, to their saying, "This is *our* child." ' But *Charlotte*, part-time researcher, pointed out, 'My daughter already knows she has to share me with other things like work. And she learns she has to share the attention of the baby minder with the minder's own child, and at the same time she has a lot of fun with her baby, which I think is very important. Later she'll go to a nursery school where she'll have to share even more.'

It is true that, as we saw in the section on mothers and their lovers, children find it difficult to share their mothers with someone else, but learning to share is rarely easy under any circumstances. Not every aspect of growth can be organized, and if a child grows up without ever having to share the attention of his mother at a deep emotional level this may make some problems for him in later life, but in exchange he will have been spared other problems, the trauma of a bitter divorce, for example.

Father's relationships with their children
The quality of this relationship varied tremendously, ranging from non-existent to whole-hearted co-operation. I found that where a known father existed, as opposed to an unknown sperm donor, the men fell more or less equally into one of three different groups – they were married to someone else before or after the conception; they were single and wanted varying amounts of contact, or they were single and wanted nothing whatsoever to do with the situation.

In the first group, there were one or two married men who dithered between wife and mistress, wanting both, hating to leave either – a situation many women are familiar with. Theatre director *Carolyn* was wanting to get pregnant before she met Martin, but because their relationship seemed promising she continued using contraception, not wanting to complicate matters too early on. He told her he was separated from his wife (which physically he was, as work and home were a considerable distance apart), and she was under the impression he was virtually a free man. Then it became clear that in fact he was still very involved emotionally with his wife – 'he was bouncing back and forwards between us, you know?' Eventually Carolyn became pregnant unintentionally (she was the woman whose diaphragm no longer fitted her accurately when she had lost a considerable amount of weight after an accident), but by that time she had already decided that she could not go along with the relationship any longer, partly because she had discovered he had been lying both to her and to his wife. Told about the pregnancy, he still could not make up his mind what he wanted to do: Carolyn had given him freedom to choose to participate in the pregnancy or to leave her completely, promising him that in the latter case she would make no claims of any kind of him. But she had added a warning 'which made him catatonic. I told him, I'm not going to lie to the child. I'm not going to go around with a sign on my back during the next nine months that says THIS IS MARTIN X'S BABY, but when the kid's old enough to ask questions I'm not going to make up any bullshit. So it's very possible that when the child is 15 or 16, or whenever he wants to do it, some teenager will come knocking on his door. I told him I wasn't going to lie to the kid any more than I had ever lied to him.

'By now I had a fair amount of information about his wife and his marriage, but she knew nothing about me at all, so if we'd split up and I hadn't been pregnant she'd probably never have known I existed. But now there was no chance of that. He was absolutely catatonic – he was seeing that not only did he have in front of him Carolyn and a child and all that that entails, but also he'd have to go back up north and spill the beans to his wife. I then discovered that his wife had always wanted a child but he never had, so you can imagine what her feelings must have been when eventually he told her about it! Gradually as time went on he began to say to me he felt OK about the child, that he was ready to be involved to some extent, that he was going to try to make his marriage work and that although his wife had been very angry about it she was prepared for him to have some sort of relationship with the child. He was very confused, and frankly it seemed to me that although realistically we didn't have a future together, neither did his wife and he.

'I really believed in his confusion at that time, but I feel in retrospect I was really taken in. We kept coming together and parting while he was trying to make a decision, or that's what I thought he was doing, and I had just persuaded him to come with me to see a therapist to help sort it all out when he told me his wife was pregnant. It was deliberate – they'd been trying ever since he'd told her about me because I think she'd said something like, well, if you're going to be a father and that's OK with you, then you'd damn well better . . . you know? I was outraged, also, because apparently he'd been telling her he had broken with me, that he was only seeing me to arrange about the child, and all that time. . . ! He'd lied to everybody – he'd never told his parents, his friends, and I felt if he's still so ashamed of it and can't deal with it with anybody, then my child is going to know that, and I'm not having that. And there was the issue of guardianship. I said to him, I don't have any brothers or sisters, and if anything happens to me the baby'd be likely to go to you. But it's not just you, it's you and your wife, and my child would go to a situation where there's a marriage that's been in trouble, there's a new child on the way – there's so much chaos, and I don't want my child to be in that situation. So I ended up having a legal agreement for one year that he's not going to see us at all, and some very good friends I've appointed as guardians will keep him in touch with what's happening.

'At some point I'm going to want him along for the baby's sake, so I can say to her, yes, this is your father, yes, you can go with him. But before I do that I want to meet his wife – there's no way I'd permit my child to go to them without my knowing just what his wife's like, how she'll treat it. I don't trust him any more, I can't believe a word he ever says.'

Catherine, actress, always knew her lover was married, and didn't intend to get pregnant with him, and certainly didn't want to marry him. But he also had his time of confusion: his wife had given birth to girls only and when she learned about his involvement with Catherine and that Catherine had had what he'd always wanted – a boy – she was extremely angry and went so far as to walk out on the entire family for a while. At one point the father decided he wanted to move in with Catherine and leave his wife, but although earlier on she might have agreed, by then Catherine was clear she did not want to live with him. When the child was born he kept up contact, 'but he doesn't come here to see us regularly, no. He knows I'll never ring his home, so I've made it terribly easy for him to come and go as he wants. A while back he decided to come to see Tommy every week and he kept it up for three weeks, but sometimes it's only every two or three weeks. Now he's disappeared again. When he comes he stays about four hours at a time, but Tommy doesn't get on with him as well as he does with other of my friends, because his father is so filled with guilt by the time he comes. I think as Tommy gets older he'll reject him because he'll find he doesn't get anything much from him. But he might not – he's very loyal towards his father. It's Tommy who takes complete responsibility for their relationship – it's come on Dad, let me show you my new toys, or come on out to the garden and I'll show you my climbing frame. He gees him up, whereas this man sort of wanders out after him looking uncomfortable. He once said to me that everything was all right at home with his daughters because he was a father and that was his home, but he doesn't know what role he has here, and I say, just a role of friendship if you like, you don't have to put a label on it.'

Museum curator *Elizabeth*'s relationship with her married lover has already been described earlier and I won't go into it again except to add one or two details. 'David sees his father much more often now he's retired not too far away, about every ten days or so. He usually stays overnight when he comes, or he might come just for supper, put David to bed and read him a story or whatever. I was away last weekend so John took David back home with him and brought him back here on Sunday and got the house ready for me to come back to. And at half-terms we've always tried to have if not the whole of half-term at least part of it together, and chunks of the holidays too. The only real problem has been discipline: two or three years ago David was going through a terribly rude stage, and he wouldn't do a damn thing he was told to do. His rudeness, his recalcitrance, it really got me down, you know? But John felt that if he came and laid down the law it was going to be very destructive of his relationship with David. But if a father is around all the time . . . on the other hand, kids play one off against the other, don't they.'

Unless they have a totally 'open' marriage like Elizabeth's John and his wife, siring a child outside their marriage inevitably brings problems if either the man or the woman want any kind of relationship to continue. Even where the mother refuses to involve the man at all, the man feels rejected or disturbed. *Laura*: 'He's very glad I'm not threatening his marriage or his family situation, but at the same time he's very upset about it – there is this aspect that he feels the child is part of him and yet he's not going to have any part in its life.'

Some of the fathers have married someone else after the conception: art gallery owner *Frances* found that her lover did this, and as I have written before he remains in useful contact with Frances and her daughter, seeing them regularly or taking his daughter on holiday with him and his wife several times a year, which seems to be a healthy and happy situation for the child. Languages teacher *Sarah*'s Peter eventually divorced the wife whom he had been separated from for many years and married someone else, to Sarah's distress. He continues to see his daughter by Sarah, although at present his new wife cannot deal with having little Sophie to stay with them. Sarah feels embittered about this and considered that Peter should not allow his new wife to interfere in his relationships with his own daughter. It is difficult to know how Sophie herself feels about this, or if

she is even conscious of what is happening – she seems
blithely content with whatever her day brings. It does seem
that in situations like this provided the adults are very
careful in how they relate to the child, keeping conflicts out
of their children's lives as much as possible and providing
them with ample love and warm attention, the children
flourish – it continually amazes me how adaptable children
are, as long as, like plants, the basic nutrients are fed to
them.

The second group of fathers, single men wanting
varying types of contact, vary far more than the married
men. The stories of most of these have already been dealt
with during the course of the book, but I will remind the
reader of some of them so that the different types of
reactions can be borne in mind. Research assistant *Janice*
shares totally with her lover in everything except responsibility for the child, which she insists on keeping for herself.
He has such a good relationship with the child – 'he's cared
for her, he's put almost as much into that as I have' – that he
probably does more for the child than most husbands do in
a marriage. *Julia*'s lover, who stayed on after the birth and
ended up living with her for three years, was never much of
a help to her, leaving her to get up in the night to look after
the child, refusing at night to turn his music off although the
child had to sleep in the single room they all lived in: he was
unable to come to terms with the fact that he was a father,
Julia said. Finally she left him, but they stayed good friends
and they still go on holiday together as a family, although
they are no longer lovers. 'He usually comes here once
during the week – not always – and usually we see him both
days during the weekend, or at least once. I think he wants
to keep it as a family, which is hard in a way – I like it too,
though it seems unreal, really. It works well enough, and she
calls him Daddy, of course, and that's very important for
her.

'He won't baby-sit any more, though. She refuses to be
left, and panics and screams even when her father baby-sits
for her, so he won't do it any more. She's all right when he
takes her out alone, but I have to be there when she comes
back or she screams her head off. I think she picks up on his

feeling that he couldn't cope with her without me there. Last time he baby-sat at night he came and fetched me, and said, I'm not going to put up with that, I'm not going through that again. So I never go out at night. That's very hard. Now she's getting older, she's 5, I've got to sort that out somehow. She's a very happy child, and gets on extremely well with other children, it's only the night thing that's a problem. Apart from that she really enjoys being with her father. She likes men, she's drawn towards them – there's a couple of men who've visited me and she's picked up they wanted a sexual relationship with me, though I won't do it – I feel very clear I don't want to have affairs while she's at home, I don't want her to wake up and find a man there – and sometimes she's actually stood there and barred the way and said, "I want my daddy, I don't want you here." But with others she actually tells them to stay the night, which is very embarrassing. I'm sure she's not aware of sex, but I think she wants that closeness in the morning, being able to climb on a man – she misses that aspect of her father being around. Occasionally we do stay at her dad's – I sleep in with her, but in the morning she'll go into his room and wake him up, and she loves that.'

Graduate student *Angela* lived with her lover Ben for a while until she decided she wanted to live alone, partly because she found him a far more conventional person than herself. They share care of the child: 'Ben still tries to make me conform to a certain standard that he considers right for a parent. . . . I'm not particularly fond of children as such, and that's one of the reasons Ben's always after me, because I don't do the sort of family things that he would want me to do. I mean I take Adrian to the park because that's the only place I can take him to play and let his aggressiveness out when it's my turn to look after him, but I'm not fond of taking him to children's birthday parties and doing those sorts of things – I just don't want to do it, and his father feels that makes me a bad mother. But the things that I do with Adrian are just different. We read together, we listen to music together, we take long walks together, and he enjoys himself when he's with me. If there's a friend's birthday party then I tell his father about it, and Ben loves those things, so he takes him and Adrian doesn't miss out on them.'

Several of the fathers are intrigued by the thought of being a father, but are too immature emotionally to accept much responsibility even where the mother is willing to let them have it. Part-time researcher *Charlotte*, for example, who became pregnant by a gay friend of long standing, says, 'He comes here about once a month, but he's in happy ignorance, really, of what fatherhood entails. He just hasn't got there yet – I think perhaps it's rather nice for him that he's got a chance to find out. I'm not putting any pressure on him and I think it would be very bad if I did. As it is it's relatively good. A while ago we were discussing if she should call him Daddy or Johnny and we felt it would be better if she called him Johnny – but now she's started calling him Daddy; I was showing her some photographs of him the other day, and she said 'Daddy!' Of course I was frightfully pleased and nearly rang him on the spot, and later when we spoke about it he was rather excited too, so I think maybe she will call him Daddy for a bit.'

When Dutch child psychologist *Anna* met the father-to-be of her child, a young Frenchman, she found 'Jean-Pierre had the same ideas as me about marriage, about love and about getting children.' When she became pregnant they happily discussed details like the possibility of him coming regularly to Amsterdam to see her and the child, but in the event it all became too complicated. 'When I first told him I was pregnant he was very proud – he was still young, only 23, and I think he didn't realize what it meant to be responsible for a child.' He came to be with her at the birth, but the love affair broke up at that point (I wrote about this in detail in Chapter 6), although he continued to come every four to six weeks to see Anna and his son. However, when she decided she wanted a second child they went on holiday together and fell in love with each other again (for Anna it was very important to be in love with a man who was going to be the father of her child), but when they returned the old problems started again. They continued to see each other intermittently after the birth of their second child: 'A few months ago we even tried to live together in Paris – but it doesn't work. He has other girlfriends and it's not good. Michel, who is 5 now, is very proud of his father and talks about him a lot, but Jean-Pierre doesn't play with him much even when he sees him – he likes it more to play with me than with his children. I am sure that Jean-Pierre likes to have me as a woman, not as the mother of two children.'

When, ten years ago, *Sonia* had her child by her lover (her first two children having been removed to Israel by her ex-husband) she had already fallen out of love with him and would have preferred not to see him at all, but for the sake of their daughter Sonia persevered in making a new kind of relationship with him. 'My daughter's happy – over the years she's asked two or three times why we don't live together or marry, and I've told her that if one lives with somebody one doesn't love there's a lot of argument, disagreement, an unhappy situation, but the fact that we live apart makes us able to be very good friends. She gets very angry with us if we ever have disagreements. She calls him Daddy, of course, and gets on very well with him. At first he was miserable and clumsy, a bit helpless and awkward and embarrassed – I just didn't want him around at all, and it was difficult for both of us. But he's much better now and it's wonderful that she has him around. They do things together, like going skating at weekends, for example. He's supportive – if he can manage it he'll baby-sit any time, and take her for a day or two which is great for me too.'

Fathers arriving out of the blue, showering the child with gifts or enjoyable trips, then disappearing again, are more familiar to divorced women than these mothers, it seems, but no doubt it happens to some. *David* told me about his own father who had left home to live with a woman not very far away: 'he'd come to see us every few weeks, and we thought it marvellous, because he'd bring us toys and give us pocket money and so on – so we thought, you know, this is the perfect man. But when he left my mother would say, oh, he gave you toys but he didn't leave any money, what about your shoes? We thought, mothers! Who cares about shoes! They're so boring with their demands! So we had this romantic view of things. It was only when we grew up that we saw the tough time she had to survive, and that he was quite irresponsible.'

The reaction of quite a few of the fathers when they heard about the woman's pregnancy was one of horror, shock, followed by a demand the women had an abortion, and then, when she refused, total rejection of the situation. Medical researcher *Felicity* had her child by a man who had just left his wife before he met her but was not yet divorced, and although he often said he wanted to marry her, 'It was always – wait for a year, let things settle first. Then when I told him over the phone I was pregnant he threatened suicide if I didn't have an abortion. I think he was just terrified. I'd told my parents, and he was also terrified that they were going to get in touch with him, which was utterly ridiculous. I think he just panicked – it was sheer panic, really. I didn't entirely give up hope until a very little time ago, when he wrote to me to tell me he had remarried. I'd kept on sending him little notes and photographs of the baby, but not hearing anything. I sent them about twice a year. Then he wrote me a very cold letter and said he'd married – whether he really had or not I don't know – and he told me to stop getting in touch. He just doesn't want anything to do with the child at all.'

Pat, midwife, had made love with an old lover after they had spent an evening out together, and had told him it was a safe time for her. 'When I found I was pregnant I went right away to where he worked and told him, and we went out that weekend to a movie and we discussed it real briefly. I didn't want anything from him, I didn't want him to be part of it – he knew, sort of, that I was lesbian, yes – and that I intended to come back West to be near my family, so it meant I was going to leave him and that he wouldn't have any chance to be a part of the child's life. And that was fine by him, he basically washed his hands of it, he didn't care. I wasn't hostile about that, I was glad I'd picked the right person that would react that way.'

Some pregnancies may have been started in the course of a deeply loving affair, but that seems to be no guarantee that the father will want to keep in touch with his child. Acupressurist *Serena*'s affair came to an end against the wishes of the father after the birth of her child, and what has deeply disappointed her is that the man, who lives in Europe – she is American – seems to have rejected the whole situation, unable to deal with it as it actually is. He came to see the baby at its birth, and, 'Yes, he wanted to make it work, he cried when he saw Michael, but I really felt like he was more into his own feelings, rather than seeing what I was going through, and he offered me no assistance, no money, nothing. And we just weren't relating any more. He went back home to Europe, and just once in three years – three years, that's all! – he's sent a little package to Michael. No letter with it, nothing. He never sends him anything on his birthday or at Christmas – if he sent even a card then I could start to talk about it to my son, he has a father. . . . I wrote a while ago about the boy to him, what his interests are, what his personality is, but I've not received an answer, and that was three months ago. I don't know if we ever will. I even sent him on one of his birthdays a little drawing that Michael had done, but there was no answer to that either. So I'm not having Michael deliberately sit down and write to his father and be ignored, it would be too painful for him.'

Psychoanalyst *Stephanie* made perhaps the briefest comment of all: 'I wasn't comfortable with the idea . . . nice Jewish girls don't go around getting pregnant out of wedlock. And then when I decided to try it I decided not to use birth control for one night, and I got pregnant. Yes, I'd thought about the man as a father – biologically he was fine, and he'd have been fine as a father figure if he'd been interested, but he wasn't. I was very clear he might not want to.'

And so that was OK, perfectly OK, for Stephanie, and for many of the other mothers too.

Where's my daddy?
This is the question that all the mothers agonize over how to answer, along with other related questions – who's my daddy? why doesn't my daddy live with us? why don't I have a daddy like other children? Some of the mothers I interviewed have not yet been faced with this question, others have already coped with it. But first, the professionals:

Psychologist Hendrike Vande Kemp's answer to my query as to what mothers who choose artificial insemination should tell their children was in line with her general opinion: 'I think a woman has no right to do that in the first place. A child deserves to have a father and so there is no answer that she can give that child.' Gynaecologist Ted Nagle agreed with Vande Kemp that it is bound to be a stressful situation for the child, and says that when couples whom he has helped conceive through artificial insemination ask his advice on what to say, 'I advise them not to tell the child. I feel it can't be anything but confusing to the kid. I feel it's much better he thinks this man who had behaved to him all his life as a father *is* his father, and not to create this crazy biological confusion, because as far as I'm concerned in many ways it's irrelevant.'

But if there is no man around then some answer has to be given to the questioning child. Psychologist Karin Meiselman: 'I'd approach it like I'd approach sex education in children, that is you wait until they ask, and I'd make sure I give them information at their level. I guess the third guideline is to tell them the truth. Not necessarily the entire detailed truth – for instance the first time they asked, aged 2, where's daddy? you don't have to bring out the turkey-baster then and there and show it to them! Maybe you say at first, I don't know where your daddy is, and sooner or later there will be questions like, Mummy, how come you don't know, didn't you see him? at which point you might say something like, I really wanted to be a mummy and I didn't know a daddy at the time so the doctor helped me to have you, and that was wonderful because I wanted to be a mummy. The important thing is to be relaxed and enthusiastic, and not to overload them or give them the wrong non-verbal messages. They will come back from time to time with more questions and then you can elaborate, and like that you avoid ending with a situation where it's all sort of frozen and the child never dares to ask again. Later you can explain more by saying something along the lines of, biologically you have a daddy, but he's not my husband, so in another way he's not your daddy.'

I asked her if where the mother had had a child by a man she knew, it was important that she builds up a good image of him, even if she didn't in fact think very highly of him as a man. 'I suppose so, if the child specifically asks about it, but I think it might develop into a problem if the mother builds him up too much – if the child eventually does seek him out and expects him to be daddy-like, they might be in for a big disappointment.'

'But if he went off when the mother was pregnant, never wrote – if she doesn't somehow soften this the child might think it normal behaviour for fathers not to give a damn about their children?'

'I guess the first thing I'd attempt to do as a mother in that situation would be to try to overcome my own anger about it. At a certain age – maybe 5 or 6 or even later – I'd try to tell the child very straight about what it was like, assuming the child was interested in knowing, and if I'd managed to overcome my own anger, I might say something like, well, I had a short relationship with this person, and he wasn't interested in being a daddy to anyone just then, and I was even a little angry with him, but I wanted to have a baby of my own, and that's how it happened. You can tell a child pretty much what the facts are without requiring him to be angry at his father, or implying the man was a total bastard.'

Jessica Curtis explained in the SMC November/ December 1984 newsletter how some of the mothers had tackled these questions. One reported that a child psychiatrist had told her that once she was clear in her own mind about what had happened 'she would have no trouble explaining it to her daughter'. Another mother in reply to her son when he said, 'I wish I had a daddy,' answered, 'So do I.' She then went on to explain to him, ' "You have a father, but not a daddy. He left you because he doesn't love mommy any more. He does love you." ' Like everyone else I spoke to, Jessica Curtis believes truthfulness is essential. She writes: 'One cardinal principle is to tell the truth . . . Grown children who were adopted or produced by artificial insemination within marriage who were not told the truth but found it out later were terribly angry, not about the adoption or artificial insemination, but about the lies and covering-up that prevented them from learning the truth in a supportive environment. They felt that their self-concepts were so changed by the new information that they had to rethink not only their lives but their very identities. They had always thought that they were the children of these two people, and to find out as adults that there was no genetic relationship at all was devastating. . . . We need to remember also that our children have a right to be angry and confused. We shouldn't whitewash the situation or deny their feelings; that will just make for more trouble later.'

Marilyn Fabe, talking about a gay male who had helped a lesbian mother he did not know personally to be inseminated with his sperm, said, 'They explained to the child when he was old enough his father was a gay male who wanted to have a child in this way, and that he donated his sperm so that mummy could get pregnant, and that he was a person who believed in her values, and that you can be very proud of him for doing what he did. I think that what you have to do is give the child, who wants to idealize the absent parent, the core of something to idealize.'

Finally, Tony Baker had some very useful things to say: 'If some of these children are getting the story that father was just somebody I had sex with so that I could have you, well, they'd think what does that mean about me, what have I inherited from this man? This is the sort of conundrum that the adolescent is going to find important – it's probably less important in early childhood, particularly if there are going to be enough adults around that the child can identify with, but when the adolescents are discovering their own identity, their own sexuality, they look to family history, they look to models, they look to – where did I come from? and if they are told the truth then I guess that must raise a very big question about who they are. The fact that mother may not be able to come up with answers because it's somebody she met for a very brief period of time, that may in fact cause an undue degree of concern and anxiety in the child.'

'*What should the AID mother say?*'

'That's a tough nut. I think developmentally the more

concrete the story the better. In other words, rather nebulous ideas associated with artificial insemination, donors, etc. – that you have a National Health-owned corporate father – I don't think is going to be very useful. I don't think they'll understand the concept of what mother was doing probably until their mid or late teens, I don't think that earlier than that they'll be able to take that idea on board – the fact that she has decided she didn't want to share her life with a man but she wanted a baby – so they're not going to be able to handle that information until they're much more mature. Perhaps at 14 or so, it depends on the child. You can discuss it earlier, yes, perhaps by 8 or 9, but it has to be in as concrete a way as possible. I think at that age he will be building a fantasy around whatever the information the mother gives. As times goes on that fantasy will change as they become more and more aware of reality, and I would hope that at some stage the mother will be able to explain exactly what was in her mind, why she planned to do things in this way rather than in a more usual way.'

'*What kind of message can a mother give her child, a boy especially, that won't let him think she feels all men are unlivable with?*'

'It's very important for the child to have a positively connoted model of a father, and that should be done at an early age in as concrete a term as possible. The attitudes and expressions that are attached in discussions about daddies and fathers should be positive ones, and as time goes by the mother should take responsibility for having made that decision not to live with somebody – it wasn't that the daddy wouldn't live with me, it was that I wouldn't live with daddy. As time goes by she should say that more and more strongly, so that the child knows it wasn't that dad abandoned me, or that dad didn't want me, and that if it hadn't been for me they'd have been together and married. And going back to AID pregnancies, I think yes, it's rather nice to talk about medical students. That will help the children see why the donors did it. And I think too a name for the father is going to be important. The less mystery the better – perhaps the mother might say, I don't know what his name is, but shall we call him X? Or what name would you like your daddy to have? This helps him to construct the fantasy that he's going to construct anyway at around 4, 5, 6 – certainly by 7. They get stereotyped models at school – you know, a family's a mother, father and two children, and meat always comes with two veg. – and it's inevitable he'll make up some sort of fantasy for himself.'

How have the mothers themselves actually handled these questions when they have arisen? As yet most of the children are very small and the more complicated questions are still to come. Psychotherapist *Stephanie*, who was never in a relationship with the father of her son Danny: 'It's so important to find out what the child is asking. It's very easy to have a prepared answer and kind of pounce when the opportunity presents itself. Just like any other loaded issue I always suggest to mothers that the child be helped to try to pursue the question a little bit themselves, and then you get an idea what it is they're really struggling with. The way I answered it for my own child was that your daddy doesn't know you and has never met you, and that made a big impression on him – my daddy never knew me!'

'*When they ask, where did my daddy go? where's my daddy? . . .*'

'It's interesting because Danny hasn't asked that yet – he's almost 3½ and he went through the social part first – why is it some children have daddies and some children don't? He said to me, some children live with a mummy and a daddy, right? So I said, right, and some children live with just a mummy or just a daddy, and he said, why? And I said, because that's the way it is, sometimes people live with one person and sometimes with another, not all children live with a mummy and a daddy – and that's what he really wanted to hear. The other day we went to a mothers' group meeting for SMC, and afterwards he asked me why I don't live with his daddy. I told him, you know, all those children there at that meeting don't live with their daddies. So he said again, oooh, why not? So I told him, well, you know, sometimes you're ready for something, or you're not ready for something (that's a term we use at home, you're not ready to go to sleep, or you're not ready to use this piece of equipment). He accepted that, he said, oh yeah, they're just not ready.'

'*How do you answer questions about AI when the mother was artificially inseminated?*'

'We've talked about that at SMC, and so far what we feel comfortable with for a somewhat older child who has some idea of biology already (who knows that a sperm cell meets an egg cell, which is the first thing you tell children usually) is that there are doctors who will help women who really want to become mummies. In all the books I've read about child development, the actual act of intercourse is not something you tell a child until much later. So if they ask how did the sperm and the egg meet, well, you say the daddy planted it there or the doctor did.'

Nurse *Lynn*, an AID mother with two daughters: 'The first time it came up was when Heather was 3 years old. It didn't come from her, it came from a friend who was here, a classmate. "What's your daddy's name?" she asked. Heather looked at me – I think for her at that point calling somebody daddy was like calling him Joe or Michael or Eddy – she didn't say anything but she was looking at me, so I felt I had to respond, and I said, "Heather doesn't have a daddy." "But everybody has a daddy." So I said, "No, Heather is a very special little girl, she just has a mummy." At that point Heather says "Yeah, I'm special, I just have a mummy." And it got dropped. Over the last two years it's come up that she's very special and she just has a mummy. Now I can see her searching for an identity, and sometimes a question comes up, like she'll be sitting reading a book and she'll suddenly say, "I wish I had a daddy," and I ask, "Why?", and she'll say, "Well, I'd like to go to the park." I'll say, "Well, mummy can take you to the park." "OK, can we go now?" "No, it's six o'clock at night, maybe we can go on Saturday."

'In fact I know quite a bit more about her baby sister's father than I do about hers – they weren't from the same donor – and I've put it all in writing, so that if something happens to me they'll be able to know everything I know. Otherwise, when the right time comes I'll tell them the truth – I've been truthful all the way along, but Heather wouldn't understand much yet.'

But Afton Blake dislikes the idea of telling a child they don't have a daddy. 'I think it's terrible to say that. Of course they have a daddy. You have to give the simplest honest answer appropriate for the age group. First question, do I have a daddy? Yes, you have a daddy. If he says where is my daddy, you say, your daddy doesn't live with us, and if he doesn't ask why not, I wouldn't say until he asked. If he does say why not, I'd say, because Mummy wasn't married to your daddy. Usually the women I've talked to who've gone through this find the children don't ask a whole lot, they ask just one single question and often the child walks away then because that's all he wants to know right at that moment. As Doron gets older, since I know a great deal about his father, I intend to make him feel good about him; I think it's very important I know a lot about the father, and I'll build it up in a real positive way – I'll say, for instance, isn't it wonderful this man was loving enough to make it possible for me to have you.'

Children's nurse *Mary*, also a mother through AID, says, 'The hardest part about AI is there's no father figure there, I mean I can't tell him your daddy did this and your daddy did that, because I don't even know what this man looks like or what his name is or anything. If when he's a teenager he needs to find out who his father is, there's going to be no way he will be able to do that. On the other hand, I feel it's easier to tell my child that I got him on my own without a father than to tell him that he had a father who doesn't care about him. I mean, which is easier to deal with? That I don't have a father, or that I have one that doesn't love me?'

Midwife *Pat*, who had Josh through an old friend when she was still uncertain about her lesbianism, had intended to tell her son about his father to help him build up a good picture of him, but now that she wants to have a second child – and since she will have to get pregnant through AID – she has decided it would be divisive if the two children were to know they had been conceived in different ways. 'Josh is just 3 now and he's beginning to ask questions. At the moment he's very confused because when he hears me talking to my lover Jackie about my father, he thinks his grandfather is his daddy too. I explain, no, that's your grandpa – he's *my* daddy. Sometimes, when he is mad with me, he says he wants his daddy, then I say grandpa isn't here right now, he's away camping, or whatever he's doing. If a bit later he asks me directly I've decided to tell him that he doesn't have a daddy. I'll tell him, you have me and you have Jackie – she lives here with us – and I'll gradually work it out with him. Right now I feel very comfortable saying you don't have a daddy, and certainly that's what I'll have to say to his brother or sister, if he has one. I will wait a long time before I tell Josh differently, until he's over 20 at least, if I ever do at all. If, say, he sees a therapist because he has problems and the therapist thought I ought to tell him then I will, but personally I think I should just hold off.'

Acupressurist *Serena*'s son, Michael, aged 3, became quite excited when he realized he had a grandfather *and* a father, also having previously confused the two. 'He's not making an issue about daddies yet, but he did say a while ago – we were sitting on the porch – oh, I don't have a daddy, and he looked at me as if to say, is that so? And I said to him, that's not so, you *do* have a daddy, you *do*. And he said, oh you mean my Boppy – that's his grandfather. And I said, no, not your Boppy, you have a daddy, and he said, I have *two* daddies then! and he got very excited about it, then he changed the subject, he was into something else. And one other time the issue came up, and I said, yes, you do have a daddy, and he lives very, very far away, so far away you have to take an aeroplane, that's how far. And that was it, he didn't ask any more. So it's going to come at me more and more. I'm going to say in all honesty that he was conceived in love, that's very meaningful for me, and I think it will be very important for him to know that, but after that I don't know – I'm going to let life say it for me. I won't be dishonest, I know that.'

Languages teacher *Sarah* used similar phraseology: 'I felt powerless to a large extent to stop life expressing itself the way it is. I shall try to do my best so that as little bitterness comes through as possible, or as mildly as possible. I'll try and correct it in other ways, to balance it out: I've only ever spoken nicely to her about her father –

even if it chokes me! – but I also think that children
generally, and she in particular, are very much more
intelligent and understanding than we give them credit for,
and I think that to some extent she can cope with the truth.
Not yet, but soon, perhaps by the time she's 5. Not about
what I really feel, but a little bit of the complexity, that I
loved him, but now he is married to someone else and they
love each other, etc.'

Medical researcher *Felicity*, the other mother who felt
bitter about the father's behaviour, says, 'What will I tell
Robert? He's asked me already, and I say his father's in
France, which he probably is. When he's older I'll tell him
the truth, and warn him when he's old enough not to let it
happen to him if he can avoid it.' When I commented it
would be difficult for her to keep bitterness out of her voice,
she replied, 'I'm not a very bitter person. I'm disappointed; I
don't think I'm bitter.' I then asked how she would cope
with the problem of not giving Robert a bad image of his
father. 'I don't know,' she said after a pause.

Tommy, actress *Catherine*'s son, sees his father quite
often, and Catherine has always been open with him about
his father: 'I told Tommy the absolute truth about how he
came about, and whether he can take it all in yet I don't
know. Yes, I've told him his daddy was married to
somebody else ever since he was tiny, because I thought I'm
not going to hide anything. I feel their relationship must find
its own way – I'm careful not to say anything unpleasant
about him, but sometimes Tommy says things like, Daddy's
really stupid, and I say why, and he says, because he says
such stupid things. But his father says them because he's
embarrassed, or he says something a bit babyish to Tommy,
and Tommy says what do you mean? If he got really silly,
rolling about or jumping about, Tommy would love it, but
he keeps saying things that are inadequate, and it just doesn't
work.'

Museum curator *Elizabeth*, whose son David is now 10,
has never had any problems, mainly because of the easy,
open relationship David's father has with his wife. 'Sometimes when David was 2 or 3 he would ask why Daddy was
going away, or where he was, but it was always normal for

him that John mostly wasn't there – it wasn't as though something had been taken away from him. He went to school just before he was 5 and he didn't have any trouble with the local kids – they don't ask questions at that age. None of his friends ask now they're older, either – they all know John, he's just David's dad as far as they're concerned. They know John's married because his wife comes here for David's birthday parties and things like that. No, I don't think the local villagers think it's very odd either – what they don't like is insecure relationships and people busting things up – as long as it's established and you keep yourself to yourself, as it were, and nobody makes any pretence about anything, then it's all right.'

Where children have been adopted it seems to be universally accepted that it is best to tell them from the beginning about their origins. *Jane*: 'She's going to know she's adopted right from the start. I'll tell her I adopted her by myself, and whatever issue she has around that I'll deal with, but she'll have many friends who don't have daddies or don't have daddies they live with. So many of my friends are lesbians who are having children on their own, and even if there is a father involved he'll not be anyone who ever lives with the child.' That this seems to be the right approach is borne out by *Margaret*, herself adopted just before the Second World War. 'There wasn't a crisis moment when I was told about my birth – I always knew it, and I didn't think it was odd there was no father. I was never aware of people making comments at school – obviously people must have known about it, but I was very happy, I never had any hang-ups – the only thing that may have been a hang-up was that later I always fell in love with men twenty years older than me! Yes, I used to fantasize about my father, that he must have been someone terribly famous, that sort of thing. The main thing is, I think it is very important that any child with an unusual background should grow up to know it from the word go. I grew up knowing – there was never a moment of shock – it all seemed absolutely natural to me.'

Role models
The subject of fathers has been explored many times
throughout this book, particularly in this last section, and
inevitably the question of role models has already been
covered to a certain extent. I want now to draw together
comments made exclusively about the importance of children having men around them on whom they can base their
own development if they are boys, or their understanding
and appreciation of males if they are girls.

This is not the place to develop an argument about
whether the differences between men and women's behaviour are inherent or learned. It seems to me that very
many of the 'normal' differences are rapidly being eroded – I
can hardly pretend any longer that my total incompetence
over all things electrical is inherent, and have to accept that I
was successfully brainwashed into thinking it was a man's
place to cope with such things by a mother who, like most
of her generation, understood very well how much nicer it is
to get other people to do these things for you. I now change
my own plugs as a matter of course, but always with a
surreptitious feeling of pride that far outweighs any pride
that I might have in considerably more complicated
achievements which, however, are not sex-loaded. But such
trivia are easily dealt with; prejudices about male and female
capabilities were looked at in Chapter 2 and needn't be
rehearsed again here, but what is important and needs reaf-
firming is that many psychological differences also, which
are generally accepted as genuine differences, may in fact be
no more than the result of social expectations. An infinite
number of little prods in the divergent directions of female-
ness and maleness are given to children from the day they are
born, and who can possibly sort out which bit of behaviour is
caused by our gender and which by social indoctrination?[5]

We might accept it no longer makes sense to say that
only men can be car mechanics or run multi-national
companies, but at the back of our minds we know there are
other values than work, and there remains the lingering fear
that a boy who hasn't been brought up seeing a real man in
action as a father is missing out on something profoundly
important, and that a girl who hasn't seen male/female

relationships at close quarters will never be able to make a satisfactory relationship herself. Earlier in this book I repeated again and again that it is pointless and unhelpful to compare these single mothers with married families as though the latter was always ideal. Let's face it, not many of them are even reasonably satisfactory! Perhaps, considering the state the world is in, it wouldn't be such a bad thing if a number of children were able to start out with a clean slate, as it were, instead of being lumbered with old habits, old expectations, old and damaging beliefs about what makes a man and what makes a woman.

Naomi Scheman answers this point succinctly: 'I think a very good argument to be made is that being brought up in the vicinity of most adult men is not good for children. There's a tremendous amount of battering and incest, and by and large adult men have not proved to be very healthy for little boys and little girls to be around. There are adult men I know with whom I would trust anybody, but if one is talking about what is the best, safest, healthiest environment to bring up a child in, then I don't think the nuclear family comes out very well in that – there's too much abuse, too much education into stereotyped sex roles. I just don't think the nuclear family is a particularly safe place for children or for women.'

Adrienne Rich has pointed out that on the whole children find men less likely to touch them warmly; men are: 'less cherishing, more intermittent in their presence, more remote, more judgmental, more for-themselves' than women, and children learn early on that women emotionally attune themselves to others in a way that most men do not.[6]

Jan: 'You know, the first thing that some people say is, oh my god, lesbians are men-haters and they've got this male child, what's it going to do to him? but I don't agree with that at all. Stella and I have wonderful relationships with men, we have a lot of men friends. Most of our men friends are gay, this is true, but we have heterosexual friends too – straight friends who are liberal non-judgmental about our lifestyle. I think there are enough men of one kind or another in our lives so that Gene will have some good role models. There are a lot of qualities about our men friends that are very good – they're sensitive, they're uninhibited, not into the macho thing where they have to prove that they're tough, and I would like our son to know that he can cry and still be a male, he can be sensitive and still feel he's himself, still feel good about being a boy. We're not raising our son up in an isolated kind of lifestyle, saying that all people live like this or trying to give him an unrealistic view of family life that is different from what society says it should be. We're hoping we can utilize our straight men friends to help in processing some of those things. We're going to try to enforce with him that there are different kinds of families – I don't think he'll grow up thinking this is the only way family life is, or that he's going to be thinking he has to be gay or that all men are gay. I would like for him to know that people are different from each other, and live differently, and not be judgmental about how people live.'

As I wrote elsewhere, although none of the mothers I have interviewed have in fact been men-haters, there must be some single mothers who have this attitude, and yes, I think there are valid grounds for concern about the effect this will have on a male child. Marilyn Fabe, researching her book, also talked to several psychiatrists and analysts about the effect of such an upbringing on a child's gender identity: she asked them, 'Will a boy raised by a woman who doesn't like men necessarily be homosexual? It seemed to be felt by those I asked, there was a good chance he will be, but the question is, is that so terrible? One psychiatrist said it doesn't so much matter if the child is raised without a role model of the opposite sex, as what the parent's *attitude* is towards the opposite sex. If a boy is raised by a mother who likes men and has a healthy regard and respect for men, that child's heterosexuality will possibly flourish, but if the woman really does not like men there's no way that that's not going to be reflected on the little boy she's raising; certain male traits that this child displays which are stereotyped or whatever aren't going to be reinforced, and in order for him to exist with this particular mother he's going to have to squelch certain aspects of himself which could lead to real conflict.'

Adina, who lives with her lover Nora, had a useful point to make in regard to the worries society at large has about the presence or absence of role models. 'You have to ask yourself how come nobody gets hysterical when a white child is raised in a white society and there are no black role models nearby for it? I was raised with a lack of any kind of role models except for the traditional Jewish heterosexual family structure, and yet I have grown up to recognize and identify that my life was very incomplete and that I need a variety of other people and cultures around me. People get upset about what they want to get upset about, because of their particular prejudice. In other words, the fact that we're very concerned that there is a Spanish role model for our child (their adopted child is coming from Central America) – nobody else seems to worry about that. The people who worry about male models for our child because we are lesbian don't worry about it. They seem to forget that most of the people our child will meet are going to be children from heterosexual families, at day care centre and at school. There'll be males as well as females at the day care centre. There are men who're interested in being involved as well – Nora's father, and a cousin, and lots of friends.'

Jane, a lawyer, also a lesbian, made a similar comment: 'In this culture it would be hard for her to grow up without men – there are men everywhere, in all the cultural roles, it's not that she won't have exposure to men. She will have members of my family who are male – I have two brothers and a father who don't live so far away – and I have some male friends, not all that many, but some, and I do think it's important for her to have good male role models, and so she will. For example, I'd like when she's ready to put her into a day care programme where there are male day care workers as well as female. I'd like her to get used to being around caring men.'

Nearly all the mothers pointed out how their children would be with men during the course of their everyday life, would read about them in books and work with them at school. Jessica Curtis, whose daughter is 2½: 'There's no lack of men – first of all her brother [who is 14] had a daddy, and he's actually living with him; sometimes she thinks her brother is her daddy, sometimes she thinks her friends' daddies are her daddy. I don't think you can sidestep the fact she's going to feel a lack, but she's going to make up a father for herself, whatever I tell her, and I know I'm going to have to live with this fantasy father for a couple of years till she gets old enough to understand properly.' *Serena*, acupressurist: 'Michael *has* some men in his life – they're not lovers of mine, but they're very good men friends and it's like family – they're of the age they could be his father, so he has some good male energy around him that he sees regularly.' *Angela*, graduate student: 'There are no problems about male models – he shares time with his father and me, and he sees his grandfather. Also they have male teachers at the childcare centre as well – it's normal now for them to have men working at these centres, which I think is very important.'

Afton Blake finds the fact that Doron necessarily spends quite a lot of time with her Spanish housekeeper a bonus rather than a minus. 'She comes here regularly, and she and Doron really love each other. The two nights I work she takes him home with her at five o'clock and he stays there having a wonderful time with her children, speaking Spanish; he's going to be bi-lingual. It's a whole different culture he gets exposed to, and he loves everybody in her family. I think it's really a blessing that he gets that, rather than feeling negatively that he's being deprived of a male or a father – there are several men in this big Spanish household all of whom adore him. He's treasured by them – he's their little blond jewel. If I were married I probably wouldn't have that, and I think my child is actually getting an enriched experience.'

It is hardly necessary to add finally that as far as picking up the skills around the house which boys traditionally learn from their fathers, both boy and girl children pick these up from their mothers instead when they live in a female-headed household. *Joanna*, Third World studies: 'Some time ago my car caught fire, and I cannot afford to have it repaired, so I have had to do it myself. So my son sees me working with a jigsaw, cutting the panelling, and replacing the burnt panelling in the car, doing the bodywork, all that, and so I reckon he gets to see what men do anyway, without a direct male role model around. He's real masculine. But he's sensitive too.' *Anna*, Dutch child psychologist: 'I do all the things in the house like the electricity, the lamps, any problems with the water, that sort of thing.' *Elizabeth*, museum curator: 'Well, as a single mum you either have to sink down and don't do anything, or you have to do everything yourself. As far as role models go I don't do much in the way of girlish things myself anyway – I suppose I tend to do things other people's dads do so, like messing about under the bonnet of the car, not that I'm much good at it! But, you know, I'll build chicken houses, and put up shelves, and that sort of thing, so I don't think it's a household with much in the way of roles anyway.'

I suspect that with so many mothers as well as fathers working outside the home nowadays, most of the automatic assumption of roles will gradually disappear, and the children of single mothers will find there is after all nothing so very unique about their upbringing. Each sex has plenty to teach the other, and if single motherhood by choice helps this process along, can it be a bad thing?

Part 3

'SHALL I, SHAN'T I?'

9
'Shall I, Shan't I?'

What the mothers say

For this final section I can only leave the mothers to speak for themselves. I asked many of them at the end of my interviews what message they had to give to women who, as they once had, were weighing up in their minds all the arguments for and against having children not only outside of marriage but also, in the great majority of cases, without the support of a partner. They had already told me about the problems, the joys, their personal experiences; what follows now are some of their final comments which have to be read in relation to the rest of the book. The mothers all hope, as I hope, that their experiences will help you to come to the decision which is right for *you*.

Mary, the nurse who works in a children's nursery with newborn babies: 'It can't be just something that you do because everyone else is doing it, and you can't not do it because you're afraid of what other people might say. It has to feel right for you. Some people just can't do it – either emotionally or because they don't have the support groups. But I think if you feel it's right for you, that you really want to do it and you can handle it and accept in advance that you're going to have to deal with some rough spots along the way. . . . I mean you can't just think, I'm going to have a baby and that's all there is to it. So far my son's been very easy, but he's been a very good-natured baby, I mean he could have been one of those babies that are up all night. You've got to go into the whole thing thinking that it's not going to be easy, because it won't be.

'You can't just make a snap decision. You have to give it a few years of mulling over it and discussing it with yourself and not really making a decision, giving it time to cook in the back of your mind. I think also you really have to know yourself. You have to know what kind of person you are. I feel that I really like myself. I think you can't go into single parenthood voluntarily with the kind of attitude like you've not got married because you can't stand men, or some other feeling like that. You just can't do that, because it's so easy to rub off your emotional feelings on to a child. You really have to know yourself inside and out, more or less. Can you handle it or can't you? You mustn't fool yourself, you mustn't say I'm pretty sure I can handle it, when you're not sure at all.

'And very important – get other things that you want out of the way, because otherwise if there's something that you really want to do and maybe you haven't taken the time to do it and you have a baby, then – well, who knows, it depends on the type of person you are – but that may come up as a resentment later on. I did a lot of travelling before, I did a lot of things that I wanted to do before I had him, and the timing was right. Everything else that needed to be done was done. I had been in my career for a while, had a good job that I enjoyed and was making good money, I had done a lot of travelling, so there really wasn't anything else that I needed to do.'

Tam, clinical social worker and therapist: 'I guess what I would say to people is, know yourself very well, and know as much as you can about what you're doing and what the implications are. I guess the more self-aware and mature and healthy the person is, like *any* parent, the better off they're going to be. The other night when I was talking to a therapist friend about it, she said that after all her years of being in therapy and of being a therapist there were still things that came up in her being a mother, parts of herself and things about herself, that she could never ever possibly have known, and I am sure that any mother would agree with that.' Art gallery owner *Frances*: 'I think having children is the most direct line to humility that you can have. There's nothing that makes you so vulnerable in this world as having a kid. There's nothing that can send me over the edge of anything the way the well-being or the not-well-being of my kid can; there's nothing that makes me feel guiltier when it doesn't work, and there are very few things that give me greater joy than the kind of connection we have when it works.'

Catherine, actress: 'I suppose I'd say to women thinking about it, that they must know themselves pretty well, know their own capabilities. Though perhaps that's a bit comfortless, because in fact I learned a lot about myself during it. You need to know you have the independence to be able to battle on alone, but again, as soon as the child's born you're not alone, you see. Also I think you've got to be sure you can be yourself, you don't want to try to fall into some image of "mother" – you must know that you can be yourself and haven't got to act out something that's not you. And you mustn't suddenly start getting desperate that you can't carry an image of a fine, handsome man standing by you with a warm hand on your shoulder as you're nursing at the breast. You can't expect any of those romantic images if you're going to do it without a man at your side. If you felt that need coming on once you'd had the baby you'd be terribly depressed, I think, and you'd rush out and look for the first man to come and share it with you.'

Carolyn, theatre director with a daughter of 1 month: 'I guess I'll find there are different problems from a two-parent household, but they probably have problems too that we don't have. I'm trying to be as realistic as I can, not to imagine for a minute that there aren't going to be terrible days – there could even be a time when I'll regret ever having done it – but I think that any parent goes through that. I definitely believe that if I'm honest with her and with myself, that it'll be OK. I know there'll be times when – you know, kids can go through a stage where all they want is to be normal, they don't want their mother to be different from any other mother, and she could be embarrassed or upset about this – but I'm not embarrassed or upset about it and she'll know that. And she'll be in a classroom of kids, each one of whom has a family situation that's different from the next one – so many people I know are adopting foreign children, there are tons of divorced people, divorced people who have remarried, divorced people who share the children who go back and forth between them, there's so many ways of living now. I know too a lot of women with children who are married but who resemble single women in the real way their lives work.'

Pat, midwife: 'I would say to your readers, try to be mature enough and talk to enough people so that you can tell what kind of a person you really are. You have to be so honest with yourself. I think everyone has a right to have a child whenever they want, and anyway, every single child-birth experience in the world today has some mistake attached to it – either it was the wrong time, the wrong husband, the wrong lover, the wrong sex, or something. You know, I just don't think you can have this ideal perfect family, because you're changing so all the time, but even if you think you're going to be a strong single parent, think again and again and question yourself constantly. Do you really want to be alone every day, and what are you giving up by not sharing the birth? I mean, seeing the childbirth experience and the child itself through someone else's eyes adds such a dimension. Doing it alone is like it's not in 3D. No. I wouldn't do it alone again myself. I'd only do it again if I was with someone.'

Jane, lawyer: 'I'd been ready to have a child for many years, and I don't believe people should wait for the perfect time, because the perfect time never comes – there's always something wrong, either at work or with your home or your relationship with somebody. What I can say about my own situation is that I have a very supportive network of friends who are having babies also, as couples or as single women, and also that some of my heterosexual friends are having babies at the same time – some in marriage, some not, so it means I have a very strong support system of people whose lives right now are going to be involved with children. It would be very hard, I would think, for somebody who is isolated, if she was the only person she knew who was single and having a baby on her own.'

Dr Afton Blake: 'Not only is your economic security important, but your own emotional maturity – I think you need to have lived alone long enough to know that you're comfortable living alone, and that you feel secure within a lone lifestyle. A child isn't going to make you feel comfortable living alone. And don't forget that you're less open to meeting people after you've had a child, your energy is so focused on the child – many women I've talked to have said this – that the time and the energy to go out and meet someone is less than it was before.'

Angela, graduate student: 'To be honest I wouldn't suggest to a woman to decide to have a child completely on her own without the support of another person. Whether that other person is male or female doesn't matter. I wouldn't suggest anyone should do it on their own, because the period around the birth and immediately after it is so incredibly difficult – I had a hard time coping with it even with his father living there with us. Afterwards, once you've settled into a routine, I suppose, if you have enough support from friends, and financial stability, which tends to be important, especially here in America, I don't see any problem with it.'

Lynn, nurse with two children: 'It's not easy being a single parent. It can be very lonely. I have a good support group, but right now I don't have a significant man in my life. I know I can go to my neighbours, but there's not that other person here for me when my coping mechanisms fail and I get really angry with the kids. I certainly don't beat them, but sometimes you know, I spank Heather when she's really obnoxious, and I sometimes wonder to myself, would I have done it if somebody else had been there and I had been able to express some of my frustration from work to somebody else. I come home to kids only, I can't say to them, I've had a bad day; well, I do, I say I've had a bad day at work and mummy's in no mood for fooling around tonight. But it's not the same thing as really being able to verbalize – you know, so and so was a real S.O.B. today – and being really able to say what happened. But on the other hand, sometimes I really feel like I have the best of both worlds. It's brought such a dimension to my life – there's a love that . . . it really bothers me when someone says they don't want children, and I think about the absolute loss they have. People say, well, you don't have a man in your life and that's a loss too. True, but there's a dimension of love that comes from these two children that I can't describe – you have to have been a mother to know it.'

Jane Mattes, founder of SMC: (this quotation was also used earlier) 'The main thing I learned is that you can't do it alone. That's the irony of ironies. That's what I tell people in the group. We run a group of three meetings for women who are thinking about it, and the thing I most try to get across is that you really have to be prepared to get help, to get support, to learn what your limits are and to find other people who can help you when you reach your limit.' Jessica Curtis, President of SMC: 'Plan ahead. Find out where you're going to get support, what finances you need. The women who have difficulties are the ones who got pregnant unintentionally and then decided to keep the baby. They're the ones who have hard times – the ones who plan ahead are basically all right.'

Rosa, Dutch specialist in child psychology: 'I think you must be open about the things that you don't like and the things that you do like, you must talk about them to other women. I think in Holland more than in other countries there is this image about motherhood – about the pink cloud, we say. You have to show you are happy and that everything is going right, even to your best friends, and that makes things more heavy than they should be. You are supposed to find everything you want in your life inside the house with your children – once you have children you are supposed to stay home and look after them. If you are living like this you have to have friends you can be open with.'

Elizabeth, museum curator and mother of 10-year-old boy: 'Certainly I never anticipated the awfulness of making sure he was being looked after properly, it's a ghastly, ghastly strain – particularly in my job. When I started I was doing conventional times, nine to five, then I was promoted to start this new museum which meant that I have a lot of evening work and weekend work – it was *awful* when he was younger. I grossly underestimated the problems, just the sheer logistics of it all, you know? the management of it all. I was completely ignorant of what was involved. But if I had the choice again I would do exactly the same thing, I wouldn't hesitate at all.'

Jenny, unintentionally pregnant at 20 when living with her lover: 'I thought you could mould children much more – I thought children were much more a product of their environment than their genes, and I found out that there's a hell of a lot more in the genes than in the environment. I mean they come out a certain sort of baby – I thought that if you created a baby in a certain sort of way that you could really have a very large influence over the sort of child they grew up to be, that you could mould your baby into the sort of baby that would go along with you and take part in your activities. But I found that wasn't so. What would I say to your readers? I'd say, don't do it, I think. I certainly wouldn't ever contemplate doing it on my own. Maybe there are some people that can do it alone, but I'm not one of them. Not at 20 or 21, anyway. Even in a relationship I don't think it's a good idea at that age. You don't really know yourself well enough to know whether you're going to want to live with this person for a long time, and how you're going to react when there's a baby. It's silly, really, because it's much better physically to have a baby at 20, but I think it's much better mentally to have them at 30.'

Acupressurist *Serena*: 'In spite of all the struggles I'm not opposed to it. I would encourage it. One of my major lessons from this is that all the real answers come from following your own intuition; there can be such peer pressure right from the beginning of single parenting – is that right, is that not right, how you should raise the child – and really and truly the only right way is the way you know it to be. You have to know that sometimes your feelings might be very different from what is the norm, and you must go along with your feelings because that's where the real answer is, and that's the way you'll be the best mother and the best friend and the best of everything for your child and for life. There are terrific doubts that come in single parenting – you keep asking yourself, am I making the right decision? They may not be so important in themselves but at the time they seem very major, specially for a first child. I think too it's real important to find out who you are before you do it. There are some people that are more suited to parenting than others, and in that case age is not the issue. Also I've searched out other single parents so I could find out what other children are like, whether some issues are special to a child of a single parent, and that's been a good support to me.'

Adina and *Nora*, who are adopting a child: (Adina first) 'I guess I would say the main thing is that motherhood is so important in a woman's life that hopefully as society becomes a little more tolerant it will find ways to create structures, family unit systems which don't follow a traditional heterosexual pattern and which will make it possible for single women without men in their lives to have children.' (Nora) 'You need to be able to be responsible for another life. You need to know that emotionally, financially you have the resources. That last doesn't mean having the money you'll eventually need for the child's growing-up right now, it means, for example, knowing how to find out about things like scholarships and grants and what's available – that's as much a resource as actually having enough money available in the bank for the child's schooling at this very moment.'

And lastly, *Sarah*, languages teacher: 'These last four years have been an enchanted time with Sophie, to see her growing, to see her developing, to share in her fun. I would say to women who are thinking of having a child, if they want it with sufficient passion they should go ahead and do it, because I think that passion will give them the guts to do it. It's all very well to say to somebody, be wise, try and love intelligently, but I think really the measure of it, unfortunately, is not so much the wisdom as the *passion* we have for something. Even though it has its sad side for me, and a lot of the time I've been very, very unhappy, I wanted Sophie with enough passion to make a good job of it, in the end. And that finally is what matters.'

Postscript

Most of the women attending the Single Mothers by Choice 'thinkers' groups decide not to have children after they have been presented with all the facts. Perhaps most of those reading this book who also are asking themselves whether or not to have a child will come to the same conclusion. I must admit that as I put together the various sections on problems I began to wonder how anybody ever has the courage to have children at all, recalling vividly the fatigue after being woken up in the night, the anguish when it looks possible that an illness may be serious, the interruption in one's career – a hundred bad times came to mind. And my experience took place within the comparative security and comfort of marriage. But when I tried to think what it would have been like *not* to have had my children, all the painful times – the memories of exhaustion, anger, frustration – all of that instantly faded away and the question seemed as absurd as asking myself if I should not have allowed the dawn to rise or the seasons to change. My children exist, and I cannot imagine that they could ever not have existed. I also know that my own life would have been immeasurably the poorer without them, and I think the world, too, would have been poorer without them.

Notes

Chapter I The 'phenomenon' of single parenting by choice
1 Adrienne Rich, *Of Woman Born: Motherhood as Experience and Institution*, Virago, London, 1977, p. 34.
2 Ann Oakley, *Becoming a Mother*, Martin Robertson, Oxford, 1979.
3 Lenore J. Weitzman, *Sex Role Socialization*, Mayfield, California, 1979, p. 34.
4 Gillian Caldwell, 'Matter of facts of life', *Guardian*, London, 8 May 1984.
5 Lillian Rubin, *Intimate Strangers*, Harper & Row, New York, 1983, pp. 10-11.
6 'Rate doubles for out-of-wedlock births', *Washington Post*, Washington, 26 April 1984.
7 Patricia Morrisroe, *New York Magazine*, 'Mommy only', New York, 6, June 1983, p. 21.
8 *Children Today*, National Children's Home, London, 1983.
9 *Information Sheet*, National Council for One Parent Families, London, November 1983.
10 Jean Martin and Ceridwen Roberts, *Women and Work: A Lifetime Perspective*, HMSO, Stationery Office London, 1984.
11 Rubin, op. cit., pp. 33-4.
12 Weitzman, op. cit., p. 26.
13 Morrisroe, op. cit., p. 27.
14 Rubin, op. cit., p. 50.
15 Rubin, op. cit., p. 128.
16 Jean Renvoize, *Children in Danger: The Causes and Prevention of Baby Battering*, Routledge & Kegan Paul, London, 1974.
17 Jean Renvoize, *Web of Violence: A Study of Family Violence*, Routledge & Kegan Paul, London, 1978.
18 Renvoize, op. cit., 1978, p. 219.
19 Rubin, op. cit., p. 51.
20 Nancy Friday, *My Mother, My Self*, Fontana/Collins, London, 1979.
21 Oakley, op. cit., pp. 263 and 265.

2 The women's movement
1 Kate Millett, *Sexual Politics*, Doubleday, New York, 1970, p. 126.
2 Betty Friedan, *The Second Stage*, Michael Joseph, London, 1982, pp. 33, 37, 46-7.
3 Michael Simmons, 'The fight against contempt and degradation', *Guardian*, London, 13 June 1984.
4 Ann Oakley, *Subject Women*, Martin Robertson, Oxford, 1981, p. 7.
5 Ibid.
6 Ibid, p. 8.
7 Ibid., pp. 143, 144.
8 Joanna Stratton, *Pioneer Women, Voices from the Kansas Frontier*, Touchstone, Simon & Schuster, New York, 1981.
9 Kate Millett, op. cit., p. 67.
10 Adrienne Rich, *Of Woman Born: Motherhood as Experience and Institution*, 1976, and Virago, London, 1977, p. 272.
11 'Romania orders baby boom', *Guardian*, London, 19 March 1984.
12 Ibid.
13 George Stanica, 'Breed, comrade women, it's your duty', *Guardian*, London, 3 April 1984.
14 Jonathan Mirsky, 'Infanticide in the one-child, one-party state', *The Times*, London, 18 March 1983.
15 Ann Oakley, *Becoming a Mother*, Martin Robertson, Oxford, 1979, p. 13.
16 Nicholas Timmins, 'Smaller families . . . in changing Britain', *The Times*, London, 26 June 1984.
17 Oakley, op. cit., 1981, p. 29.
18 Oakley, op. cit., 1981, p. 30.
19 Betty Friedan, 'The new way for women – and men', *Cosmopolitan* (first published in the *New York Times Magazine*, 1983), London, August 1983, p. 100.
20 Ibid., p. 165.
21 Oakley, op. cit., 1981, pp. 318-19.
22 Chris Reed, 'Is the President a push-over?', *Guardian*, London, 15 March 1984.
23 Brenda Whisker, Jacky Bishop, Lilian Mohin and Trish Longdon (eds), *Breaching the Peace*, Onlywomen Press, London, p. 5.
24 National Children's Home, *Children Today*, London, 1983, p. 9.
25 Georgine Ferry, 'Women in Hungary – changing minds', *The Times*, London, 1983/4 (exact date unknown).
26 Oakley, op. cit., 1981, pp. 335-8.
27 Stephanie Dowrick and Sibyl Grundberg (eds), *Why Children?*, The Women's Press, London, 1980, pp. 79-80.
28 Millett, op. cit., p. 185.
29 Lillian Rubin, *Intimate Strangers*, Harper & Row, New York, 1983, pp. 21-4.
30 Jean Renvoize, *Incest: A Family Pattern*, Routledge & Kegan Paul, London, 1982.
31 Oakley, op. cit., 1981, pp. 109-10.

32 *Letterbox Library* from Children's Books Co-operative, 1st floor, 5 Bradbury Street, London N16 8JN (they will send you a catalogue on application).
33 Millett, op. cit., p. 52.
34 Friedan, op. cit., p. 28.
35 Oakley, op. cit., 1979, pp. 267-73.

3 Man as stud
1 Adrienne Rich, *Of Woman Born: Motherhood as Experience and Institution*, Virago, 1977, p. 11.
2 Judith Cassetty (ed.), *The Parental Child-Support Obligation*, Lexington Books, Lexington, Mass. 1983, p. 121.
3 Lillian Rubin, *Intimate Strangers*, Harper & Row, New York, 1983, p. 50.
4 Nancy Friday, *My Mother, My Self*, Fontana, 1979.
5 Rubin, op. cit., pp. 53-6.
6 Mary Ingham, *Men*, Century, London, 1984, p. 46.
7 Marilyn Fabe and Norma Wikler, *Up Against the Clock*, Random House, New York, 1979.
8 Deborah Moggach, 'The redundant male?', *The Sunday Times*, London, 20 May 1984.
9 Susanne Boscher, *Jenny lives with Eric and Martin*, Gay Men's Press, London, 1983.
10 Rich, op. cit., p. 64.
11 Clare Dyer, 'When a father has no rights', *The Sunday Times*, London, 19 January 1982.
12 Dyer, op. cit.
13 Cassetty, op. cit., p. 62.
14 Cassetty, op. cit., p. 65.

4 Why women make the choice
1 Lillian Rubin, *Intimate Strangers*, Harper & Row, New York, 1983, pp. 120-5.
2 Stephanie Dowrick and Sibyl Grundberg (eds), *Why Children?*, The Women's Press, London, 1980, p. 9.
3 Rubin, op. cit., p. 112.
4 Patricia Morrisroe, 'Mommy only', *New York Magazine*, 27 June 1983, p. 6.
5 Rubin, op. cit., p. 151.
6 Dowrick, op. cit., pp. 67-8.
7 Dowrick, op. cit., pp. 24-5.
8 Dowrick, op. cit., p. 69.
9 'Rate doubles for out-of-wedlock births', *Washington Post*, 26 April 1984.
10 Marilyn Fabe and Norma Wikler, *Up Against the Clock*, Random

House, New York, 1979, pp. 282-5.
11 Ibid.
12 Ibid., pp. 286-7.

5 Family

1 Judith Cassetty (ed.), *The Parental Child-Support Obligation*,
   Lexington Books, Lexington, Mass. 1983, p. 292.
2 *Parliamentary Debates, House of Commons Official Report, Family
   Proceedings Bill (Lords), Examination of Witnesses*, HMSO, London,
   22 March 1984, p. 106.
3 Ibid., p. 106.
4 Cassetty, op. cit., p. 292.
5 Don Edgar and Freya Headlam, *Working Paper – One-parent Families
   and Educational Disadvantage*, Institute of Family Studies,
   Melbourne, October 1982, p. 2.
6 *Guardian*, 'Europe's divorce rate soars and birth figures tumble', 2
   June 1984.
7 Cassetty, op. cit., p. 287.
8 Cassetty, op. cit., p. 121.
9 John Eekelaar and Eric Clive, *Custody after Divorce*, SSRC, Centre
   for Socio-legal Studies, Oxford, 1983.
10 Stephanie Dowrick and Sibyl Grundberg (eds), *Why Children?*, The
   Women's Press, London, 1980.
11 Ibid., p. 22.
12 Kate Millett, *Sexual Politics*, Doubleday, New York, 1970, pp. 35, 36.
13 Ann Oakley, *Becoming a Mother*, Martin Robertson, Oxford, 1979,
   pp. 214-16.
14 Ibid., p. 218.
15 Ibid., p. 227.
16 Jean Renvoize, *Web of Violence: A Study of Family Violence*,
   Routledge & Kegan Paul, London, 1978, pp. 219-224.
17 Ibid.
18 Cassetty, op. cit., p. 288.
19 Catherine Guy, *Asking About Marriage*, National Marriage Guidance
   Council, NMGC, Bookshop, Little Church Street, Rugby, CV21 3AP,
   1983.
20 *Teenage Pregnancy in Britain*, Birth Control Trust, 27-35 Mortimer
   Street, London, WIN 7RJ, 1984.
21 'The revolution is over', *Time*, New York, 9 April 1984, pp. 48-54.
22 Patricia Morrisroe, 'Mommy only', *New York Magazine*, New York,
   6 June 1983, p. 29.
23 Cassetty, op. cit., p. 287.

6 Action

1 Lillian Rubin, *Intimate Strangers*, Harper & Row, New York, 1983, p.
   141.

2 Denise Winn, *The Sunday Times*, 'How dangerous is the birth jab?', 26 August 1984.
3 Ann Oakley, *Becoming a Mother*, Martin Robinson, Oxford, 1979, pp. 82, 86.

7 Problems and joys
1 Jean Renvoize, *Children in Danger: The Causes and Prevention of Baby Battering*, Routledge & Kegan Paul, London, 1974.
2 Judith Cassetty (ed.), *The Parental Child-Support Obligation*, Lexington Books, Lexington, Mass., 1983, p. 284.
3 National Council for One Parent Families, Information Sheets Nos. 35 and 5.
4 Don Edgar and Freya Headlam, *One Parent Families and Educational Disadvantage*, Working Paper No. 4, October 1982, Institute of Family Studies, Melbourne, Australia, October 1982, p. 1.
5 Cassetty, op. cit., p. 120.
6 Michael Horsnell, *The Times*, 'Raising first child to 16 costs average working parents nearly £70,000', 23 September 1983.
7 Cassetty, op. cit., p. 63.
8 Jean Martin and Ceridwen Roberts, *Women and Work: A Lifetime Perspective*, HMSO, London 1984.
9 Heather Joshi, 'Unfair shares', *Guardian*, 8 May 1984.
10 Spencer Rich, 'Women dent male domination of executive jobs in US', *Guardian*, 12 April 1984.

8 The children, and more about men
1 Patricia Morrisroe, 'Mommy only', *New York*, 6 June 1983, p. 21.
2 Don Edgar and Freya Headlam, *One Parent Families and Educational Disadvantage*, Working Paper no. 4, Institute of Family Studies, Melbourne, Australia, October 1982, p. 6.
3 Lenore J. Weitzman, *Sex Role Socialization*, Mayfield, California, 1979, p. 14.
4 Stephanie Dowrick and Sibyl Grundberg (eds), *Why Children?*, The Women's Press, London, 1980.
5 Lillian Rubin, *Intimate Strangers*, Harper & Row, New York, 1983, pp. 12-13.
6 Adrienne Rich, *Of Woman Born: Motherhood as Experience and Institution*, Virago, London, 1977.